Dominican-Americans and the Politics of Empowerment

New World Diasporas

Florida A&M University, Tallahassee
Florida Atlantic University, Boca Raton
Florida Gulf Coast University, Ft. Myers
Florida International University, Miami
Florida State University, Tallahassee
University of Central Florida, Orlando
University of Florida, Gainesville
University of North Florida, Jacksonville
University of South Florida, Tampa
University of West Florida, Pensacola

Dominican-Americans

and the Politics of Empowerment

Ana Aparicio

University Press of Florida

Gainesville   Tallahassee   Tampa   Boca Raton
Pensacola   Orlando   Miami   Jacksonville   Ft. Myers

A record of cataloging-in-publication data is available from the Library of Congress.
ISBN 0-8130-2925-2

The University Press of Florida is the scholarly publishing agency for the State
University System of Florida, comprising Florida A&M University, Florida Atlantic
University, Florida Gulf Coast University, Florida International University, Florida
State University, University of Central Florida, University of Florida, University of
North Florida, University of South Florida, and University of West Florida.

University Press of Florida
15 Northwest 15th Street
Gainesville, FL 32611-2079
http://www.upf.com

Focus on the visible coastline of politics and [you will] miss the continent that lies beyond.

    James C. Scott

Contents

Tables

Foreword

Diasporic groups do not simply come into being and reproduce their sense of a unique corporate self through an identification with a real or imagined homeland. Nor are these groups exclusively defined through their varied transnational ties that transgress and redefine nation-state borders. Instead, as Ana Aparicio shows in this book, diasporic identities are concocted and no doubt contested in the rough and tumble of *local* politics that have to do with inherently *local* issues. And as she also shows, Dominicans in New York—and even more so second-generation Dominican-Americans as they take over the reins of community organizing—actively cultivate alliances with other groups such as Puerto Ricans and African-Americans, thus rendering Dominicans' and Dominican-Americans' diasporic experience multiplex, entailing shifting modes of salience for the construction of multiple identities.

In this thoroughly researched book, Aparicio grapples with the received academic wisdom on immigrant groups in the United States and their transnational relationships, while presenting a wealth of ethnographic and qualitative data based on her own activist research. And it is the power of this research that gives credence to Aparicio's critical interventions. She considers but then seriously questions models of immigrant incorporation, particularly for the second generation, that is, the children of Dominican immigrants to the United States. One such theory which Aparicio critiques is "segmented assimilation." This theory arose in order to replace simplistic "melting pot" and "assimilation" theories. Its promoters emphasize the ability of immigrant groups to make strategic choices in terms of their incorporation into U.S. society, and they suggest that the most successful course of action is to maintain a "co-ethnic" identity and culture that emphasize the group's nationality and ethnicity. Yet, as Aparicio argues, this view assumes internally homogeneous and bounded communities and cultures for both the receiving society, including its dominant sectors, and the immigrant groups themselves. Lost here is any sense of multiple identities and symbolic border crossings. At the same time, the theory's overemphasis on choice and agency, as Aparicio rightly points out, downplays the determinative role of structural forces affecting class and identity position-taking.

One reason for Aparicio's advantage here is that much of the research on immigration and immigrant groups in the United States is not based on ethnographic investigations. For Aparicio, an ethnographic (and historical) approach could best appreciate the fluidity inherent in the situations she encountered. Through these methods she is able to add to but significantly challenge (1) theories of immigrant group transnationalism by showing the local nature of much political organizing even while these groups sustain what Aparicio calls their "multiplicity of involvements" in both the home and host societies; (2) theories of identity by showing how identity shifts with context; and (3) theories of second-generation political organizing methods by showing how Dominican-Americans reach out to other groups in order to empower their communities.

It is quite possible that Aparicio has not only charted a new theoretical direction in immigration studies, but that she has described a new model of immigrant group organizing based on the Dominican-American experience in New York. It remains to be seen if other groups employ this model that Aparicio has so skillfully rendered here.

Kevin A. Yelvington
Series Editor

Acknowledgments

Since embarking on the journey that led to this text, I have been blessed with remarkable friends, family, mentors, and colleagues. It is a privilege to be able to extend my gratitude to them all. I began the research on which this book is based at the Graduate School and University Center, City University of New York. I owe much to Leith Mullings, Donald Robotham, Ramona Hernández, and Michael Blim. Leith was and continues to be an unfaltering and dedicated advisor and mentor; her commitment to activist scholarship and social justice is a tremendous source of inspiration. Don and Ramona extracted a world of ideas from fragmented drafts and helped me explore the nuances within my work; for that and so much more I am very grateful. Others at CUNY who also offered various forms of support include Sarah Aponte, Ellen DeRiso, Roger Hart, Louise Lennihan, Felix Matos-Rodriguez, John Mollenkopf, Ida Susser, Silvio Torres-Saillant, and Ana Celia Zentella.

I am fortunate to have a circle of supportive and inspiring friends and colleagues as well. Jemima Pierre and Melanie Bush read through earlier drafts and offered critical feedback. During various phases of my work, many others have also helped flesh out ideas and offered encouragement and inspiration; they include Madeline Belkin, O. Hugo Benavides, Lawrence Blum, Rod Bush, Raymond Codrington, Kawana Cohen, Kathleen Coll, Hector Cordero-Guzmán, Jason Cortes, Darius Daniel, Arlene Dávila, Dana Davis, Carlos Decena, Amy DenOuden, Heather Duncan-Fairman, Evelyn Erickson, Tracy Fisher, Marcial Godoy, Kenneth Guest, James Jennings, Patricia Landolt, Suzanne Oboler, Gina Pérez, Milagros Ricourt, Raquel Z. Rivera, Cesar Rosario, Bill and Irma Rose, Dara Rose, Jessica Rose, George Sánchez, Suzanne Scheld, Jocelyn Solis, Shirley Tang, Tanya Tiangco, Andrés Torres, Mary Tse, Ronald

Walters, Kevin Yelvington, and Rafael "Papo" Zapata. For their critical and detailed reviews of the manuscript, I extend many thanks to Edmund T. Gordon, Raquel Z. Rivera, Tim Sieber, Silvio Torres-Saillant, and an anonymous reviewer for UPF. I thank project editor Jacqueline Kinghorn Brown and freelance copy editor Kirsteen Anderson for invaluable editorial assistance. Special thanks are also due John Byram, of the University Press of Florida, and Kevin Yelvington for believing in this project and for including it in the New World Diasporas series. For their unconditional love and support I thank my mother, Maria Aparicio, and my family, Gabriela Aparicio, Margoth Aparicio-Williams, Joaquín and Dolores Martínez, Kaeleb Williams, Sumira Williams, Isabelle Williams, Carmen and Jorge Flores, Ana Argueta, Joaquín Flores, Francisco R. Ponce, Manuel Martínez Jr., José Neftalí Muñoz, Elvira and José Muñoz, Rene Martínez, Will Gock, Karim Williams, Manuel and Marta Martínez, Xavier Cornejo, Kendra Cornejo, the Aparicios and Greens of California, and countless others.

This book could not have been written were it not for the work of many activists in New York. In order to maintain their anonymity I cannot list them by name, but I extend my gratitude and respect to every one. In the midst of organizing a multitude of programs, rallies, marches, and conferences, they graciously let me into their lives. I thank them for seeing me as more than a researcher, for encouraging me, feeding me, and shuttling me home after late-night meetings. I also thank them for allowing me to share in their celebrations and to partake in their moments of sudden grief. It was with great sadness that I joined many activists and local residents at the funeral of a youth organizer from one of the organizations that was the subject of my study. They inspire and motivate me, especially when things seem overwhelming. My work is easy compared to the mountains they climb year after year. Their dedication to social and political transformation is remarkable. I thank them all for grabbing my hand, for insisting that I take up my pen to write their stories.

Very many people contributed to this book; it truly does "take a village." It is only because those who came before me endured hardships, sacrificed so much, and dared to struggle that I can write these words now. And it is because so many activists in Washington Heights remain committed to social justice and community empowerment that I have a story to weave within these pages. It is because of all of these people that I find reason and remain optimistic about the work of anthropology. I hope that my journeys and decisions in this field do justice to all they continue to do.

Introduction

As a teenager growing up in Washington Heights, New York, Carlos Pierre,[1] a twenty-four-year-old second-generation Dominican-American, attended public schools alongside Black and Dominican peers. When he was in school, he says

> I didn't feel any connection to those [newly arrived] Dominicans. . . . It's just that they were just coming here. I didn't have anything in common with them, or, you know, that's what I thought back then. They were into merengue and even bachata and I was like, "Whoa, what the hell is this?" You know, give me my hip-hop and I was good, you know. I felt that I had more in common with Blacks growing up, you know. We were here, living and growing up in New York [City]. They were coming from the island. I knew we weren't the same. There was something different with us Dominicans growing up here and Blacks, you know.[2]

Carlos' reflections on his identity changed once he went away to college and started working with other Latinos. During his early years in college, he began thinking about joining a fraternity. His first inclination was to join a Black fraternity: "You know, I wanted to feel that community, that feeling of brotherhood." But as he started to meet and hang out with other Latinos who grew up here, in the United States, he opted to join a Latino fraternity. He explains,

> I am identifying myself as a Dominican who grew up in the U.S., you know. Not exactly a Dominican-American really or an American of Dominican descent. It's all in there and I know people see that all the time. . . . Yeah, you know, I definitely am Black and I have a lot in common with African-Americans, but I started to see that, also, there was the

Latino part of me that also needed a place, you know. I started to learn about Pedro Albizu [Campos] and Che [Guevara] and Emiliano Zapata, and all these other people I had no clue about before. I knew about Malcolm X and Black leaders but I didn't know about my other roots. I became Latino in a new way then . . . and Dominican.

Carlos now works with young Dominicans—both the newly arrived and those born and raised here—through a youth program in Quisqueya United, one of the largest organizations in the neighborhood of Washington Heights. This neighborhood is home to the largest concentration of Dominicans in New York City, the city that boasts the second highest number of Dominicans globally (second only to Santo Domingo, the capital city of the Dominican Republic). Carlos speaks vividly of his experiences and identities, which include categories of Blackness, of becoming and belonging to a new community of Latinos, and of rediscovering his Dominican-ness. He also maintains a political-ideological connection to African-Americans and other Latinos, emphasizing to youth in the organization the importance of seeing connections. He and other staff members of the organization have shown films on the Black Panthers, the movie *Pa'lante, Siempre Pa'lante* about the Young Lords Party, and Spike Lee's movie *X* about Malcolm X. Carlos' youthful appearance (he is often mistaken for a teenager) and his ability to "speak the language" of youth in the organization—Spanish and English, but particularly Neuyorican Spanglish and Dominicanish (see Báez 1999), and Black English—has drawn many youth in the organization to the youth council, in which he is a lead staff person. His ability to identify with (and as) Latino, Dominican, and Black creates no direct contradiction; these identities represent, as he says, "my community of support. This is where I'm going to be. These are my people."

When thinking of people such as Carlos Pierre, and other Black immigrants and second-generation youth, one must contend with cartographies of race, racialization, the power and re-creation of the nation, and community. Akhil Gupta and James Ferguson suggest, "In the pulverized space of postmodernity, space has not become irrelevant; it has been reterritorialized . . . [and] it is this that forces us to reconceptualize fundamentally the politics of community, solidarity, identity, and cultural difference" (1992: 9). Today's immigrants and their children work to create networks in personal and institutional settings and to construct local politics that extend beyond strict boundaries of race, ethnicity, and nation. In fact, through their work, many are challenging these boundaries. Contemporary immigrant groups in the United States are altering local politics and transforming the communities and cities in which they live. This study examines the ways in which Dominican-Americans living in Washington Heights participate in local politics. Central to this study is the exploration of the extent to which Dominican-American community building and politics involve second-generation Dominicans as well as other racial/ethnic groups. It is a story about Dominican-American organizers in the neighborhood that is considered, in the words of one local organizer, "*the* Dominican Mecca" in the United States. However, this is not an account of fixed identities built around a static ethnic or racial lexicon "native" to the group under discussion. Rather than offer a detached and decontextualized analysis (á la Glazer and Moynihan 1963), I consider the way Dominican-American organizers continuously reevaluate the world and locale around them and alter their politics. That race and ethnicity become key factors (or tools) in their routes toward empowerment is understandable. As Manning Marable (1994) explains:

> In the United States "race" for the oppressed has also come to mean an identity of survival, victimization, and opposition to those racial groups of elites that exercise power and privilege. What we are looking at here is not an ethnic identification or culture, but an awareness of shared experience, suffering, and struggle against the barriers of racial division. . . . [The] second distinct sense of racial identity is both imposed on the oppressed and yet represents a reconstructed critical memory of the character of the group's collective ordeals. Both definitions of race and racial identity give character and substance to the movements for power and influence among people of color. (31)

It is within this context that we must understand Dominican-Americans and the politics of empowerment. The character of Dominican-American community organizing has changed since the first wave of Dominican immigrants arrived in New York in the 1960s. Through the generations, local organizers have altered the geopolitical focus of their efforts. That is, they have moved from sole emphasis on "homeland politics," or the transnational sphere, to include organizing to confront local issues in the city of New York. Dominicans have a strong history of civic participation. In New York, in an attempt to build their power, they have expanded their organizational efforts to include other people of color, namely Puerto Ricans and African-Americans. A number of factors converged in the 1980s and 1990s that allowed the Dominican community in Washington Heights to establish a foothold in local politics. First, community organizers retreated from an exclusive concentration on "home politics." Following this development, Dominican organizers began to focus on establishing organizations to take on local issues. In this process they reached out to Puerto Rican and African-American activists and established leadership in New York. And finally, a new generation of Dominican-Americans, raised and educated in public institutions in New York City, came of age and solidified the new direction of Dominican-American organizing.

Contrary to mainstream perceptions (see Suro 1998), the political transformations fostered by Dominicans have proven significant and have led to a multitude of local, community-based institutions (see Georges 1984; Ricourt 2002; Hernández and Torres-Saillant 1998). I examine the patterns of community organizing in the Dominican neighborhood of Washington Heights, New York, particularly from the 1980s to the present, focusing on the ways that second-generation Dominicans are envisioning themselves and their communities as a new American citizenry. In this reading, I extend the realm of politics beyond the formal electoral process to examine the numerous ways Dominican-American activists struggle for power and control of their community.

At first glance Dominican-American organizing in Washington Heights appears to be exclusively Dominican identified. I suggest that behind the appearance of "co-ethnic" community organizing and empowerment lies the reality of coalition building across racial and ethnic lines. Second-generation Dominican-Americans are at the forefront of many developments toward this end. This study seeks to bridge the gap between two bodies of literature, one focusing on first-generation immigrant politics and the other examining the second generation. While examining Dominican-American organizing and politics, it is important not to omit or marginalize the role of young Dominican immigrants and the second generation in these processes.

This study also examines the ways in which and the reasons why some Dominican activists in New York City have developed a particular framework of identity—as Dominican-Americans or as people of color or both—through their political mobilization and institution-building projects. Central to this study are the ways in which identity politics is understood and used in organizing efforts. The extent to which Dominican-American organizers build coalitions across racial and ethnic lines in this process raises questions about assumptions prevalent in contemporary theories on immigrants and the second generation. Through the use of ethnographic material, this text builds upon and challenges several postulations common in the literature on contemporary immigrant communities. Research on immigrant politics tends to em-

phasize transnational organizing, while that on the second generation and segmented assimilation privilege co-ethnic identity and action. This study follows
the trajectory of this literature in moving beyond "straight-line assimilation"
and "melting pot" theories of immigrant incorporation. The text also aims to
move beyond these paradigms to present a more dynamic portrait of the ever-
changing face of Dominican-American politics.

Embarking on an examination of the political developments of community
organizing in Washington Heights requires that we pay attention to the historic, economic, and political circumstances in which this community operates. We must also begin to look at these factors as forces or macro-level
processes with which local activists and organizations are in dialogue. Community organizing does not develop in a vacuum. Dominicans who arrived in
Washington Heights in the latter part of the twentieth century have faced particular social and political conditions, including gentrification and housing
shortages, government abandonment of the social safety net, erosion of the
manufacturing industries in the United States, and a racialized educational
system. Local activists and organizations have gradually but surely come to
focus their efforts on these locally produced issues. The strategies they use in
organizing to confront these issues and the modes of identification they call
upon to do so are at the core of this study. Within this reading of Dominican-
American organizing I will address issues raised in the literature on contemporary immigrants: transnationalism, segmented assimilation, racialization, and
community politics.

The questions guiding this text therefore include, What constitutes Dominican-American organizing in Washington Heights? With whom have they
collaborated in this community-building process? How does identity come to
bear on the manner in which they organize? How does the new cadre of Dominican activists—composed in large part of the second generation—confront and organize local politics? To what extent do they work with co-ethnics
and other people of color? And finally, is contemporary activism in Washington Heights grounded in specific geopolitical spaces and identities? To what
extent is political organizing transnational, translocal, or New York–based?

Identity and Power

An identity and a community, as imagined as these may be (Anderson 1983),
constitute a political space. People continuously reconstruct their communities and reconfigure their identities as members of those communities. Some

would argue that people not only alter their identities and community perspectives (that is, who makes up their community and what community they belong to) over a span of time, but that they also change their self-ascribed identities and roles according to the situations in which they find themselves. This notion of a situational identity is often discussed when speaking of the children of immigrants—that is, the second generation—thought to live "betwixt and between" the world of their parents and the world of their adopted country. Far from being schizophrenic self-ascribed definitions, however, the identities around which an individual or a group organizes and from which they draw collective strength are designated after prolonged study and involvement in micro- and macro-level processes. In the United States this necessarily involves an awareness of racial hierarchies and the power and consequences of the process of racial coding. People can at times choose to use particular identities in their attempts to attain a certain goal. Today's immigrants of color select from the limited racially coded options available to them; these choices of identity do not however single-handedly determine the outcome of their efforts.

In the case of organizing and contemporary politics, identity appears to have taken center stage as people organize to confront the state (Castells 1982, 1997; Hale 1997). Studies on identity politics demonstrate that the relationship between politics and identity is historically specific, contextual, and multilayered. It is also constantly shifting in practice and in meaning. It is based on this understanding that I use concepts gleaned from studies of ethnicity, race, and community building.

The Transnational Paradigm

In recent years scholars have focused considerable attention on the ways in which today's immigrants alter concepts of assimilation and identity. This scholarship encourages us to reevaluate our assumptions about immigration, assimilation, cultural hybridity, community, and political participation and suggests that such processes are manifested in new ways in the lives of today's immigrant communities compared to those of earlier immigrants. The role of immigrants as active agents is at the forefront of such theories. Immigrant organizations and the geopolitical sites of their activities and political positioning have been at the center of contemporary literature on the new immigration. Current theory highlights the nature of agency and activism of immigrant groups, noting the significant role immigrant organizations have on "home politics." Scholars such as Basch, Schiller, and Szanton Blanc (1994) and Duany (1994) have advanced interpretations of immigrant communities. They have defined immigrants' invariable pull to "home" as *transnationalism,* interpreting this kind of purposeful involvement with their country of origin as *the* tool (and political strategy) through which immigrants gain a sense of empowerment.

Scholars writing about transnationalism argue that contemporary immigrants are identifying and positioning themselves between "home" and "host" countries; that is, although their daily existence occurs in their "host" country, their social, political, and economic existence continues to be in their "home" country. Some would argue that immigrants are reconfiguring their place, circumventing marginalized spaces in their "host" countries by building their social, political, and economic capital in their "home" countries. In this process, they create a new sense of community, nation, and identity. In a recent text about Dominican immigrants in Boston, Peggy Levitt (2001) describes this new space as a "transnational village." According to Levitt, people on both geographic ends of this village form part of one social and political space, with most efforts aimed at developing the neighborhoods that émigrés left in the Dominican Republic. These types of studies offer insights into a historically overlooked pattern of immigrant politics.

The idea that immigrants somehow abandon all connections to their familial, social, and political relationships in their home country once they settle in a new host country has been confronted and disproven. On the other hand, scholars focusing on transmigrant activity do not sufficiently analyze the extent to which immigrants organize in ways that are not transnational. Recognizing these limitations, Levitt and Waters (2002) also suggest that there is a need for further research to determine the extent to which second-generation immigrants participate in this transnational space.

Contextualized within and beyond theories of transnationalism and community organizing, this study shifts the direction of research on immigrant politics to include an analysis of relationships that immigrant organizations have with local (that is, U.S.) politics and people of color, while reconsidering previous interpretations of community and immigrants' identities and connections to their country of origin. I explore the nature of local organizing activities, examining the roots and routes of political efforts evident in the Dominican-American neighborhood of Washington Heights. Many of the organizations established by this population have, since their inception, worked to confront and change issues they face in New York: funding for public education, local environmental hazards, health concerns, bilingualism and English as a second language instruction, underemployment, lack of representation in local government, civic participation, and so on. The role of the second generation in these organizations has been crucial for the development of community organizing. Although local organizers and the major organizations—including those on which this study is based—have their distinct missions and fields of activity, they all appear to share similar goals of involvement in local and U.S. politics. These organizations have charted roads toward institution building in Washington Heights, engaging in and developing community and community-building efforts in multiple and converging ways, often invoking "home" in a manner that contradicts some of the focal points of current theory.

To date, there have been few accounts of the Dominican presence in local politics. In the studies that exist, Dominicans are generally seen as either transnational actors (see Levitt 2001; Grasmuck and Pessar 1991; Duany 1994) or local Dominican-American actors (see Hernández and Torres-Saillant 1998; Ricourt 2002; Georges 1984). Of the two paradigms, the transnational has been used more frequently to define the Dominican community. For example, two recent qualitative studies on Dominican-American politics declare that Dominicans comprise a truly transnational village (see Levitt 2001; Grasmuck and Pessar 1991). My research suggests a rather different focus and conclusion. I build on the work of those who dedicate much-needed attention to the local-actor perspective. The local-actor perspective does not necessarily deny the existence or importance of transnational work. Scholars focusing on local work choose to provide much-needed analysis of the ways in which new immigrants work to build communities, institutions, power, and culture in the United States.

Dominican-American organizers have established a strong local presence in New York, embarking on a new era of "power from the margins," to borrow Milagros Ricourt's phrase (2002). Authors such as Ricourt (2002), Ricourt and Danta (2002), and Hernández and Torres-Saillant (1998) discuss the different ways that Dominicans participate in local political and cultural spheres. They agree that Dominican immigrants are establishing power in politics and community development. They concur that this is a politically astute community with substantial background in organizing and civic participation. Nonetheless, their work, along with that of others who examine immigrant community politics, does not analyze the role of the second generation in local organizing. They have left the question of the second generation, their identities, and their political behavior open for further investigation.

The Second Generation

A new body of literature has emerged under the auspices of scholars such as Alejandro Portes, Rubén Rumbaut, and others. Though it does not address the second generation's role in local politics, this new literature seeks to address questions regarding the "new second generation," their identities, and their prospects for social mobility in the United States. Scholars such as Portes, Rumbaut, Zhou, and Waters have developed a theory of segmented assimilation in their studies of the new second generation. Central to their theory is a discussion of the second generation's identity choices. Portes and Rumbaut identify three possible avenues of assimilation that contemporary second-generation immigrants can take: They can assimilate into white America (a seemingly impossible task for most contemporary immigrant groups); they can identify with and assimilate into "native minority" groups, namely Puerto Rican, African-American, and Mexican-American, a choice that leads to "downward assimilation"; or they can remain rooted almost exclusively in their immigrant group, maintaining a "co-ethnic" identity.

Proponents of segmented assimilation theory argue that it is in the best interest of the new second generation, and of their immigrant communities, to maintain a "co-ethnic" identity and lifestyle that revolve around their own national ethnic group. They give a positive prognosis in terms of successful economic and social mobility for those who remain attached to the "co-ethnic." Although these authors appropriately dispel any remaining fragments of a straight-line assimilation approach and insist that race was a crucial factor in the assimilation of earlier European immigrant groups, I argue that these contemporary analyses are limited. Implicit in their work is the assumption that people maintain strict adherence to a bounded, unchanging, homogeneous community—either that of white America, that of native minorities, or that of co-ethnics. Furthermore, in their assessments of "native minority" groups, they present a picture of a permanent underclass. These contemporary accounts also suggest that identity choices are the most important factors in social and economic mobility for the new second generation. Moreover, they do not adequately consider the ways in which second-generation populations inhabit numerous spaces, or identities, simultaneously. As I will argue later in the text, the spaces occupied by second-generation Dominican-Americans include other people of color, and this has been a crucial component of the manner in which Dominican-Americans have constructed local power and political capital.

To summarize, mainstream literature on immigrant communities in the United States, particularly that examining organizing efforts, points to the transnational or co-ethnic strategies utilized by both first- and second-generation immigrants. In this study I seek to move beyond these approaches by exploring the process by which activists become involved in local politics and the ideologies that lead to and support their participation in these efforts.

Dominican-American Politics: Coming of Age in New York

During the period between the 1970s and 1990s, when Dominicans became the majority population in the northern Manhattan neighborhood of Washington Heights, New York City was undergoing massive economic upheaval. Working-class New Yorkers were hit especially hard by the erosion of the manufacturing industries in the northeastern United States. Yet ethnographic work demonstrates that people are creative and find ways—within the context of the social, economic, and political restrictions they face—to participate and intervene in this process. It was during this period that Dominican activists began to feel that the task of organizing and obtaining resources for the community rested on their shoulders and that they were best equipped to represent the Dominican immigrant community in local politics. They began to participate in local civic projects to garner power. Although such participation can constitute a form of resistance, it can also easily become a form of accommodation (Kelley 1996; Sacks 1988; Jones 1987).

While most Dominican leaders who participated in this study express their commitment to working to benefit the community, they have charted two distinct paths toward this end. Some have accommodated to local political machinery in order to obtain grants and other resources for local community development and service delivery. I refer to those who emphasize this direction as the *ethnic entrepreneurs.* I label those in the other organizing trend as the *community mobilizers.* Community mobilizers base their work on the assumption that community empowerment requires work from a grassroots level and that empowerment can be accomplished only if local residents take it upon themselves to demand resources and simultaneously challenge state policies.

All community leaders believe it is important to focus their efforts on local issues. They all believe that the state must provide more resources to enable Dominican economic, social, and political growth. And regardless of the organizing ideology to which they subscribe, organizers understand the importance of working with other people of color. Their methods and ideologies may differ, but a critical reading of the modes of political engagement and participation would suggest that people, no matter their circumstances and position in society, struggle to have a say in their own lives, their communities, and the processes that affect them. And they do so using various strategies and ideologies. It is therefore not surprising that Dominican-American activists would use various strategies in their efforts to garner power for the community.

To focus on community-based organizing is to tell the story not only of these organizations and their constituents, but also of the possibilities for a new democracy built from the ground up. Marable's (2002) assessment of civic participation among the working poor and unemployed is pertinent in this discussion of immigrant community organizing and contemporary social movements. He notes, "In the postindustrial cities of America . . . the decisive battleground has shifted from the workplace to the living space," and many disenfranchised people "express their political activism through civil society rather than in trade unions or formal electoral political parties. These small-scale, ad hoc, grassroots organizations represent a 'great well of democracy,' an underutilized resource that has the potential to redefine our democratic institutions" (2002: 222).

It is imperative that we continue to examine and understand contemporary immigrant organizing. Not only will we learn about the "new immigrant politics," but we also stand to learn about the new possibilities for democratic movements in this country. The issue of "the color line," as William E. B. DuBois analyzed it a century ago, resonates today. Its relevance and enduring legacy are particularly clear when we embark on a study of politics and power in the United States. An examination of the new immigrant politics necessitates an excavation of race and racialization and of the ways in which racialized groups challenge these processes.

Ethnicity, Race, and Community Mobilizing

In the past ten years there has been an increase in the literature that examines panethnic identities and coalition building. Scholars working in this vein examine the ways in which immigrants of color broker identities with other marginalized groups in the United States (see Jennings 1994; Espiritu 1992; Ricourt & Danta 2002; Torres & Ngin 1995). They argue that groups organize around these panethnic identities for the explicit purpose of empowerment (Bonus 2000).

Social scientists have tended to explore identity from either a primordial or an instrumentalist stance. In an attempt to move beyond the limitations of these approaches, Rick Bonus' (2000) ethnography of Filipino-American politics highlights Rodolfo D. Torres and ChorSwang Ngin's (1995) primary thesis that when people identify themselves as one collective or when they associate themselves with other racial/ethnic groups, they do so for political empowerment. Torres and Ngin define this identification as "ethnicity for itself." They argue that today's racialized immigrant and "native minority" groups (or "racialized Others") forge commonality under a unifying (racialized) ethnic category, such as Latino or Asian-American, to promote and protect shared goals and to create a space of inclusion and civil rights (17), an analysis in which Manning Marable (1994) concurs. This process is one of renegotiating and redefining the group's relationship with the dominant society. It is also a process that can lead to alliances across traditionally defined racial and ethnic lines. Bonus explains that this "instrumentalist view" allows us to understand the development of a panethnic/pan-racial identity. He suggests that this type of identity arises from the "circumstantial manipulation of identities" by individuals gathering as one to suit their collective interests. Bonus' discussion of the ways in which these processes have taken shape within the Filipino-American population of California points to identity formation as a "set of claims about ethnicity and nationhood" (Bonus 2000: 16). These issues, along with how identities enter local political efforts, are taken up in this text.

Guide to the Text

The book is organized around key issues of identity,[3] political mobilization, and community building. Before delving into the ways these processes take shape in Washington Heights, I offer, in chapter 1, an analysis of recent research on immigrants and the new second generation. Matched by a now-voluminous and ever-expanding documentary literature, the growth of communities of post-1965 immigrants and their children marks a historical watershed. There has been a recent surge in scholarship on immigrant communities. As noted earlier, one of the foci of this literature is contemporary immigrant politics and immigrant transnational activities. Another focus is the second generation and their ethnic "choices." This chapter sets the stage for understanding Dominican-American politics in Washington Heights, New York, by bridging the gaps in current literature.

Chapter 2 offers an overview of the physical and social landscape of the neighborhood that served as the site of my research. Washington Heights' history, its resources, and its contemporary demographics provide the context within which local Dominican organizing operates. Chapter 3 outlines the political developments in the Dominican Republic and in the United States that serve as the backdrop to migration trends and Dominican-American community building and political participation.

Chapter 4 presents a chronological account of major organizing trends in Washington Heights, paying close attention to developments since the 1980s. In this chapter I challenge the transnational framework presented thus far to describe the Dominican immigrant community and offer a chronological analysis that explores the development of community power in conjunction with Dominican collaborations with other people of color. I argue that a series of factors converged during the 1980s that allowed Dominicans to imagine a Dominican political space developed in consultation and in solidarity with other organizers of color in New York.

Chapter 5 highlights the work of the Dominican-American leadership. Today's leadership is diverse in age, gender, class background, and, most important, in ideology. Though all the leaders described in this text focus their energies on New York– or U.S.-based issues affecting the Dominican community, they have generally emphasized one of two ideological paths to meet the needs of and garner power for Dominicans. This chapter illustrates these two ideological tendencies—ethnic entrepreneurship and community mobilizing—through the use of life histories, political statements, and community-organizing events.

Chapter 6 delves into an analysis of the new second generation and the ways they identify themselves, their communities (as Dominican, Latino, Black, and people of color), their racialized place in this society, and their work in politics. The manner in which they use different identities and establish coalitions across racial and ethnic lines is a driving force in this analysis.

Second-generation Dominicans are using a variety of methods and allies to address local needs and concerns. In chapter 7 I present two projects in which

Dominican-Americans are involved. Their involvement in these interracial/ interethnic collaborations tell us about the ways in which Dominicanness, local Dominican politics, coalitions, and diaspora come together as Dominican-Americans contend with conceptualizations of race, nation, and power in the United States.

A Note on Terminology

Numerous phrases used in this text require early definition. One of the key distinctions made in the literature on immigrant communities is that of first, 1.5, and second generations. The first generation is commonly understood to be the group who embarked on the emigration process as adults. Their children are referred to as either the 1.5 or the second generation. The 1.5 generation, as explored by Gustavo Pérez-Firmat (1994), defines those young immigrants who were born in one country and then spent their formative years in the country to which their parents immigrated. Scholars such as Sánchez (1993), Portes (1996), and Waters (1996) conclude that this generation stands in a unique position, as they spent some time in their country of birth but their teen years were shaped by life in a new land. *Second generation* is a term used to refer to those born to immigrant parents in the host country. The second generation is distinguished from the 1.5ers because their entire life experience is through the lens of a life lived in the host country.

For the purposes of this study, I do not distinguish between the 1.5 and second generations. Instead, I use *second generation* to describe Dominicans who arrived in the United States as children, as well as those born in the United States. For my analysis, the distinction between these groups is not necessary, particularly in light of the fact that as young people of color in the United States, they face the same processes of economic disenfranchisement, racialization, and sociopolitical marginalization regardless of their generation-based status. While the ideologies they adopt may be influenced by their experiences of life in one particular society (that is, either the Dominican Republic or the United States), I argue that it is their experience as young people of color in the United States that is most pertinent in their understandings and ideologies around race and politics in the United States.

I do, however, distinguish the second generation from the first generation. When using the term *first generation,* I am referring to the immigrants who embarked on their journey to the United States as adults. I also use this term to distinguish between the "old guard" immigrant leaders who were activists in the Dominican Republic and the "new second-generation" leaders whose politicization began and developed primarily in the United States. I do not make these distinctions to suggest that they are disparate and disconnected populations with distinct ideologies. That would displace arguments of the macro-level context of political developments of a community through time. I make the distinction only for the sake of clarifying the ages and historical trajectories of these actors. Rather than seeing these two generations as disconnected and acting upon generation-specific ideologies, I examine the ways that they have developed politics in Washington Heights together. The two generations continue to interact considerably in local and national Dominican politics.

The uses of the terms *Dominican* and *Dominican-American* also require brief definition. *Dominican-American* is generally used to identify individuals who employ an ideology that leads them to focus their organizing in and for Dominicans in the United States. The term *Dominican* does not, however, imply the inverse. That is, defining someone as Dominican does not suggest that he or she is a transmigrant disengaged from civic life in New York. When discussing transnationalism or people involved in this process, I refer to them as Dominican transmigrants. The distinction between *Dominican* and *Dominican-American,* therefore, denotes the strong political inclinations of the person so labeled, with the latter term denoting strong identification with U.S. organizing.

Another set of terms that needs clarification is *African-American, Black,* and *Latino. African-American* and *Black* are used interchangeably at times, though *African-American* is popularly employed to distinguish U.S. Blacks from other Black populations. I use *Black* to talk about all the people of African descent in the Americas, including African-Americans, West Indians, and Dominicans. The term *Latino,* like Dominican-American, is used in this book as a political identity. It describes people with roots in Latin America or the Spanish-speaking Caribbean now living in the United States. There is still ample debate surrounding the use of this term (see Oboler 1995). Because it encapsulates so many different national groups with distinct histories, this category can obscure many important aspects of individual national groups; for example, Dominican history and immigration experiences differ greatly from those of the Cuban population. Using the term *Latino* can, unfortunately, gloss over such important distinctions. Yet, as I will demonstrate later,

Latino is an important political identity for Dominican-Americans organizing with or seeing themselves as a part of a broader body politic in the United States.

It is with these terms and many other tools in hand that I present just one of the many stories of resistance, community building, and empowerment found in the neighborhood of Washington Heights.

1

Scholarly Demarcations

New Typologies

Immigration, immigrant groups, and their modes of incorporation (including political incorporation) have long been subjects of social science inquiry. Some scholars have placed their studies within the context of urban studies and globalization (Alba 1985; Muller 1993; Rischin 1962), others within the field of community studies (Whyte 1943; Handlin 1951; Gans 1962; Mahler 1995), while still others have emphasized civic participation, transnationalism, or both (Kasinitz 1992; Jennings 1994; Hernández and Torres-Saillant 1998; Trueba 1999; Torres and Velázquez 1998). This text draws on all these interrelated bodies of scholarship to provide a multi-stranded account of Dominican organizing in Washington Heights. This chapter presents an outline of the major theories around which issues of contemporary immigrant communities, their identities, and their politics have been constructed. As noted in the introduction, we are currently at a historical juncture with regard both to the post-1965 immigrant populations in the United States and to the scholarship about these new groups. The new, ever-expanding literature on the new immigrant groups and the second generation is beginning to set roots in the canon. This is an important moment to assess, critique, and reinvigorate scholarly demarcations and the typologies proposed to describe new immigrant communities.

The questions guiding my assessment of the recent literature include, What theories have social scientists constructed to explain the manner in which contemporary immigrant communities establish political activity? How have scholars typically categorized immigrant organizing? To what degree does this literature account for the ways in which immigrant communities, such as the Washington Heights Dominican-American population, enact politics located in U.S. society? How has the literature explained race and its relevance for today's immigrant communities, particularly with respect to the second generation? And, finally, to what extent have scholars writing about new immigrants and the second generation examined the ways these populations identify and work across ethnic and racial lines?

Much of the contemporary literature on immigrant communities dispels the assumptions of straight-line assimilation theory and the melting-pot metaphor in describing the incorporation of immigrant groups into U.S. society. Since 1965, the majority of immigrants have been people of color. They arrive from Latin America, the Caribbean, Asia, and Africa in larger numbers than before. They settle in major cities throughout the United States, facing very different economic and political topographies than did earlier waves of immigrants. Racial discourse, though salient in debasing earlier southern and eastern European immigrant groups, has a particular sense of permanence for contemporary immigrant groups. That is, whereas earlier immigrant groups were extended avenues to white privilege through programs such as the GI Bill of the post–World War II era (see Sacks 1994; Ignatiev 1995), institutionalized racism is unlikely to permit today's immigrants the same privileges born of whiteness. Faced with marginalization, immigrant groups do not easily "melt into" U.S. society, but neither do they remain passively accepting of their secondary status in this society. Contemporary scholars examining immigrants highlight these points and analyze the strategies they believe immigrants employ under such conditions.

Transnationalism

During the past decade, scholars of immigration have developed a new analytic perspective to describe the ways in which immigrants adjust to their new countries of residence. Their analyses center around the concept of transnationalism. Social scientists employing this perspective (see Basch, Schiller, and Szanton Blanc 1994; Duany 1994) have established working groups, created funding for a new body of scholarship, and published numerous articles and books on the subject—enough perhaps to call it a new wave of research or even a new school of thought. They challenge the notions inherent in assimilation discourse, which proclaims that immigrants eventually become part of the great "melting pot" of the United States (Portes and Bach 1985; Basch, Schiller, and Szanton Blanc 1994). Today's scholars recognize the ways in which race and racism, as well as economic and employment trends, affect immigrant groups differently. Based on this understanding, they posit that contemporary immigrant groups are not only unable to follow the same assimilationist path of earlier waves of European immigrants, but that they also make attempts to accrue power across borders by acting as transmigrants (Basch, Schiller, and Szanton Blanc 1994; Grasmuck and Pessar 1991).

Taking off from Gloria Anzaldúa's critical political theory of borderlands (1987), researchers such as Gilbertson (1992), Duany (1994), and Schiller, Basch, and Blanc-Szanton (1992a, 1992b) suggest that contemporary immigrants straddle two geopolitical regions in distinct and creative ways, that they live betwixt and between two or more nation-states. Their studies point to the ways in which immigrants forge and sustain multi-stranded social relations —relations that link their societies of origin and settlement in particular and meaningful ways. Nina Glick Schiller, Linda Basch, and Cristina Blanc-Szanton state that contemporary immigrants are, in fact, "transmigrants" in-volved in transnational processes "when they develop and maintain multiple relations—familial, economic, social, organizational, religious, and political— that span borders. . . . The multiplicity of migrants' involvements in both the home and host societies is a central element of transnationalism. Trans-migrants take actions, make decisions, and feel concerns within a field of social relations that links together their country of origin and their countries of settlement" (1992a:ix).[1] This body of research on transnationalism dis-places the assumptions of earlier work on immigrants and assimilation. Re-searchers argue that today's immigrants are not bound by static notions of the nation-state. This conceptualization of transnationalism includes an under-standing of the processes through which immigrants build social, political, and economic fields that cut across geopolitical boundaries of the nation-state. Though the somewhat romanticized notion of "border-free" movement exists only for a select wealthy or powerful few (see Torres-Saillant 2000a), the literature frequently portrays all immigrants as members of this new "trans-migrant" class, even to the point of describing their lives as existing in a "trans-national village" (Levitt 2001). Silvio Torres-Saillant suggests that this reading of contemporary immigrants and state control overlooks the lives of many immigrants who struggle to survive economically and socially in their new home countries (2000a).

Nonetheless, scholars such as Schiller, Basch, and Blanc-Szanton state that immigrants today are active transmigrants and "take actions, make decisions, and feel concerns, and develop identities within social networks that connect them to two or more societies simultaneously" (1992a: 1–2). These authors identify six premises that, they believe, situate transnationalism in time, space, world systems, and sociological theory: The first is that "bounded social science concepts such as tribe, ethnic group, nation, society, or culture . . . limit the ability of researchers to first perceive, and then analyze, the phenomenon of transnationalism" (5). The second is that the transnational reality is "inextricably linked to the changing conditions of global capitalism and must be analyzed within that world context" (5). The third element of transnationalism is that, like all cultural processes, it is "grounded in the daily lives, activities, and social relationships of migrants" (5). The fourth defining element hinges on the notion of identity constructs. The authors explain that transmigrants "live a complex existence that forces them to confront, draw upon, and rework different identity constructs—national, ethnic, and racial" (5). Given this process of identity and ideological shifts, they suggest that we must "reconceptualize the categories of nationalism, ethnicity, and race" (5). This fifth element of transnationalism demands that we "reformulat[e] our understanding of culture, class, and society" (5). The sixth element of transnationalism rests on the understanding that transmigrants are in dialogue with "hegemonic contexts, both global and national" (5). Transmigrants are affected by these contexts but, perhaps more important, they also reshape these contexts (Schiller, Basch, and Blanc-Szanton 1992a).

Politics and the Transmigrant

An essential element of today's transnationalism, which one can argue, distinguishes it from past eras, is the multiplicity of involvements that transmigrants sustain in both home and host societies. This framework urges us to begin to understand and document the agency exhibited by such individuals and populations.

Demonstrating this population's agency is critical when we consider that immigrants are enmeshed in and in dialogue with the structures created by world capitalism. The limited labor markets open to these new immigrants have made it almost impossible to secure social, political, or economic bases in the mainstream United States (see Hernández 2002). Many working-class (and working poor) immigrants have found employment in the service sector;

clerical jobs; low-wage manufacturing or garment industries; or the underground economy of sweatshops, street vending, child labor, and piecework, which offer low pay, few if any benefits, and employment insecurity (Kwong 1996; Waldinger 1989). If we take the example of New York City, where many immigrants continue to relocate, it becomes apparent that economic and social "integration," or "assimilation," has not been the possibility it was for early twentieth-century European immigrants in the United States. Transnational theorists would contend that exclusion from better economic and social positions in the United States has led today's immigrants to opt to improve their positions and involvements in their home societies by becoming active transmigrants.

In efforts to document immigrant agency through transnational activity, scholars have provided qualitative accounts and case studies of various immigrant populations, focusing considerable attention on immigrant ethnic and political associations (see Basch 1987; Basch, Schiller, and Szanton Blanc 1994; Georges 1987; Graham 1997; Kasinitz 1992; Sassen 1987; Schiller et al. 1987). This literature often points to two main functions of such organizations: (1) reproducing and maintaining "ethnic distinctiveness," and (2) maintaining communication with and activities in the home society (Basch, Schiller, and Szanton Blanc 1994; Kasinitz 1992). For example, in his account of West Indian voluntary associations in New York City, Philip Kasinitz (1992) states that such associations have "taken only small and tentative steps toward becoming involved in New York political affairs" (122), while key leaders attempt to solidify a "West Indian" identified presence in local politics. Pamela Graham (1997) describes the ways in which Dominican (elite) immigrants have begun to involve themselves in local, New York political endeavors. She points to the U.S. census of 1990 and ensuing political debates in New York City over redistricting. Her study examined the manner in which Dominicans participated in the debates that culminated in the creation of a new city council district in Washington Heights.

The dramatic growth of the Dominican population in the neighborhood of Washington Heights sparked a citywide debate and subsequent geopolitical alterations. The creation of the Dominican-dominant City Council District 10 was clearly a significant factor in the local elections of 1991, in which the first Dominican was elected to city office. Larger political and economic forces structure the experiences and activities of this and other immigrant populations.

Scholars researching immigrant organizations conclude that regardless of the site of political activity, immigrant groups maintain an exclusive national ethnic identity. Furthermore, transnational endeavors afford immigrants an empowering role in contemporary politics. However, an analysis of the history and continuing development of immigrant organizations invites an additional interpretation. Within the body of literature on immigrant organizations and enclaves are a number of studies that point to the heterogeneous nature of community and community politics (Schiller et al. 1987; Guest and Kwong 2000). I argue that in the past twenty-five years many Dominican-American organizers have forged alliances to build a broad political network. This network includes people of color, including people identified as "native-born minorities"—African-Americans, Puerto Ricans, and Mexican-Americans. Furthermore, many Dominican organizations have been focusing their activities around issues in New York. The election of immigrants to city and state government—with Councilman Guillermo Linares and Assemblyman Adriano Espaillat as the principal examples from the Dominican community—is one result of such organizing shifts. These developments flip the old assimilation model on its head. Studies have not yet examined the degree to which such processes reverberate in the experiences of the children of immigrants, the second generation.

The Second Generation

If we were to accept that the first generation focuses on empowerment via transnational efforts, could we draw the same conclusion for the second generation born or raised in the United States? Is the second generation rooted in an identity and mode of action that extend into their parents' country of origin? To what extent are they rooted in an immigrant co-ethnic community? Do they move beyond these communities? What do the results of these identity choices mean for the contemporary process of assimilation? And what do these processes tell us about race and power in the United States?

An emerging body of interdisciplinary research is directing our attention to the new second generation (DeWind, Hirschman, and Kasinitz 1997; Grasmuck and Pessar 1996; Portes 1996; Valenzuela 1999; Waters 1996). Continuing in the same line of thought as studies of transnationalism, this new literature correctly challenges the idea that immigrants follow set modes of incorporation and assimilation through the generations. Scholars suggest that the earlier straight-line assimilation model is not a valid tool with which to measure immigrant progress today. On the contrary, in order to achieve upward mobility in social, economic, and political realms, today's second generation has to make strategic choices of ethnicity, particularly given contemporary patterns of socialization and their effects on new immigrants. For this population, given its racial composition, assimilation into middle-class white America is not feasible in the way it was for European immigrants (see, for example, Sacks 1994; Ignatiev 1995). Assimilation today must take a different route, according to this literature. Alejandro Portes (1996) states that asserting and maintaining a strong, virtually exclusive co-ethnic niche is the most productive strategy for contemporary racialized immigrants and their children. That is, although the second generation cannot blend into middle-class white American society, they can achieve an important degree of upward mobility if they hold on to their ethnic identity and community. It is within these cultures and self-ascribed identities that today's racialized second generation finds the social and moral capital necessary to succeed.

In light of limited economic and social options and racial discrimination, the second generation will have to make strategic ethnic choices to overcome the barriers set before them. Portes and Zhou (1993) assert that within this process, called "segmented assimilation," the second generation has three options for social mobility:

1. "acculturation and parallel integration into [the] white middle class";
2. "permanent poverty and assimilation into the underclass"; or
3. "rapid economic advancement with deliberate preservation of the immigrant community's values and tight solidarity" (Portes and Zhou 1993: 82).

Portes (1996) correctly argues that the first option is virtually unattainable for immigrants of color. He argues that the second option leads to "downward assimilation," in which the second generation grabs hold of an "oppositional identity" and stance that curtails the options of those within this subculture. He argues that it is within the third option that the second generation will be able to create a path to successful mobility in this country. Many second-generation populations residing in immigrant neighborhoods in cities such as New York live in poverty and in close proximity to native-born people of color —including Puerto Ricans and African-Americans, populations that Portes and colleagues identify as part of the underclass. To advocates of the segmented assimilation model, such environmental circumstances can easily paralyze the mobility of second-generation youth and their communities. In contrast, maintaining a close identity with the immigrant community will allow second-generation youth to advance in their educational careers, stay away from drugs and other vices, obey their parents, and become honorable and successful citizens.

In an article describing the educational success of Vietnamese second-generation youth, Min Zhou and Carl Bankston (1996: 200) explain, "Despite close proximity to urban ghettos and attendance at often troubled urban schools, many of these children have been able to succeed in school through the use of the material and social resources that their families and ethnic communities make available."

The characteristics they believe "shield" these impoverished youth from the "ghetto underclass" that surrounds them lie within their ethnic groups and families:

> In disadvantaged neighborhoods where difficult conditions and disruptive elements often are found, immigrant families may have to preserve traditional values consciously by means of ethnic solidarity to prevent the next generation from assimilating into the underprivileged segments of American society in which their community is located. . . . Ethnic social integration creates a form of capital that enables an immigrant family to receive ongoing support and direction from other families and from the religious and social association of the ethnic group. Consequently, community standards are established and reinforced among group members, especially among younger members who may otherwise assimilate into an underclass subculture. (Zhou and Bankston 1996: 218)

There is no question that support from a close-knit community and family unit is an important factor in the life of youth (see Kozol 1991; LaGuerre 1984). And Portes correctly identifies the roles of discrimination and xenophobia (Portes and Rumbaut 2001a). For example, Portes and Rumbaut (2001b) document that Mexican immigrants consistently earn less than other immigrants and native-born populations with the same education and labor skills. They explain that nativist discourse and discrimination "undermine successful adaptation" (279). Second-generation immigrants must contend with these processes of discrimination. "Challenged to incorporate what is 'out there' into what is 'in here' and to crystallize a sense of who they are, they translate themselves and construct a variety of self-identities" (190). As they contend with external processes of discrimination, racialized youth will attempt to construct self-identities that help them make sense of the world around them.

Despite these contributions, numerous elements of the theory of segmented assimilation beg reanalysis. The assumptions underlying various aspects of this theory have already been contested in the social sciences. The concerns I have about this new literature revolve around three important concepts: the assumption of bound and static communities; of race, poverty, and the underclass; and of the nature and significance of identity choices and interethnic/interracial identification (see also Pierre 2004).

Bound Communities

Transmigrant communities span two or more nation-states. Proponents of segmented assimilation assume that immigrants automatically belong to only one cohesive co-ethnic community, with the second generation deciding whether or not to cross that identity border. Although both concepts allow for immigrant agency and individual choice in selecting the way they define their community, there is still a need to revisit the idea of community borders and cultural change.

Inherent in the concept of co-ethnic community maintenance is the implication that an immigrant group consists of a single, unified cultural body with set cultural components transferred from one generation to the next. These scholars (see, for example, Zhou and Logan 1989) frequently overlook the various class and power struggles that affect an ethnic niche or enclave and those within it (Kwong 1997; Guest and Kwong 2000). The assumption that new immigrant groups automatically establish egalitarian, prosperous ethnic enclaves is currently a matter of considerable debate (see Guest and Kwong 2000; Sanders and Nee 1987). For example, Peter Kwong (1997) demonstrates that key political and economic figures within the Chinese immigrant community in New York have controlled and exploited their less prosperous co-ethnics in a variety of ways.

Early understandings of the concepts of community and of culture assumed a homogenous, static, isolated population (see, for example, Mead 1949; Malinowski 1922). The idea that entire communities were bound and did not change permeated much early anthropological writing (Wolf 1982). In contrast, scholars such as Oliver Cox (1948) and W.E.B. DuBois (1935) pointed out that not only were specified groups of people, or communities, heterogeneous and stratified, but they were in a state of constant change, often due to internal and external influences. These external influences included processes of capitalism, capitalist exploitation, and institutional racism— forces that continue to shape society and local communities today (Castells

1997; Mollenkopf and Castells 1991). However, contemporaries of Cox and DuBois presented analyses that ignored macro-level processes. The mainstream perspective focused instead on ethnic groups and their internal composition and function; this perspective continued in the later work of scholars studying immigrant neighborhoods (see, for example, Whyte 1943; Gans 1962). The paradigm that ignores the ongoing effects of macro-structural processes also predominates in today's literature on second-generation immigrants.

As early as 1969, in his introduction to *Ethnic Groups and Boundaries*, Frederick Barth warned social scientists of the dangers in assuming preconceived, biologically based definitions of ethnic groups. In early anthropological literature, scholars frequently defined an ethnic group as a population that was biologically self-perpetuating; shared basic cultural values; made up a field of communication and interaction; and had a membership that identified itself, and was identified by others, as a distinguishable, separate group (Barth 1969: 10–11). Barth contested this popular understanding of groups and society. He declared that this perception of ethnic groups failed to problematize or imagine a different concept of boundaries and their formation, thereby impeding our understanding of society and culture. Instead, Barth offered a concept of ethnic groups that included analysis of how members of such groups identified themselves *in relation to others*. From this vantage point, interactions between people came to center stage.

Barth (1969) went on to elaborate processes of group interaction, describing, for example, the ways in which members of one ethnic group might *individually* select membership in different ethnic groups. Although Barth's work set the stage for agency in ethnic identification (because individuals could choose to "pass," accept a minority status, or emphasize their ethnic identity), his formulation did not leave much room for hybridity or the formation of multiple identities in the context of racialization and exclusionary practices—a feature I argue exists in Dominican-American organizing in Washington Heights.

Although scholars of segmented assimilation allow for the possibility of second-generation individuals changing their ethnic identity, the implication is that they would move from one particular and bound community or ethnic group to another. Furthermore, there is an assumption that each ethnic group shares one unified culture to which all members adhere and that this ethnic community and its culture are self-perpetuating and remain the same over time.

Poverty and the Underclass

As already noted, scholars examining the new second generation acknowledge the roles that race, racism, and contemporary economic developments play in shaping the dim prospects many impoverished immigrants of color confront. In the introductory pages to the seminal text *The New Second Generation* (1996), Alejandro Portes acknowledges that "members [of the new second generation] confront the same reduced circumstances in the American labor market affecting domestic minorities. Most second-generation youth are also nonwhite and hence subject to the same discrimination endured by their predecessors" (5). However, proponents of segmented assimilation theory do not examine the long-term effects of such macro-level processes on immigrants and the new second generation. Instead, they focus on understanding immigrant communities' inherent cultures. Portes states that "immigrant families and communities commonly possess material and moral resources that confer advantages on their young as they seek avenues for successful adaptation." Given the limited opportunities presented them, their social mobility "depends decisively on the resources that their families and ethnic communities can bring to bear" (Portes 1996: 5).

Segmented assimilation theorists posit that inherent in the cultures of immigrant communities are the tools members need to circumvent these marginalized social positions and succeed in the wider society. However, they fail to fully examine the role structural and sociopolitical factors might have in maintaining poverty among the so-called native-born minority groups. Instead, they offer a description of an underclass steeped in poverty and in a culture that limits its members' mobility, placing the emphasis on group culture, rather than structure, as the root of poverty. The authors are clear in their view that if today's second generation identifies with and becomes part of the minority underclass culture, their communities will not gain the social or economic mobility of immigrants that came before them. Not only does this perspective erroneously assume successful social mobility for all previous white immigrants, but it also attributes the success or failure rate to self-identity, self-esteem, and other individual characteristics.

Linking poverty to a deficient culture—as is evident in discussions of the underclass—is not new in social science inquiry. Neither are the critiques of this assessment of impoverished groups. The assumptions about the underclass—which authors such as Portes (1996) identify as Puerto Rican, African-American, and Chicano—are the same as those of Oscar Lewis more than four decades ago. It is, once again, "old wine in new bottles" (Mullings 1977). The idea that the "oppositional identity" of native-born minority groups limits their chances of mobility implies a kind of culture of poverty (see also Pierre 2004). These arguments underplay the social science data demonstrating that social conditions, rather than innate propensities, lead to differences in group behavior and life chances. So began Eleanor Leacock's 1971 critique of the culture of poverty arguments.

The culture of poverty theorists based their argument on a few major assumptions. The first was that an autonomous subculture exists among the poor. The second was that this subculture and its poverty are self-perpetuating and self-defeating and that there exists a sense of resignation or fatalism within the subculture. Following this, culture of poverty scholars posited that individuals in this subculture were unable to plan for the future, choosing rather to seek satisfaction of their immediate needs. These (decontextualized) characteristics were then linked to and presented as though they alone caused low educational motivation and achievement, high unemployment, poverty, and despair. Take, for example, Daniel Patrick Moynihan's report, *The Negro Family: The Case for National Action* (1965). Moynihan argued that the "tangle of pathology" which characterized the Negro community "was 'capable of perpetuating itself without assistance from the white world.' Its basis was to be found in the Negro family, which 'once or twice removed ... will be found to be the principal source of most of the aberrant, inadequate, or antisocial behavior that did not establish, but now serves to perpetuate the cycle of poverty and deprivation'" (11).

Although contemporary scholars developing the theory of segmented assimilation may not make claims as crude as those of Moynihan, their model implies similar claims about native-born people of color living in poverty.[2] I argue that the main assumptions of the culture of poverty—delineated and critiqued by Eleanor Leacock (1971) and others in the 1970s—are found in a slightly revised form in today's literature on the second generation. While modern scholars recognize the role of lack of job opportunities in pushing youth to one identity or another, they nevertheless accept Wacquant and Wilson's (1989) thesis of the "hyperghetto," the "veritable human warehouses where the disappearance of work and the everyday reality of marginalization led directly to a web of social pathologies. Proliferation of female teenage pregnancy, high involvement of youngsters in crime, and the disappearance of work habits and discipline are common traits in these areas" (Portes and

Rumbaut 2001b: 59–60). And they warn that identification with such a culture will not benefit second-generation youth and their communities.

Contemporary authors writing about the new second generation continue to reproduce these assumptions, though theories about intergenerational poverty and social isolation have undergone a radical critique (see, for example, Vincent 1993; Maxwell 1993). The structures that create poverty continue, so poverty persists. In a postindustrial society where jobs are scarce, unemployment or underemployment are increasing, and the social safety net has been nearly abandoned by the state, poverty will persist.

As Delmos Jones (1993) insisted, however, poor people not only attempt to survive through poverty, but they consistently attempt to move beyond poverty. Unfortunately, attempts to achieve are not always positively correlated with success. Through ethnographic work, he demonstrated that this is not due to inherent flaws in the culture(s) of the poor, who work at the local level and challenge supralocal institutions in their attempts to secure access to education and work for themselves and their children (Jones 1993; see also Sharff 1998). Many scholars have demonstrated that the idea that the success or failure of ethnic groups rests on internal family and community characteristics is quite problematic. Contemporary scholars' adherence to the idea that Black, Puerto Rican, and Mexican-American communities represent inherently pathological subcultures of poverty is not only flawed, but continues to portray stereotypes as scientific fact. Ideologies and theories that stigmatize people of color continue to play a central role in maintaining class, race, and ethnic inequality and injustice. As Mullings states in a challenge to stereotypic portrayals of Black women, "by constructing them [that is, stereotypes] as 'natural' rather than social and historical, these representations justify the continued oppression" (Mullings 1997: 125).

Proponents of the segmented assimilation model only briefly outline race, racism, and structural factors as elements to consider when analyzing the reasons why contemporary immigrant groups face difficult conditions. They then move into theories about the central role of culture and moral resources found (or missing) within individual cultures in determining social and economic mobility. As in Oscar Lewis' writing, the structural issues they allude to early on, therefore, become virtually invisible by the final analysis. That is, although they acknowledge the way in which racism denies contemporary immigrants access to assimilation into the white middle class, they fail to examine the way in which racialization processes construct the parameters around which today's second generation will attempt social, economic, and political mobility. Furthermore, although they point out that the U.S. economic system and labor markets are not as prosperous as they were a century ago, they fail to examine the extent to which this situation significantly curtails upward social mobility for any urban working-class population.

Identity

Another issue that one must reexamine in light of recent literature about the second generation is the degree to which identity choices influence or determine social mobility. Scholars such as Portes and Waters emphasize the importance of identity selection in predicting the social mobility of today's racialized immigrant groups. This exclusive emphasis on identity choices can easily lead us in the direction of suggesting that cultures or groups of people are inherently adept or inept at achieving success in this country. Take, for example, the theory that identifying with African-American culture will lead today's second generation to a path of downward assimilation and limited social mobility, whereas maintaining a strong identification with their immigrant community will lead them to achieve social and economic mobility. These assumptions ignore the role that macro-level processes have in circumscribing the experiences (and life chances) of today's immigrant groups. Many of today's second-generation populations, with roots in Latin America and the Caribbean, are racialized by society as "Black" or "Latino." They face institutional discrimination and contend with its long-term effects.

As I will demonstrate, given the diversity in residence patterns and daily social interactions of the second generation in urban centers like New York, Portes and colleagues' inflexible view of culture and racial and ethnic classification becomes problematic. That is, if the second generation attends school and maintains networks that are racially and ethnically heterogeneous, how do they retain their identity as co-ethnics at times, while simultaneously embracing relationships and identities with members of other ethnic and racial groups —those identified by these authors as "native minorities" or "the underclass"? Their framework does not allow for an understanding of such variance or its context and ultimate significance. Carlos Pierre, the twenty-four-year-old Dominican organizer in Quisqueya United, illustrates this complexity when he declares himself Dominican, Latino, and Black, seeing no contradictions in this conglomerate of social and political alliances.

How others identify you becomes an important element in personal and political arenas. Consider another example, that of José Mendoza, a seventeen-year-old second-generation Dominican living in New York. He is described as "black but not quite black enough for many African-Americans, very Latino but not light enough to matter to most Hispanics, American in every way but at the same time inexorably foreign" (Escobar 1999: A21). In self-referential instances, someone like José can be Dominican, Latino, Black, Afro-Latino, American, or any combination of such identities. And I will demonstrate that in other instances where ascribed identities affect their relationships and experiences with other groups—for example, in encounters with the New York Police Department—self-identification may be irrelevant, as was the case with Abner Louima and Amadou Diallo (for further examination, see Pierre 2004). Current research on the second generation has not fully considered such issues.

Relationships and ties to native-born minority groups, an affiliation some suggest is not embraced by first-generation immigrants (Waters 1996; Kasinitz 1992), may prove to be an important and empowering option for this second generation, particularly in organizations. My research demonstrates that many Dominican-American organizers use this strategy to help inform their work. The relationships Dominican-American activists develop with other people of color—whether they take the form of momentary interethnic/interracial coalitions, prolonged panethnic/pan-racial identities, or anything between these points—are an important, and perhaps essential, element of Dominican-American organizing. This possibility complicates the co-ethnic strategy emphasized in recent immigration literature discussing both the first and second generation.

Conclusion

In sum, many of the assumptions inherent in contemporary immigration and second-generation studies have been contested in anthropology and elsewhere. Community-studies scholars have challenged the idea that ethnic groups (or any group) are bounded within temporal, cultural, or geographic spaces. We have also moved toward an understanding of the ways in which supralocal institutions and macro-level processes affect the lives of people in all locales, an understanding particularly relevant for immigrants and people of color (those identified as "native-born minorities" by Portes). And scholars examining grassroots organizing have noted the important opportunities that interethnic/interracial collaborations present to all involved. Nonetheless, social theorists writing about the second generation assert that maintaining a strong, virtually exclusive co-ethnic niche is the most productive strategy for contemporary racialized immigrants and their children, because it allows them to capitalize on otherwise unavailable material, moral and social resources.

In a 1973 position paper, Anthony Leeds laid the groundwork for a revised conceptualization of community, or locale, studies (see also Jones 1987). He advanced the same underlying arguments that DuBois ([1899] 1961) and Cox (1948) had set forth decades earlier: In analyzing any site, we must develop models that allow us to view "(a) the institutions of the territorial state, (b) the social unit—the community, and (c) the human-geographical unit—the locality, in a single frame of reference and as a single, systemic totality" (Leeds 1973:15). This analysis focuses on the link between the microcosm and the macrocosm, and on the relations between local populations and larger economic, political, and social processes. Not only are local units connected to these processes, but their interactions (and at times, their direct interventions) can significantly alter the locale and affect what happens in external institutions as well. In fact, we must focus our attention on the interactions within and between localities, and on the ways that supralocal institutions affect the locale and the opportunities available to their members.[3] When studying immigrants in cities today, we need to look at the ways they are affected by and interact with global economic and political developments, local and state institutions, and other local populations.

It now goes without saying that a highly complex web of contested and ever-changing individual and institutionalized relationships characterizes any given locale. This constitutes the base from which a locus of power forms. Such local power can be used either in cooperation with external agencies and institutions or as a tool with which to resist "against the encroachments of the supralocal institutions. It is also the basis for the emergence of the true community" (Leeds 1973: 24). In response to their relationships with these and other forces, people in distinct communities based on race, geography, or "imagined" solidarity (Anderson 1983) have forged social movements to combat oppressive forces and to create paths to access much-needed resources. Although scholars of the "old left" have focused on social movements fashioned by the proletariat, others, such as Piven and Cloward (1977), have targeted the many ways that impoverished communities mobilize to act in response to state policies. Contemporary scholars (see Castells 1982, 1983, 1984; Gregory 1998; Hale 1997; Jennings 1994, 2003; Kelley 1996; Sharff 1998) have now turned their attention to the ways that people in grounded geographic communities struggle to create grassroots mobilization aimed at altering the physical landscape of their communities, the communities' access to resources (employment, housing, government funding, and so on), their relationships with larger state and federal institutions, and the impositions of various macro-structural processes in the lives of their communities (see Kelley 1996).

Those who advance these conceptualizations and utilize a historical process analysis (Rosaldo 1993) enable us to understand how communities and their efforts at mobilization change over time. This particular framework is crucial in any study of immigration today. As historical and political climates change through time, so too do communities. The theories concerning the creation of the nation-state and of contestation, malleability, permeability, and imagined community and cohesion are easily adopted in studies of local immigrant communities. Scholars have looked at how people in one locale consider themselves part of a larger community, how they create differing notions of community, and how, through constant renegotiation and conflict, their community continually changes. In various articles about community organizations in New York, Delmos J. Jones (1982, 1987, 1993) outlined the ways that people organize themselves as a political community to demand resources for members of their neighborhoods. Ida Susser has analyzed similar processes of institutionalization and local agency through her work with women in New York (1986).

People continue to work to affect change within and outside the regulated parameters established by these institutions (Beck 1982; Piven and Cloward 1971). José E. Cruz writes, "Empowerment begins when the perception or experience of social, economic, and political inequity leads citizens to organize and mobilize" (1998: 12). In what ways do Dominican activists in Washington Heights engage in this process? What role does the second generation play in this endeavor? And to what extent do they change how the Dominican-American community, particularly its organizers, identifies itself vis-à-vis other communities of color in New York? It is to these questions that I will address the history and ethnography contained within this text.

2

El Alto Manhattan

The Setting and Research Context

Before we can understand organizations established by Dominicans in Washington Heights, we must first know the neighborhood in which they carry out their work. In order to fully appreciate the histories and development of community-based organizers in any locale, one must understand the broader context with which they are in dialogue. Dominican activists had clear agendas and developed organizations in Washington Heights during particular moments in the history of New York and the United States. They consistently interacted with the local neighborhood, other non-Dominican communities, the city of New York, the larger state, and in some cases, the Dominican Republic and its leadership. In this chapter I offer an overview of the neighborhood setting—its geographic and sociopolitical landscapes. This includes a brief introduction to the organizations that form the subject of this study.

Washington Heights: Becoming el Alto Manhattan

In the two weeks leading up to the weekend of February 27, 2000, Washington Heights was marked with declarations of a Dominican-American political presence. Large white posters with blue and red lettering announced an upcoming conference, at which participants would draft a "Dominican-American agenda." Walking through Washington Heights that winter, it was impossible to miss the poster campaign throughout the neighborhood. Dominican

Nation, a group of young second-generation Dominicans, had been organizing this conference for three years. That winter, groups of young, primarily male organizers from the organization armed themselves with posters and heavy-duty staplers and marched through the area to announce the upcoming conference, posting the signs on lampposts across the neighborhood. The grassroots effort aimed to bring together Dominicans from all sectors— elected officials, members of community-based organizations and churches, business owners, scholars, activists, and "everyday people"—to discuss issues confronting the community and to collectively draft an action plan to address their numerous concerns (see chapter 4).

The goal of the poster campaign was to draw in Dominican masses from around Washington Heights. And in the minds of the activists of Dominican Nation, Washington Heights spanned Manhattan from 135th Street up to the bridges connecting Upper Manhattan to the Bronx. Identified as el Alto Manhattan by many and Quisqueya Heights by others, the Dominican portion of Upper Manhattan was easy to distinguish—one needed only to follow the blue, red, and white road paved by Dominican Nation's conference posters.

Washington Heights is located on the northern tip of Manhattan Island, atop hills and between rivers. Washington Heights is named after General George Washington, who lived in the area while directing the battle against the Hessian troops during the Revolutionary War in 1776. The city of New York demarcates the neighborhood by various districts: School District 6, Community District 12, and City Council Districts 7 and 10. Community District 12 encompasses the neighborhoods of Washington Heights and Inwood. In fact, people often include Inwood in their description of Washington Heights. The city of New York created City Council District 10 after the 1990 U.S. census revealed the massive growth in the Dominican population in the neighborhood (see Graham 1997). Given the census analysis, local leadership argued for redistricting to divide what was previously one electoral district into two.[1] The new district was carved through the center of Washington Heights, with the old District 7 bordering it to the east and west. The new district also included Marble Hill, a southern section of the Bronx located just north of Washington Heights/Inwood. The new district was overwhelmingly Dominican, a fact that helped catapult a Dominican into the elected leadership of New York City government; in 1991 Guillermo Linares became the first Dominican to represent the neighborhood on the New York City Council.

Washington Heights' officially defined geopolitical borders frame the neighborhood between 155th Street and 200th Street, and between the Hudson and

East rivers. As I have already suggested, however, everyday cultural and socio-political borders stretch the neighborhood twenty additional blocks north and south of these official divisions. This is due in large part to the fact that the Dominican population and its flourishing businesses share families, networks, language, and other resources across this broad physical space. Dominicans claim and transform businesses and public spaces throughout this area. Their daily activities extend into northern sections of Harlem and all of Inwood. In a recent *New York Daily News* article, journalist Leslie Casimir traveled through the public space Dominicans inhabit in northern Manhattan:

> On any given summer weekend, Sylvia Perez swears she's back home, surrounded by the sights, sounds and tastes of her native Dominican Republic. She can smell the pork sizzling in cauldrons of oil. She hears the lilting merengue and the nostalgic chatter of her fellow Dominicans. Perez spends many of her weekend days relaxing in a concrete lot at [Riverbank State] Park . . . where a merengue riverside party has been drawing hundreds of homesick Dominicans for more than a decade. . . . With large stereo speakers blasting away, the area is transformed into a New York version of the popular stretch known back home in Santo Domingo as El Malecón—The Seawall. . . . The crowd manages to make the best of the Dominican Republic come to life here—a joyous place far away from the cramped walkups in Washington Heights. The partygoers are miles from immigration problems and the financial stress related to supporting families on two shores. At this Malecón, the Hudson River serves as the backdrop, standing in for the Caribbean Sea. Shiny sport-utility vehicles and vans—all loaded down with musical instruments like metal guiras and bottles of the national rum, Brugal—jam the riverside. "This is a small piece of Dominican land," said Perez's son, William, 30, who was born and raised in Washington Heights. "We have created this paradise." (Casimir 2000b: 22)

It is clear that Dominicans utilize areas of Harlem regularly. Though not always applauded or warmly accepted by the longtime African-American residents of the neighborhood, Dominicans use and transform areas officially part of Harlem, such as Riverbank State Park, into Dominican spaces. Activists and politicians also recognize parts of Harlem as Dominican. They often practice politics across this wide geographic span of Dominican life in New York (as apparent in Dominican Nation's conference poster campaign of February 2000). Throughout my period of fieldwork, organizers and youth from various organizations carried out voter registration drives in the neighborhood, including in areas officially part of Harlem. During the 2000 Dominican presidential elections, local chapters of the parties of presidential hopefuls organized massive caravans through Washington Heights, often stretching the parade-like troops from 135th Street up into the heart of the neighborhood, 181st Street. In the summer of 2001, one of the leaders of Dominican Nation, Osiris Robles, organized a caravan as part of his campaign for the city council seat Guillermo Linares was vacating. The caravan, totaling more than seventy cars, began just south of the official Washington Heights–Harlem border. In light of this locally specific understanding of the neighborhood, in this text, when referring to Washington Heights I include all the neighborhoods that local residents define as part of Quisqueya Heights or el Alto Manhattan. Unless specified otherwise, I am referring to Washington Heights proper, Inwood, and West Harlem from 135th Street north.

Urban Landscapes: Resources and Change

Washington Heights has gone through various periods of urban development, with the most significant physical and social developments occurring during the past century. The neighborhood remained semirural and sparsely populated until the end of the nineteenth century. Development in the area occurred in sudden spurts, with different sections receiving attention during the early and middle decades of the twentieth century, and major economic and urban redevelopment being initiated in the past decade. Historian Steve Lowenstein cites the pre–World War I era as the time when the southern and eastern apartment buildings were erected, and the 1920s and 1930s as the period when most of the houses in the northern and western sections were built (Lowenstein 1989). This real estate development coincides with other historical developments; namely, the completion of two prominent subway routes and the influx of new waves of European immigrants. The IRT, now more commonly known as the 1/9 subway line in Washington Heights, completed in 1904 and extended into Inwood in 1906, cuts across the easternmost sections of the neighborhood. The building that occurred during the first two decades of the twentieth century coincided with the movement of many Irish, German, and eastern European immigrants into the area along the IRT subway route from the southern regions of Manhattan to the north.

During the Great Depression urban development slowed in the area. However, as part of President Franklin D. Roosevelt's Works Progress Administration, the city constructed the Eighth Avenue "A" subway line. This new line connected the western and remaining northern sections of Washington Heights to the city, allowing people with a bit more wealth to build and acquire residences in the more scenic western and northern sections. By the end of this era of major development, Washington Heights was a sea of buildings, and as Ira Katznelson (1981) points out, a diverse community of immigrant groups —Greeks, Jews, eastern European, and Irish—and class-based divisions, with the wealthier residents living west of Broadway and to the north, and the working-class immigrant majority residing in the southern and easternmost sections of the neighborhood.[2]

Washington Heights is home to a significant amount of park space; about one-third of the neighborhood's landmass is preserved as parkland. The New York City Department of City Planning lists twenty-six park sites, totaling 626.52 acres, in Manhattan Community District 12; all of the district's parks are maintained and supervised by the New York City Department of Parks and Recreation. Washington Heights houses more park space than any other neighborhood in Manhattan, with Inwood Hill Park in the north, Fort Tryon Park in the west, Highbridge Park in the east, Riverbank State Park and Riverside Park in the southwest, and various local parks and recreation spaces throughout the area. These parks provide local residents with refuge from Manhattan's perpetual traffic of people, vehicles, and general city chaos. Residents use the parks for general recreation, birthdays and other celebrations, concerts, and athletic league competitions. A recent wave of immigrants from Central America who live or work in the neighborhood have established soccer leagues, which hold games on weeknights and weekends in the local parks, with women and children picnicking, socializing, and occasionally cheering from the sidelines. Many of the parks—including Riverbank State Park, a park that extends over the southern border of Washington Heights into West Harlem—host annual Dominican festivals and other community celebrations (see Casimir 2000b).

Neighborhood residents complain that neither the city nor fellow community members contribute enough of their energy and resources to maintaining these parks in suitable condition. Walking through these parks, one can easily find beautification projects next to areas of neglect and deterioration. In Fort Tryon Park, for example, flowerbeds are evidence of attempts at beautification, yet one need walk only a few minutes in another direction to find paths paved with broken glass, garbage, and even fields of abandoned auto parts. Residents have discussed such extremes of maintenance during monthly meetings of the

Community Planning Board 12. The neighborhood's parks suffer the consequences of the city's disinvestment in its public spaces. In 2000, the Parks and
Cultural Affairs Committee of Community Planning Board 12, the local community planning and policy board,[3] drafted the following resolution:

> Community Board 12, Manhattan, calls upon the Mayor, the Borough
> President, its local Council Members and candidates for these offices to
> commit to allocating and spending 1% of the City's annual expense
> budget on the operations of parks Citywide to ensure: regular mainte-
> nance of all facilities, sufficient personnel to ensure safety and enforce-
> ment, programming to engage our youth and seniors, and the efficient
> and equitable use of the City's resources.

Although I have not studied issues regarding public spaces in depth, participant observation suggests that although this neighborhood has not been
able to generate the private or individual donations necessary to refurbish the
parks, the public's perception and use of the local parks have shown some signs
of improvement. During the eight years I have lived in the neighborhood, I
have observed more people using the parks' trails and playgrounds, as well as
the open spaces that are ideal for large events and concerts. Many local
groups—including school and youth groups—organize periodically to help
clean up portions of the parks.

In addition to natural park space, Washington Heights is also home to a
variety of other resources, including three branches of the New York Public
Library, twenty-one day-care facilities with space for 1,070 children, three
Head Start facilities with space for 140 children, countless licensed home
child-care centers, seven residential facilities for adults and families with a mix
of 509 beds and single units, twenty-three food programs and drop-in centers,
nine facilities for seniors, and innumerable religious centers and places of
worship. Of the quarter-million people living in the neighborhood, approximately 33 percent are under the age of twenty-one, most of whom are still in
the public school system. Seventeen public elementary schools, in which
16,782 students are enrolled; six public intermediate or junior high schools, in
which 8,119 students are enrolled; and two public high schools, in which 3,220
students are enrolled, serve the scholastic needs of the area (New York City
Department of City Planning 1999). One of these schools, Gregorio Luperón
Preparatory School, was designed to serve newly arrived Spanish-speaking
immigrant youth. The school's principal and staff have roots in community
movements in the Dominican Republic and New York, and many teachers and

staff from this school are heavily involved with events organized by Dominican Nation.

There are also a total of fourteen private schools: ten elementary schools with 3,060 students, one school serving 434 students in K–12th grade, and three senior high schools enrolling 960 as of 1999. Given that most high school students of Dominican descent living in Washington Heights attend public schools, the one general high school located in the neighborhood—which serves both the immigrant and U.S.-born or English-proficient students—can accommodate only a fraction of the resident student population (see López 2003). (The second public high school, with fewer than 500 students, serves newly arrived Spanish speakers only.) Many students therefore travel to schools in Harlem and the Upper West Side of Manhattan. Although students in the two organizations with which I worked attended a variety of schools, the majority were enrolled in the immigrant-focused preparatory school in the area; another public school in the neighborhood, in Manhattan Community District 7; or one public high school in Manhattan Community District 9.

Bringing Quisqueya to the Heights

Since the early 1960s Washington Heights has witnessed a surge in the Dominican population, which is the fastest-growing new immigrant group in the city. The population has grown considerably since the first major wave arrived in the early 1960s, in the post-Trujillo, post-U.S.-military-invasion era. The Dominican population residing in the city continues to grow (see table 1 for recent immigration trends). There are currently more than half a million Dominicans living in New York City (see table 2).[4] According to the 2000 U.S. census, the Latino/Hispanic population comprises 74 percent of the total population of Washington Heights; Dominicans represent 72 percent of that population and 53 percent of the total neighborhood population. Yet these figures are probably low because they do not include undocumented immigrants who may be living in the neighborhood or those who did not participate in the census count.

Puerto Ricans still outnumber Dominicans citywide, accounting for 10 percent of the total population and 38 percent of the Latino/Hispanic population in New York City. However, despite a significant and steady increase in the Latino population in the country and in New York City, the Puerto Rican population residing in the city is dwindling while the Dominican population continues to expand dramatically (see table 2). Between 1990 and 2000 the

Dominican population in New York City grew by over 200,000. This growth can be attributed to both new arrivals and to an increasing birth rate. Again, these numbers do not include undocumented workers residing in New York. In fact, other sources indicate the number of Dominicans in Washington Heights may be more than twice the official census count. The Dominican population is a relatively youthful group; those under the age of twenty-one accounted for approximately 36 percent of the population in 2000 (see table 3). Many in the second generation are becoming increasingly important actors in local organizing. These young people are shaping the community's perspectives on race and politics.

The Dominican population continues to grow in all the boroughs of New York City, particularly in Manhattan, Brooklyn, Queens (Ricourt and Danta 2002), and more recently the Bronx. Through their various migrations, they are undoubtedly changing the physical, social, and political landscapes of the neighborhoods they adopt as their own (Duany 1994, 1998; Hernández and Torres-Saillant 1998; Grasmuck and Pessar 1991). Dominicans have established numerous organizations in their new places of residence, and in Washington Heights organizers have founded and developed some of the largest and best-known nonprofit organizations. By addressing local issues through these organizations, Dominican-American activists have begun to take their place in New York politics.

Table 1. Immigration from the Dominican Republic, 1988–1998

Year	Immigrant arrivals in New York
1988	16,313
1989	14,625
1990	18,780
1991	16,515
1992	25,239
1993	24,667
1994	26,115
1995	19,945
1996	18,912
1997	13,410
1998	9,656

Source: U.S. Census, 2000.

Table 2. Racial and Ethnic Demographics in the United States, New York City, and Washington Heights, 1990 and 2000

Population	United States, 1990	United States, 2000	New York City, 1990
Total	248,698,332	281,421,906	7,322,564
White[a]	199,819,876	211,460,626	3,831,907
Pct.	(80.3%)	(75.1%)	(52.3%)
Black[a]	29,927,500	34,658,190	2,107,137
Pct.	(12%)	(12.3%)	(28.8%)
Hispanic	21,900,001	35,305,818	1,737,927
Pct.	(8.8%)	(12.5%)	(23.7%)
Non-Hispanic	226,798,331	246,116,088	5,584,637
Pct.	(91.2%)	(87.5%)	(76.2%)
Puerto Rican	2,651,811	3,406,178	861,122
Pct. of total	(1.1%)	(1.2%)	(11.8%)
Pct. of Hispanic	(12.1%)	(9.6%)	(49.5%)
Dominican[b]	520,151	908,531	342,357
Pct. of total	(0.2%)	(0.3%)	(4.7%)
Pct. of Hispanic	(2.4%)	(2.6%)	(19.7%)

Source: U.S. Census, 1990, 2000, 2004 CPS.

[a]Non-Hispanic

[b]The figures given for the Dominican population are highly contested. As it reevaluates demographics, the U.S. Census Bureau itself provides numerous documents with different statistical assessments of this population. For example, a 2002 census press release indicated that in 2000 there were 765,000 people of Dominican heritage living in the United States; a 2004 press release gave the revised figure of 908,531. A report by Ramona Hernández and Francisco Rivera-Batiz (2003) states that according to U.S. Census data the number of Dominicans living in the United States in 2000 was 1,041,910. Similar discrepancies exist for the 1990 New York City data, with the New York City Department of City Planning stating that there were 225,017 Dominicans in the city, while census figures give the number of 342,357. The same holds true

	New York City, 2000	Washington Heights/ Inwood, 1990	Washington Heights/ Inwood, 2000
	8,008,278	205,851	216,234
	3,576,385	80,970	61,655
	(44.7%)	(39.3%)	(28.5%)
	2,129,762	49,639	28,980
	(26.6%)	(24.1%)	(13.4%)
	2,160,554	136,541	159,456
	(27.0%)	(66.3%)	(73.7%)
	5,847,724	69,310	56,778
	(73.0%)	(33.7%)	(26.3%)
	813,539	20,037	14,411
	(10.2%)	(9.7%)	(6.7%)
	(37.7%)	(14.7%)	(9.0%)
	555,033	88,059	114,584
	(6.9%)	(42.8%)	(53.0%)
	(25.7%)	(64.5%)	(71.9%)

for the 2000 figures for New York City. The original census estimates suggested that 424,847 Dominicans resided in New York City; revised census estimates then gave 555,033 as the official number; the New York City Department of City Planning placed this number at 369,186; the 2003 Hernández and Rivera-Batiz report places this number at 554,638; and finally, a 2001 report issued by the Mumford Center for Comparative Urban and Regional Research at the State University of New York at Albany stated there were actually 602,714 Dominicans in the city. Furthermore, no accounts can be completely accurate, as it is difficult to gather information on the undocumented portion of the Dominican population living in the United States. What all the numbers do accurately suggest is that this population is growing rapidly.

Table 3. Washington Heights/Inwood Hispanic Population by Age Group

Age group (in years)	Total population 1990	Total population 2000	Percentage of total Hispanic population in specific age brackets 1990	2000
Under 5	12,470	12,211	24,544	25,881
5–9	12,074	13,670	(18%)	(16%)
10–14	10,687	13,077		
15–17	6,068	7,558		
18–19	4,368	5,361		
20	1,987	2,738	25,345	31,449
21	2,235	2,715	(19%)	(20%)
22–24	7,300	8,226		
25–29	12,786	13,093		
30–34	13,528	13,313	45,146	47,351
35–39	11,532	12,719	(33%)	(30%)
Subtotal			95,035	104,681
			(70%)	(66%)
40–44	9,894	11,868		
45–49	7,865	10,607		
50–54	6,768	8,860		
55–59	4,858	6,382		
60–61	1,798	2,367		
62–64	2,272	3,115		
65–69	3,157	3,991		
70–74	1,997	3,171		
75–79	1,577	2,078		
80–84	716	1,313	41,506	54,775
85+	604	1,023	(30%)	(34%)
Total			136,541	159,456
			(100%)	(100%)

Source: U.S. Census, 1990, 2000.

The Field of Dominican Politics in Washington Heights

Issues of identity politics, local organizing, and Dominican-American community building were evident throughout my period of fieldwork. Underlying all this work was an understanding of and confrontation with supralocal powers and processes. When I first began conducting fieldwork in the neighborhood in 1996, theories of transnationalism guided my assumptions; I imagined myself stepping into a community of political transmigrants, of activists shuttling politics back and forth between the Dominican Republic and New York. The path on which local organizers would take me, however, led in a very different direction.

Dominican-American organizers have created new forms of politics that focus on building power in order to address issues that the Dominican community faces in New York and in the United States. This became clear even to the casual observer or die-hard transnational scholar in February 2000, when Dominican Nation's national conference took place. On February 27, 2000, my day "in the field" began at five in the morning on the campus of City College of New York (CCNY) of the City University of New York (CUNY), a public city institution.[5] The night before, organizers of Dominican Nation had left their office, based at CCNY, around two in the morning. Many arrived on the campus once again at sunrise on the morning of the twenty-seventh. Once there, they involved themselves in a frenzy of last-minute logistical work, formal greetings, and speech preparations. We were there to celebrate a national conference aimed at forging a Dominican-American national agenda. Dominican Nation began preparing for and planning this conference in 1997. In the months preceding the conference, issues of community building, politics, and identity had been addressed in numerous ways. As I will detail in chapter 4, the Dominican Nation steering committee members had traveled to Washington, D.C., to meet with leadership from the National Council of La Raza, a Mexican-American policy and advocacy organization. They also solicited support from a prominent Puerto Rican political figure, the former president of New York's Hispanic Federation. This Puerto Rican organizer helped to plan Dominican Nation's national conference; he offered his organizing experience as well as access to his expansive network of organizers, foundations, and politicians. They communicated with and solicited participation from Dominicans' local leaders, such as those affiliated with Congressman Charles Rangel's office and the office of Manhattan Borough President C. Virginia Fields; from various organizations of color, such as the National Council of La Raza; from the Hispanic Federation of New York; and from Haitian organizations, such as Movimiento de Mujeres Dominico-Haitianas (MUDHA). Understanding the nature of this diversity of contributors and collaborators allows us a glimpse into the multiple ways Dominican organizers in Washington Heights use identity and political strategies to advance their efforts toward political empowerment. And as Manning Marable and Leith Mullings (2000: xiv) insist, "Politics begins at the moment when any group recognizes for itself its specific objective interests and aspirations, and seeks agency to realize those interests." The goals of the Dominican community in New York are numerous, though political empowerment seems to be the goal of all activists.

Methodology and the Field: Establishing Involvement

I began my research with an attempt to elaborate and refine current research on contemporary immigrants and community-building efforts. I was struck by academia's growing concentration on all that is transnational. As stated earlier, contemporary literature on immigrant communities emphasizes the transnational, or home politics, aspects of immigrant organizing, with the first generation as the focus of inquiry. I was interested in documenting the degree to which organizing in Washington Heights conformed to these paradigms, particularly given the growing second-generation population.

The original research design was aimed at examining the manner in which second-generation Dominicans influenced or altered community activism and community organizations in Washington Heights. The political nature of such participation was a given, as earlier research had already illustrated the ways in which community-based organizations in immigrant communities served as crucial intermediaries between the community and government (Gans 1962; Sánchez 1993; Handlin 1951, 1959; LaGuerre 1984). My goal was to uncover the processes by which and the reasons why second-generation Dominican-Americans in Washington Heights were becoming active in organizing and why they seemed to emphasize local issues. In my attempt to offer a diachronic and dynamic analysis of Dominican immigrant organizing in Washington Heights, I took on the task of researching the other side of the coin as well; that is, examining the ways that older, first-generation leadership had established organizational efforts. I had originally assumed a zero-sum game, in which I placed the first generation in the now well-recognized category of transmigrant politicos and understood the second generation to be focused on the local New York political environment. The fieldwork experience was to teach me more than I could have ever anticipated. When I arrived in the field, I thought I was operating with the open system of thought that David Nugent (1982) says is crucial for anthropological analysis. Throughout my period of work and research in the community, however, my field of vision expanded quite dramatically.

Although the official period of research for this study began during the summer of 1999, I had established close contact with the leadership of both organizations a few years earlier: with Dominican Nation in 1996 and with Quisqueya United in 1997.

Quisqueya United

Quisqueya United was established in the late 1980s, although the discussions about establishing this kind of organization began a few years earlier. During this era, one group, consisting primarily of individuals emanating from radical movements in the Dominican Republic, founded various organizations that would mobilize people in Washington Heights but still retain a consciousness about changing politics in the Dominican Republic. Another group of young activists saw the need to bring all existing Dominican clubs together. Although the historical memory of various actors is inconsistent, all concur that discussions about creating the organization that became Quisqueya United began in 1984 and that between 1985 and 1986 the core of the organization was established. Quisqueya United was founded on an initial plan to bring all the existing social, political, and recreational clubs under one large umbrella organization run by Dominicans in Washington Heights. One of the founders explained,

> We saw that here's the 27 de Febrero [a political/social club], here's El 30 de Marzo [another political/social club], and here's this and here's that, and they all had space which went underutilized. So we thought that through [Quisqueya United] we could serve as a funnel to begin utilizing these spaces and transforming these organizations to provide additional community services. So [Quisqueya United] was formed as an umbrella to network these organizations.

During Quisqueya United's earliest years, staff was primarily volunteer. In 1987, after it received its first major grant of more than $88,000 for a pregnancy prevention program, the current director was hired by the founding board of directors. This director, Abraham Pierino, is still the executive director of the organization. In 1988 the New York State Department of Substance

Abuse received money to fund programs to prevent HIV/AIDS among young people and awarded Quisqueya United $50,000. This new grant enabled the executive director and the director of programs to hire one more full-time staff member and two young, second-generation activists—Martín Guevara and Farabundo Márquez, both nineteen years old at the time—to work part time.

These two second-generation organizers started a youth after-school and leadership club in the basement of Quisqueya United office space. During these early days they brought in many young people, mostly young men. Gabriel Aponte, one of the lead directors of the after-school program today, explained,

> They were young just like us. I was 16 so, you know, it was like we could relate to each other. . . . We would sit there and play dominoes, play Monopoly . . . in those days we were at [Quisqueya United] at 12 at night.

The organizers report that the extent to which the youth present at that time felt "at home" and surrounded by people to whom they could relate was important in helping to build the organization. Staff and constituents recognized the need to develop more youth outreach. The executive director's work consisted of networking and acquiring additional funding to expand the organization's staff and programs. Although for some time volunteers led many of the programs in the organization, today all full-time staff are paid, either by the organization or, for temporary work, by an outside agency—for example, the New York City Summer Youth Employment Program and Work Experience Program.

After receiving some major grants in the late 1980s, the agency secured the narrow four-story building that continues to serve as its central offices. It also runs programs from three other sites in Manhattan and a recently established site in the Bronx. My fieldwork focused on the agency's youth programs, a particularly popular and strong area of the organization's work.

Dominican Nation

Dominican Nation was founded by a very young group of Dominican students living in Washington Heights. At the time they began meeting, these students ranged in age from thirteen to twenty-four. The leadership of this group had close ties with the first generation of left-wing militant activists from the Dominican Republic living in New York, particularly those involved with the Partido de Trabajadores Dominicanos (PTD), then a Marxist Dominican workers' Party, in the late 1980s. The same Dominican Marxists were part of the group that founded Quisqueya United.

During the summer of 1987, some of these youth activists traveled to the Dominican Republic's capital city, Santo Domingo, to meet with students on the island. The goal was to discuss the nature of youth activism and analyze the way that young people were treated in both societies. After a series of events and meetings, the New York contingent of this binational youth force established Dominican Nation in New York. Organizers held informal meetings where people discussed issues they felt needed to be addressed: education, after-school and recreational programs, and so on. The groups went on yearly retreats, either to a site in upstate New York or to meet with youth in the Dominican Republic, to discuss how they could work to establish programs and actions that would address pressing issues. Since 1996 they have operated primarily out of a student union office at the campus of CCNY.[6]

Although the New York chapter activities take place for the most part on college campuses, the majority of the organizers are college students and young professionals, and the constituents are still in high school. One of the main goals of the organization is to show the positive side of Dominican youths' lives and to foster grassroots strategies of empowerment. The organization's unofficial motto is "el futuro nos pertenece" [the future belongs to us]. In an effort to fulfill this prophecy, the organization established a program aimed at building an educated, dynamic community in New York. Dominican Nation has developed numerous youth, community, and educational programs, most of which emerged from the ideas of the organization's constituents and leadership. Although activities and initiatives have changed somewhat over the years, Dominican Nation's core programs include pre-university curriculum, theater and arts, leadership, and athletics (primarily basketball and volleyball). In recent years, they have also attempted to organize periodic community forums where community members focus on one issue they face in the neighborhood.

The pre-university, theater, and athletics programs take place on Saturdays. The events were held at Gregorio Luperón High School in Washington Heights during the early years. But in mid-November 1996, the events were relocated to the ballroom of CCNY and, for a brief period, to the gymnasium of a neighborhood church.[7] The decision to move the activities to a college campus was applauded by all participants. Many students report that being around the college campus gives them a sense of possibilities. Organizers have pointed to the fact that through working in the CCNY library and walking around the campus, students begin to see college as a viable option. Organizers note that these students are frequently discouraged from attending college and that being on the CCNY campus allows them resources and power so that they can ultimately make their own informed decision on postsecondary education.

As noted earlier in this chapter, in 1997 leaders of Dominican Nation (still a relatively young second-generation leadership) developed a national advocacy and policymaking agenda. During the period of my fieldwork they organized a national conference for the purpose of drafting a national agenda for Dominican-Americans. Since this conference, they have maintained a perspective of community development based on a number of premises. These include encouraging participation from all sectors of the Dominican community; forging alliances and consulting with other people of color throughout the city; and developing a new outlook to political action on a national level.

On Fieldwork, Subjectivities, and Political Engagement

I came to know organizers in Washington Heights in 1996 and 1997. In 1996 I traveled to the Dominican Republic to conduct research on the issue of politics and transnationalism. I interviewed key leaders in the PTD and the Partido Revolucionario Dominicano (PRD). Among the people with whom I spoke was the secretary of international affairs for the PTD. That summer he introduced me to two teachers who were directing Dominican Nation. One of the individuals, Osiris Robles, was a cofounder of the organization. He continues to maintain close contact with some of the leftist leaders from the old Marxist guard of the PTD. The other Dominican Nation organizer was Altagracia Santiago. In her early twenties, Altagracia joined the ranks of Dominican Nation after meeting Osiris as a student at CCNY; she soon became the volunteer director of the organization's pre-university program (in addition to maintaining full-time employment as a public school teacher). This particular summer she was in the Dominican Republic with a study-abroad program organized by CUNY. When I returned to New York I met with the leadership of the organization; soon thereafter they invited me to a youth leadership meeting. During my first visit to that Friday-night program, approximately thirty youth and four volunteer staff were present. After their regular meeting, I introduced myself and spoke about my interest in learning about Dominican youth and activism. Although they did not ask many questions during this first visit, they eventually asked me about my work, requesting details on the nature and goal of my research and how it might develop into something that could benefit the community. I have continued as a researcher and volunteer staff member in Dominican Nation for periods of time—a privilege for which I extend much gratitude.

I first met and interviewed staff and leadership of the other organization that became part of this study, Quisqueya United, in 1997. However, I first heard about the organization in 1994. At that time I was involved in organizing Muévete!, a Puerto Rican youth conference in New York City.[8] This was the second annual conference put together by a young group of New York Puerto Rican and non–Puerto Rican Latino and Latina activists. The conference addressed numerous Puerto Rican historical and contemporary political and cultural issues, such as the plebiscite in Puerto Rico, hip-hop, graffiti, and Puerto Rican arts in the community. Organizers attempted to attract the young Puerto Rican population and, in the process, also attracted large numbers of other Latino and Black youth. During this conference organizers publicly thanked two leaders of Quisqueya United, Martín Guevara and Farabundo Márquez, for their contributions to the conference. This was a significant introduction into the ways in which young Dominican and Puerto Rican organizers in New York City collaborated on community-specific projects. I did not meet the Quisqueya United leaders until two years later.

I met the two directors of a Quisqueya United Beacons site in the summer of 1996 through mutual friends who worked with them in solidarity efforts with Cuba.[9] In 1997, I was part of a city- funded education research team undertaking an evaluation of the New York City Beacons Initiative, an initiative I discuss more fully in chapter 4. I began making regular visits to the Washington Heights Beacons site, run by Quisqueya United. My role as evaluator, though formal, did not impede the creation of more informal and friendly relationships with key figures in the organization. Their knowledge of my history as an active contributor to various youth and activist efforts in New York and of my network of colleagues allowed for a congenial working relationship. After I completed the evaluations project, I lost touch with Quisqueya United.

When I began the research for this study in 1999, I reestablished communication with the directors of the Beacons site. Because we had met previously and because I had been involved with the activities of Dominican Nation, they were aware of my work and invited me to meet with them once again. During my first informal meetings with leaders at the site, they often joked that the evaluator was back, this time without the mask of scrutiny. They introduced me to their youth leadership group, their youth council, and, later, to their youth and community employment group. It is with the staff and membership of these groups that I had the privilege to work.

My official fieldwork, which began in the summer of 1999, came to a close sometime in late spring 2001. During these two years I conducted ethnographic and archival research in Washington Heights. I also traveled to the Dominican Republic with the leadership of Dominican Nation. My ambiguity about the end of the fieldwork period is reflective of my own political interests in the organizations with which I worked. Conducting ethnographic fieldwork with activists and organizations represented a unique opportunity to delve personally into some grassroots work, which I expect to continue in the future. My involvement in community organizations in Washington Heights has now taken a new road and I no longer take copious and exhaustive notes while "in the field," but I continue to learn from the organizations and the dedicated activists who run them.

During the official period of fieldwork, qualitative approaches included participant observation, structured and semi-structured interviews, focus groups, and family and life histories. Through extensive participant observation at various events, such as ongoing programs and activities, formal and informal meetings and events, weekly television programs, and conferences, I examined the foci of organizing among the generations of local Dominican activists. I conducted in-depth interviews and life histories with the directors and staff of two key organizations, open-ended questionnaires, focus groups, and informal interviews with membership of these organizations, and in-depth interviews, life histories, and community history interviews with local activists. I spent much of my time working with different groups within the organizations, usually after the school day finished at three in the afternoon and on Saturdays.

I complemented these qualitative approaches with archival research. In addition to interviews with first- and second-generation activists in the community, my analysis of local efforts was enriched by the collection of community documents and city data. Coupled with interviews with current leadership, these sources provided a comprehensive understanding of the history and continuing development of community organizations and their relationship to other communities of color and to local, New York, national, and translocal or transnational politics. The data collected through these diverse methods are weaved together throughout the text.

My involvement as a researcher in both Quisqueya United and Dominican Nation was clear from the beginning, as was my commitment to contribute to community organizing and youth programs. Due to the close contact I maintained with the two organizations, I was able to develop relationships of trust and camaraderie with staff and members that has made this research endeavor more complete and rewarding.

It is a daunting task to attempt to tell the history of activism and the stories of activists in Washington Heights. There were many times my legitimacy was challenged because I did not grow up in the neighborhood (I am of the Queens and Long Island Latina variety); my parents are not Dominican (to some, particularly older male leaders, this meant that I could never truly understand Dominican politics); and I am not a "veterana" (when I began the official fieldwork period, I was twenty-six years old). While these facts are all true, the extent to which they limited my ability to document and understand political activism in the neighborhood was not something I worried about. I was, and still am, more concerned with portraying truths in community politics, with respectfully documenting a long trajectory of activists and activism in Washington Heights, and with presenting an analysis that will help us understand the paths that Dominican-American activists are charting, which will allow us to view the roads that began decades ago and will surely carry much weight in the future.

My experience in the field was not what I anticipated as a newcomer to the discipline of anthropology. No one could have forewarned me of the complex nature of the processes of research and activism. I would not have understood the many responsibilities to which I had just committed myself. This project became exhaustive, complex, and enriching, extending its reach to the professional, personal, and deeply political realms of my life. In the midst of this whirlwind of activity and careful observation and maneuvering, I was able to develop one interpretation of the history and continuing development of youth and community activism in Washington Heights. It is this interpretation that I present here and that I hope will contribute to the eradication of malicious or unprofessional misreadings of the community in both popular and academic discourse. I do not pretend to know all that has led to activism as we see it today in Washington Heights, nor do I expect anyone to take this text as the only story of community politics. This is my reading based on fieldwork and active participation in community organizing in the neighborhood.

In the process of conducting this research, I was fortunate in many ways, not the least of which was finding a responsive, active, engaged, and welcoming group of people who forgave my daily intrusions and allowed me to ask questions and, in my own small way, assist them in their work. My working relationship with members of the two organizations allowed me to develop a level of camaraderie and trust for which I feel very honored. The degree to which these working and friendship ties extended into life and work beyond this research made for a very distinctive (and privileged) perspective on local politics. I felt particularly grateful when I noticed that these local leaders' interactions with other researchers tended to be more formal and, I suspect, temporary. The director of one organization expressed resentment toward the many researchers, particularly Columbia University journalism students, who "took information" from the organization and never returned to share the results of their research. Having established first a personal commitment to local youth organizing and then maintained a daily presence in the sites of research, I enabled organizers and participants to view me differently than most other researchers. I was touched at the way people welcomed me as part of their organizations and their lives, allowing me to participate in their personal celebrations as well as their moments of grief. The life histories I collected were also very personal and intense, though they had the feel of deep conversations with longtime friends. This was made possible, in part, by my extended presence, assistance, and political activity in the community. I can only hope that my interpretation of local organizing and politics adequately represents what was happening on the ground. In many ways, this book is about my travels with people and through a community I've now adopted as my own.

3

Politics and the Dominican Exodus

Mass migration from the Dominican Republic to cities such as New York occurred within the context of major economic and political upheavals in the
Caribbean region. It is not possible to understand Dominican organizing
without first addressing this history. This chapter provides a brief sketch of the
history that shaped the Dominicans' exodus from their home country to the
shores of New York City. The first major wave of Dominican immigrants arrived in the 1960s after the 1961 assassination of dictator Rafael Trujillo led
to political instability and eventual U.S. occupation in 1965–1966, when the
United States established a consulate's office to issue passports and the 1965
immigration reform laws were passed. In the late 1970s and 1980s this immigrant population began to concentrate in northern Manhattan.

Today, Dominicans clearly constitute the majority in Washington Heights,
leading many to refer to the neighborhood as el Alto Manhattan or Quisqueya
Heights, Quisqueya being the precolonial Indian name for Hispaniola. Since
they began arriving in New York, Dominicans have established community
centers, social clubs, and local chapters of political parties and organizations.
Many who arrived as political exiles had formed part of the Marxist revolutionary groups in the Dominican Republic. When they first arrived, they were
primarily involved with organizing to change the political scene in the Dominican Republic. With the realization that the Dominican community was
setting roots in New York, however, coupled with the growth and influence of
the second generation in local organizing, this first generation of activists
helped to establish some of the best-known organizations in Washington

Heights. This chapter aims to explore the history behind these Dominican movements—revolutionary politics and the migratory waves.

Sugar, External Debt, and Mass Migrations

As I noted previously, Washington Heights has been home to various immigrant groups throughout the twentieth century: Irish, Jewish, Greek, German and German-Jewish, and more recently Dominicans. The majority of Dominicans now living in the United States arrived within the past four decades. Various factors—namely government policies, economic trends, and mass mobilization—created the conditions for this recent exodus.[1] When discussing Dominican emigration, one cannot overlook the relationship that the United States has fostered with (and sometimes imposed on) this Caribbean country. More specifically, U.S. policy has fostered external dependency on and influence over the Dominican economy and state development policy. The effects of such processes of neocolonialism include high rates of poverty and out-migration.[2] Migratory flows throughout the Caribbean and Latin America are integrally related to these policies and processes of exploitation and dominance (Dietz 1986; Santiago-Valles 1994).

Economic and political turmoil in the Dominican Republic from the 1960s onward propelled much of the Dominican out-migration. Political developments and ensuing civic responses are intimately connected to economic processes and prospects. The case of the Dominican Republic is no exception. The economy of the Dominican Republic once depended on agriculture. And as Grasmuck and Pessar (1991: 26) note, it is "impossible to understand contemporary Dominican society without taking into account the development of the modern sugar plantations in the latter part of the nineteenth century." From the 1880s to the 1960s, the Dominican Republic was economically integrated into the world economy through exports of sugar, cacao, and to a lesser extent, coffee. Dominican export agriculture affected all segments of the Dominican population. With the virtual collapse of the agricultural sector and the installation of free trade zone manufacturing and informal sectors, out-migration became a means of economic survival for major sectors of the population.

Many of the essential characteristics of the Dominican sugar industry developed between 1900 and 1920. Between 1916 and 1924 this industry, one of the constant pillars of the Dominican economy, was brought under North American control. U.S. military occupation prefaced this economic takeover.

From 1916 to 1924 U.S. Marines occupied the Dominican Republic, assisting North American corporations in the appropriation of Dominican land for sugar cultivation. The U.S. military occupation also facilitated the rise to power of General Rafael Leonidas Trujillo as dictator in 1930 (Moya Pons 1995).

The U.S. occupation and economic takeover also initiated an era of sugar production that focused almost exclusively on export (del Castillo et al. 1974: 151, cited in Grasmuck and Pessar 1991: 26). During this period, landowner-ship became concentrated in the hands of a few. Local forms of subsistence agriculture were impeded through confiscation of land and excessive and un-equal bases of competition. Sugar industrialists opted to import cheaper labor from freed slave societies in the Antilles, leading to domestic unemployment (see Cassá 1982; Báez Evertsz 1978). When sugar prices dropped on the world market in the late 1920s and early 1930s, these industrialists began to rely more heavily on the even cheaper labor coming from Haiti. Haitian labor has con-tinued to play a central role in the harvesting of sugarcane in the Dominican Republic (Sunshine 1988; Báez Evertsz 1978; Plant 1987).[3] Many of the dis-placed subsistence farmers found themselves not only without land, but with-out adequate, steady employment.

The results included rural displacement and a growth in the agrarian labor surplus. Subsistence agriculture became virtually impossible for many rural landowners, and many small-scale landowners and agricultural laborers be-gan to migrate into the cities of the Dominican Republic; a select few from the elite classes also left for New York. The migration to New York, however, esca-lated precipitously after 1961, with the death of dictator Rafael Trujillo.

On May 30, 1961, Rafael Trujillo was assassinated by military personnel; Ramfis Trujillo, the dictator's son, took control of the country the following day, and the assassins went into hiding. Ramfis eventually rounded up all the purported Dominican assassins, their families, and their friends, ordering their torture and execution; some chose to commit suicide rather than face Ramfis' style of justice.[4] In October 1961, workers financed by the anti-Trujillist National Civic Union went on strike. Street riots erupted in Ciudad Trujillo (then the name of the capital, Santo Domingo). On November 19, 1961, under U.S. military guard, Ramfis Trujillo fled the Dominican Republic. As Trujillo left, the U.S. Atlantic fleet arrived in Santo Domingo's harbors. The Dominican military still exerted control over the country, attempting four coups d'état over the next three years. Popular uprisings developed into a civil war, and on April 28, 1965, the U.S. Marines arrived in Santo Domingo and took control of the country. One year later Joaquín Balaguer, under the auspices of the U.S. government, took over the government, beginning a new regime that would not end until the 1990s.

Migration from rural areas to urban centers such as Santo Domingo and Santiago escalated during the post-Trujillo era, as did the exodus to places such as the United States and Venezuela. Among the displaced were the families of some of the activists with whom I worked. Marcos Villegos, a longtime activist in Washington Heights, lived in a rural area of Peravia Province, just west of the capital, until 1964. In 1964, when Marcos was seven years of age, one of his older sisters decided to go to school in Baní, the capital of Peravia. She took Marcos to live with her. Her education and employment ultimately helped to support the family that remained in rural Peravia. Marcos was also expected to contribute to the family's subsistence. He remained in the city of Baní until he emigrated to New York City in 1980, at the age of twenty-three. Although Marcos was only four when the Trujillo era ended, he and his family lived through the economic repercussions of that period. He also became involved at a young age in organizations—particularly the Movimiento Popular Dominicano (MPD) and La Línea Roja, a group that grew out of the Movimiento Revolucionario 14 de Junio (MR-1J4)—that addressed some of the political chaos that followed Trujillo's assassination and continued in his successor's regime.

Fearing a successful socialist or communist revolution supported by the population, as had occurred in Cuba, the United States rallied its military to squash popular protests and rebellion in the country. "'No more Cubas' became the rallying cry of U.S. foreign policy in the 1960s. . . . The United States also showed itself ready to use covert and overt action against what were seen as 'new Cubas in the making.'" (Sunshine 1988: 52). During this period, both Dominican and U.S. authorities perceived Dominican out-migration as a safety valve, a strategy to curb political discontent and mass mobilization (Hernández 2002). John Bartlow Martin, the U.S. ambassador to the Dominican Republic at the time, took the initiative to grant a larger number of U.S. visas to Dominicans. Prior to this period, out-migration was nearly impossible, as few Dominicans were able to leave the Dominican Republic during Trujillo's dictatorship. Dinorah Rosa, a twenty-seven-year-old organizer in Dominican Nation, explained how her great-grandfather's position in Trujillo's military enabled her grandfather and his mother to move to New York:

He moved to New York when he was six [years old]. . . . My grandfather's father was the head of the police and the military at different times through the years of the Trujillo dictatorship. . . . His mother was one of the first people that had been allowed to move to the U.S., and that was sort of like a political caper. . . . [It was in] the early 1950s. You had to be allowed. Yeah, she was given permission.

Granting easier access to out-migration after Trujillo's regime was clearly an attempt to curb radical political mobilizations, to acquire a cheap labor force for U.S.-based industry, and to foster improved bilateral relations (Mitchell 1992; Grasmuck and Pessar 1991; Hernández 2002). In 1962 U.S. ambassador Martin established a new consulate building and appointed a new consul and three additional vice-consuls in the Dominican Republic (Martin 1966). Immediately following these actions, the number of immigrant visas issued by the U.S. consulate in the Dominican Republic increased; from 1961 to 1962 the number doubled, and from 1962 to 1963 it almost tripled (Mitchell 1992).

Out-migration continued during the Balaguer era. From 1966 to 1978, President Joaquín Balaguer's administration introduced an industrialization strategy based on protectionist measures, tariffs, tax exemptions, a legal dual-exchange market, and cheap financing for foreign-owned and foreign-run industrial activities. After 1974, due to the overall worsening of commodity export prices, the national economy declined. The capital-intensive production promoted by the government left many Dominicans without employment or economic prospects. The rising unemployment rate was exacerbated by the simultaneous deterioration in the real wages of those still employed. Then in the early 1980s, the severe depreciation of sugar, which was still the Dominican Republic's principal export, resulted in millions of dollars in lost foreign exchange for the struggling republic (Moya Pons 1995; Sunshine 1988). Unemployment rates continued to surge. The resulting poverty was a major causative factor in the exodus of Dominicans. The migration stream that began in the late 1960s increased throughout the 1970s and rose once again in the mid-1980s. New York City has been the destination of choice for many. To date, this city is home to more than half a million Dominicans. Washington Heights is home to the second largest population of Dominicans in the world, second only to the Dominican capital of Santo Domingo.

The Dominican Population in Washington Heights

On their arrival in New York, many Dominicans worked in the garment industry. One of the activists with whom I worked arrived in Washington Heights in 1980 at the age of twenty-three when, having fled political persecution in the Dominican Republic, he joined his wife and infant son in New York.[5] His wife helped him to obtain employment on numerous occasions. His earliest jobs were in manufacturing and in manual labor:

> [My first job was in] the textile industry. I worked as the flow boy. I would help the women. They would say "Bring me this," and I would get it for them. From there I went to a printing press. . . . From the printing press [I went] to a hat business; that was the best place in terms of salary. . . . By Lexington and Fifty-Sixth or Fifty-Seventh Street there is a bakery. There, I used to wash the floors and wash the dishes. . . . They paid me very well.

Between 1970 and 1990, manufacturing jobs in New York declined significantly (Sassen 1991), causing many Dominicans to shift into the low-wage service sector or the informal economy (Hernández and Torres-Saillant 1998; Hernández and Rivera-Batiz 1997; Grasmuck and Pessar 1991). These jobs are some of the least secure, least remunerated occupations. In 1993, approximately 1.4 million immigrant workers in New York City accounted for 47 percent of the metropolitan workforce. These immigrant workers are "nearly *twice* (1.8 times) as likely to earn minimum wages as native-born workers: 11.7% of immigrant workers receive minimum wage earnings vs. 6.4% of native-born workers" (Fiscal Policy Institute n.d.: 1). Dominicans represent a large portion of this low-wage workforce, accounting for 17.9 percent of all low-wage immigrants in the city of New York; they are the "single largest immigrant group receiving low wages in NYC and likely to be the largest among minimum wage workers" (Fiscal Policy Institute n.d.: 1). Not surprisingly, the overwhelming majority of Dominican households (78 percent) have a combined household income of less than $15,000, and 87 percent of individuals have a personal income of less than $15,000. Consequently, at least 39 percent of Dominican households in New York City live below the poverty line (Hernández 2002; Hernández and Rivera-Batiz 1997). Despite such economic hardships, Dominicans continue to migrate to New York, associating migration with socioeconomic advancement, or *progreso*, particularly for their children.

Among the earliest arrivals were exiled revolutionaries, like Marcos Ville-gos, from organizations such as MPD, MR-1J4, and Línea Roja. It is no coin-cidence that the early Dominican progressive movement in New York was composed of people who survived political persecution in the Dominican Republic in the 1960s and 1970s. These political immigrants brought with them a drive to engage in politics and create democracy from the ground up; their field of vision was focused on fighting imperialism and fostering eco-nomic, social, and racial justice in many countries. Marcos, one of the political refugees, indicated that

> the majority were ex-combatants from the Guerrrade abril [April War] and from the Constitutionalists. The majority of these people arrived in New York between 1966 and 1968. They established a Dominican Human Rights committee here. Many organizations lasted a very long time. . . . Línea Roja founded ACDP [Asociación Comunal de Dominicanos Progresistas] because it followed a very clear path, which was to establish strong vehicles for the Dominican community here in the U.S. but to serve the purposes of national liberation in the country. . . . We had to organize and obtain good services for that community that is not going to leave.

It was the latter ideology that would redirect Dominican organizing in New York. Armed with an understanding and an active history of civic participa-tion and struggle, they developed an important form of politics on the north-ernmost shores of Manhattan Island. I will turn to this ever-changing political cartography in the following chapter.

4

Setting Down Roots, Expanding Routes

In this chapter I present a chronology of organizing in Washington Heights'
Dominican community, with special emphasis on the 1980s and 1990s, the
pivotal years of Dominican-American community building in New York City.
Stretching back to politics and patronage in the Dominican Republic, organizing in Washington Heights has changed along with external political developments. Having endured Trujillo, a U.S. military occupation, Balaguer, and ensuing economic and civil disruptions, many early immigrants arrived in New
York with the idea that they would earn money and return to the Dominican
Republic. But what they brought with them helped them create and develop
political and social capital in Washington Heights. They arrived with a history of involvement in grassroots organizing and civic participation; other
racialized groups with a long trajectory of political involvement in New York
met with them as they set down roots and developed political routes in the
city. Dominican immigrants established political organizations almost immediately. Initially, they organized clubs and associations whose goals revolved around building a democracy in the Dominican Republic to which
they could return. I review the factors that led to a shift in this ideology among
local organizers and to a strong interest in developing community-based organizations aimed at tackling local issues.

I argue that despite local activists' ability and interest in fostering civic engagement in New York, Dominican-American community development took
off only after (1) local organizers reached out to local institutions and politicians; (2) organizers built a network that included non-Dominican people of

color; (3) young Dominicans, including the college-educated second generation, became involved in civic life in Washington Heights; and (4) political figures and institutions outside the community offered resources (particularly financial). The existence, activities, and power of today's Dominican-American organizations are due in large part to the convergence of all these factors.

To a significant extent, larger political, social, and economic forces have structured the experiences and activities of the Dominican immigrant population. Government policy in both the Dominican Republic and the United States has had a direct effect on the nature of the organizing shifts in Washington Heights, particularly in the early decades of organizing. The development of community activism and organizational activity in the Dominican community has changed accordingly.

Within the milieu of local activism occurring in Washington Heights during the mid- to late 1980s, various organizations were established to address the needs of the ever-growing Dominican population in the neighborhood. Local community boards and the city government promoted the growth of youth and community initiatives. Having established that their community was in dire need of services and advocates, first- and second-generation Dominican leaders founded some of the most active organizations in the neighborhood.

It was young first- and second-generation organizers who paved the way for the proliferation of local grassroots and social-service organizations in Washington Heights. The roots of organizational growth emerged from the community's strong desire to become involved in local organizing and to exert some influence over decisions made in and for the community. Many began their political careers on the local school board. Some then advanced to more prominent positions under Mayors Ed Koch and David Dinkins. Additional developments in the 1980s and 1990s created unique prospects for Dominican organizing. Among the organizations established during this era were the two on which this research is based: Dominican Nation and Quisqueya United. This chapter discusses the history of organizing trends in Washington Heights, a chronology that situates contemporary organizations within the neighborhood's activist lineage. The historical accounts presented in this chapter explicate the nature of the emerging grassroots politics in the community and the growth in interethnic/interracial collaborations. There is no question that Dominicans, as a community in Washington Heights, have declared their arrival in local politics. Local organizers work hard to garner resources and rights for Dominicans. But, as I will demonstrate in this chapter, the backdrop to this growth of Dominican-focused political activity is complex. It encompasses a growing involvement of the second generation, an ideology that permits—and at times advocates—interethnic/interracial collaborations, and a network that includes elected officials and other political power brokers.

Organizing across Borders: Dominican Transnationalism in the Early Years

As discussed earlier, the mass exodus of Dominicans from the Dominican Republic to New York began after the assassination of dictator Rafael Leonidas Trujillo and the creation of a U.S. consulate in the Dominican Republic in 1962, which liberally issued passports and visas in order to reduce potential unrest and militancy in the country.[1] The U.S. Immigration Reform Act of 1965 also created the conditions under which emigration could occur. Many Dominicans who immigrated at this time did so for economic reasons. Others arrived as de facto political exiles, remaining in close contact with political organizing efforts based in the Dominican Republic. As one local organizer recalled,

> El movimiento progresista en el movimiento de dominicanos organizados en Estados Unidos . . . la base originaria de ese movimiento todos fueron compañeros sobrevivientes de las persecuciones y de los atropellos en la República Dominicana. . . . Tenían una organización [en Nueva York]: Asociación Dominicana. Tenían una asociación que se llamaba María Trinidad Sánchez. Tenían una que se llamaba Enriquillo. . . . No puedo dejar de mencionar a Alfredo White. Alfredo White estableció el primer centro comunitario de dominicanos aquí en Washington Heights, pero la mayoría de los dirigentes de esos grupos aquí fueron, la mayoría fueron ex-combatientes en la guerra de abril del lado de los Constitucionalistas y la mayoría de ellos . . . llegaron aquí a raíz de que [Joaquín] Balaguer llega al poder. O sea, la mayoría de ellos llegaron aquí entre 1966 y 1968. Entonces establecieron un comité dominicano de derechos humanos, el comité de dominicanos del comité dominico-haitiano de amistad. . . . Había un movimiento aquí bastante activo. De nuevo, su mística era de organizar a la gente no solamente para jugar domino pero organizar a la gente para que la gente se movilizara.

> [The progressive movement within the Dominican movement in the United States . . . the original foundation of this movement were com-

rades who survived the persecutions and abuses in the Dominican Republic. . . . They had an organization [in New York City]: Asociación
Dominicana. They had an association called María Trinidad Sánchez.
They had another called Enriquillo. . . . I can't forget to mention Alfredo
White. Alfredo White established the first Dominican community center here in Washington Heights, but the majority of the leaders of those
organizations here were, the majority were ex-combatants in the April
War on the side of the Constitutionalists, and the majority of them . . .
arrived here [in the United States] once [Joaquín] Balaguer came to
power. In other words, the majority arrived here between 1966 and
1968. At that time they established a Dominican committee for human
rights, a Dominican committee of the Dominican-Haitian Committee
of Friendship. . . . There was quite an active movement here. Again, their
ideology was to organize the people not just to play dominoes but to
organize the people so that the people would mobilize.] (Translation by
author)

Two organizers—Marcos Villegos and Emiliano Luis Montenegro—who
helped to establish some of the most prominent organizations in Washington Heights were part of this militant Dominican émigré population. Both
Villegos and Montenegro formed part of the leadership of the radical Marxist
Línea Roja in the late 1970s and the 1980s. Both fled the Dominican Republic
to escape poverty and political persecution. Both men, like most political refugees of the time, arrived in the United States as young adults in their late twenties. And they arrived with a leftist, community-based orientation to civic participation, grounded in anti-imperialist Marxist ideology. This political capital
helped to shape Dominican community organizing. Many from the current
ranks of local leadership arrived at this time (and entered the New York City
public education system), or are children of those who emigrated during these
years.

During these early years of mass migration, many Dominicans—including
political activists—assumed that their stay in New York would be temporary.
They believed that after saving money and after the political upheaval on the
island abated, they would return home. Armed with this belief, many sought
employment and enrolled their children in New York schools but continued to
receive news about politics in the Dominican Republic and mobilized accordingly.

By the beginning of the 1970s, the Dominican population living in Washington Heights and on the Upper West Side had significantly expanded.[2] As the population grew during the 1970s, there was a proliferation of all kinds of organizations: social clubs, hometown associations, recreation clubs, and political clubs. In 1973 Ira Katznelson conducted a survey in Washington Heights in which he found that 14 percent of Dominicans interviewed belonged to one or more social or political organizations (Katznelson 1981). The more visible and active groups at the time were political clubs, whose emphasis continued to be directed toward influencing politics in the Dominican Republic. Many activists were also involved in political efforts that extended to various Latin American countries, namely Cuba, Nicaragua, and later in the decade, El Salvador. This suggests that a more complex reading of political motivation, discourse, and strategies is in order.

Some political exiles led local chapters of leftist Dominican political parties. Organizers from Línea Roja formed a chapter of the radical group in their new home. They elected leaders and representatives to meet with comrades in the Dominican Republic. This group remained active until the mid-1980s. When Marcos Villegos, a local organizer and cofounder of Quisqueya United, arrived in New York in 1980, his first stop was the home of Emiliano Luis, a fellow Línea Roja organizer in New York. In 1981 he was named one of the leaders of the New York chapter. The purpose of the political clubs was to keep those living in New York abreast of affairs on the island and to rally political and economic support for causes of their island compatriots. These clubs also provided a mechanism of social support by keeping people in close contact with one another while adjusting to life in New York.

After the 1965 U.S. invasion, unrest continued in the Dominican Republic until 1976–77, when the PRD took control of the government. Overt repression of revolutionaries in the country diminished. Although many activists in the Dominican Republic and the United States protested the PRD's signing of an economic development agreement with the International Monetary Fund and the military continued to assassinate young militants in the Dominican Republic, uprisings on the island subsided. After this period Dominican activists living in New York began to debate return migration versus long-term residence in New York and to discuss whether to develop a political base in New York, to empower the Dominican community in New York through active participation in grassroots mobilization around local issues, such as housing and representation in the local school system (Georges 1988; Linares 1989). (I discuss this debate later in the chapter.) Many key political figures, however, still had their lens directed toward the Dominican Republic. An interest in homeland politics remains an important aspect of many organizations, and one cannot overlook the reasons for the specific political agendas and orientations of the early political clubs in Washington Heights' Dominican community. As one organizer indicated, "These [clubs] were our refuge. We had a role in helping to democratize the island. We were here, but our hopes for revolutionary change in the Dominican Republic could not die. It just couldn't."

The political situation in the Dominican Republic propelled Dominicans to organize these clubs. The 1960s and 1970s were particularly difficult times for leftist movements in the Dominican Republic. As one political exile explained,

> Eran difíciles momentos, difíciles en el periodo del [mil novecientos] setenta y dos al setenta y ocho.... En esa época los principales dirigentes estudiantiles fueron asesinados y más de 4,000 personas en las cárceles, aproximadamente unas 70 o 80 personas desaparecidas.... Hoy en día los jóvenes no creen que criticar y ejercer el derecho a pensar [es cosa grande].... [Ellos creen] que es algo natural y debe ser así. Yo me alegro que piensen así. Pero en mi tiempo pensar tenía un precio muy alto. Hasta de la manera que te vistiera [tenía peligro]. Por ejemplo, si te ponías un pantalón negro y una camisa verde simplemente porque te lo regalaron y no tenías mas nada ibas preso y cogía bastante palo y te torturaban para que tu digieras que tu conocías los del 14 de junio. Si te ponías un pantalón negro y una media roja te hacían lo mismo para que digieras qué era lo que tu sabías del MPD. Y cuando ocurrían luchas entre grupos del ejercito, ellos mismos mataban a un compañero, pues está pendiente que un grupo de jóvenes caían preso y cumplía sentencia. Un compañero de trabajo de la escuela que cumplió siete años, siete años que cada vez que habla de eso llora. Hace un montón de tiempo pero son siete años de su vida por haber hecho nada. Lo agarraron, lo hallaron en la casa, llevaron la supuesta evidencia. Le dieron una arma, que encontraron supuestamente en la casa. Con esa arma fue que mataron a un sargento en San Francisco de Macorís, y él pagó por eso, algo que no hizo.

> [They were difficult times, difficult in the period between (nineteen) seventy-two and seventy-eight.... During that time the principal student leaders were assassinated and more than 4,000 people were in prison; approximately 70 or 80 people disappeared.... Today young people don't think that to criticize and to exercise the right to think for

oneself [is a big thing].... [They believe] that it's something natural and should be that way. I'm happy that they think this way. But in my time, thinking had a very high price. Even the way that you dressed [could be dangerous]. For example, if you put on black pants and a green shirt, simply because someone gave them to you and you didn't have anything else, you would be arrested and you would get beaten up and they would torture you so that you would say that you led, that you knew people from the June 14th [movement]. If you put on black pants and red socks they would do the same to you so that you would say that you knew about the MPD. And when there were fights between military groups and they killed [one of their own], well, it is likely that a group of young people would be imprisoned and serve a sentence. A companion here at work in the school served seven years in prison, seven years, the mention of which brings him to tears. That was a long time ago, but that was seven years of his life [he lost] for having done nothing. They grabbed him, they found him at home, and they took the supposed evidence. They gave him a weapon, which they said they found in his house. It was with that weapon that they had killed a sergeant in San Francisco de Macorís, and he paid for that, something he did not do.] (Translation by author)

Stories and events like these reached Dominicans living in Washington Heights. They were part of the raison d'être of political clubs.

As the Dominican population in New York expanded through the early wave of migration, so did the need for social clubs and organizations. Scholars have drawn attention to the many ways throughout history that immigrant groups have established these hometown associations and social clubs in order to maintain contact with co-ethnics and with their home country, and simultaneously, to help them adjust to U.S. society. Those who emphasize the transnational relationships of immigrants suggest that such organizations are a way in which immigrants, denied power in the political mainstream of the host country, bypass formal political channels and establish a different kind of power. Disenfranchised from the political discourse in the host country, they may choose to maintain some engagement with their home country. Hence, politics serves as a tool for regaining a sense of power and control. In fact, the character of Dominican organizing in New York City in the 1960s would support the transnational, or home politics, theory. Crucial to an understanding of Dominican transnationalism, however, is an analysis of the political climate in the Dominican Republic at the time this organizing was most fervent. It is also important to assess the political ideologies of the activists involved in transnational politics; many were involved in solidarity movements in multiple countries throughout Latin America, regardless of their own country of origin. The literature on transnationalism has not sufficiently highlighted this broader context of transnational politics. Political developments would later alter the sense of urgency with which this community addressed international solidarity issues.

Political and social clubs still operate in Washington Heights, often attracting the newly arrived. In the spring of 2000, when the Dominican presidential campaign was in full swing, New York–based offices of political parties from the Dominican Republic organized caravans, fundraisers, and speaking engagements throughout Washington Heights. There is no question that homeland politics has a space in Washington Heights. However, Dominicans in Washington Heights have also developed organizations to empower, provide services for, and obtain resources for Dominicans living in New York City.

Becoming New York Locals

The shift from organizing almost exclusively for homeland politics to organizing to empower Dominicans locally spanned the better part of the 1980s. The 1980s was a turning point for Dominican-American community building and empowerment in New York (Georges 1984; Ricourt 2002; Torres-Saillant 1998a). Its development rested on the convergence of a series of factors. First, upon wrestling with the *aquí-allá* (here-there) debate, a large contingent of Dominican community organizers let go of exclusive focus on home and began orienting their work toward New York–based issues, establishing locally focused organizations. Second, many young organizers began to graduate from New York City public schools and CUNY. This new second generation of activists took the networks and political experiences garnered in these institutions into their organizing in Washington Heights. Third, Dominican-American activists established local organizing and connected to other people of color in New York, primarily Puerto Rican and Black organizers and elected officials. And finally, established leaders and external institutions began to offer resources to organizations in the Dominican-American community of Washington Heights; among these was the Dinkins administration of the late 1980s and early 1990s. These factors helped channel Dominican organizing in a new direction, initiating a critical era of activism for the Dominican-American community.

Sojourners No Longer: Dominican-Americans Organize Locally

Even two decades after the first wave of Dominican emigrants arrived in New York, many organizers still believed that their stay in New York was temporary. But as revolutionary prospects diminished in the Dominican Republic, local residents and activists debated the permanence of the Dominican community in the United States and began to redirect their organizing efforts.

Along with local Dominican residents of Washington Heights, Dominican activists debated the issue of return migration. Was the Dominican immigrant population going to return to Hispaniola, or did activists need to plan for another scenario? In local organizations and in everyday settings, residents and activists debated prospects for this community, their projections hinging on the realization that they were not a group of transient sojourners that would return en masse to the Dominican Republic. Local activists—both the first generation of radical émigrés and the second generation raised in New York—began to accept the fact that the Dominican population in New York was setting down roots in the United States and it was their duty to secure a degree of civic participation and empowerment for them. One informant explained that guiding their efforts in these early days was a political ideology that included questions of inclusion and exclusion and racialization in the United States:

> During that time it was en vogue to discuss Stalin's book *The National Question*. We discussed if Dominicans living here were part of the multinational nation or if we were a minority exploited in the United States. That caused a division in the group. There was one group that said, "We Dominicans are here, we're staying, y pa'l carajo con la República Dominicana" [to hell with the Dominican Republic]. The other sector, to which [Emiliano Luis] belonged, said, "There's a group that will stay but there's also a group that will go back. We have to be responsible for both groups." The first group was more firm, and they left Línea Roja. . . . They founded ACDP . . . the focus would be [on] organizing the community, the tenants. That was going to be the focus.

But intent alone did not catapult Dominicans into major organizations. Initially, Dominican organizers attempted to gain entry into preexisting organizations in Washington Heights. Although there were many community-based organizations providing services to residents of Washington Heights, Dominican activists felt that these did not adequately address or meet the needs of the newly arrived Dominican population. As one local activist ex-

plained, the organizations established by others in the early 1980s did not include Dominicans in their boardrooms or in their program development.[3]

By the 1980s some of the more prominent community activists had cur-
tailed their organizing around politics in the Dominican Republic and agreed
that they needed to organize and address some of the issues they confronted
as New Yorkers (clearly racialized subjects, hyphenated or otherwise). One
Quisqueya United leader explained,

> We made a conscious decision that we were going to focus here, because
> in the mid-eighties there was a very strong awareness and somewhat of a
> debate in the community, so were we here permanently or temporarily
> as a group? Because if we were here temporarily, then obviously the
> agenda had to be different, we had to prepare to leave. And many of us
> knew that we were here permanently. That meant we had to create insti-
> tutions that could support our permanent presence.

These organizers analyzed the nature of existing community organizations
in Washington Heights and concluded that although there were many, none
represented—nor attempted to represent—the Dominican presence and none
attempted to serve the needs of the Dominican community. There were many
existing Dominican social and political clubs, but these did not address New
York–based concerns. Local activists began to meet to discuss how they might
contribute to the development and empowerment of the Dominican population residing in New York City.

The new generation of U.S.-educated activists joined with fellow activists
who had been involved with organizing for home politics in discussing the
future of the Dominican population residing in New York. Younger Dominican activists were first to recognize the need to structure programs that would
address the needs of the Dominican community. The issues raised during this
time—including the near-exclusion of Dominican-Americans from established institutions—led many activists to focus on building routes to empowerment in the United States via grassroots activism and institution-building
efforts.

The issues that activists addressed included the nature of belonging and
entitlement in the United States. Michael Ocampo, one of the founders of
Quisqueya United and current director of a community development program, explained,

> Something was emerging at the time.... There was an obvious commu-
> nity presence ... in [Washington] Heights, needs coming up, young

people coming out of college looking to make their mark on the day. . . . The first manifestation was some people ran for [the local community] school board and won. . . . They had a presence for the first time. So the community had begun to show its face. . . . I was painfully aware of something called the Washington Heights–Inwood Task Force that was formed in the late seventies by [Mayor Ed] Koch. Everyone but Dominicans [was included], there was one Latino there, but he was a landlord. There was also a task force and a lot of committees. Early on in that work, or as a result of that work, there were three things done in this community, which is the part that is really a milestone . . . in the development of this community. Three agencies were formed in 1978–1979: Northern Manhattan Improvement Corporation, the Washington Heights–Inwood Development Corporation, and the Washington Heights–Inwood Coalition. . . . They were formed to address really discrete stuff [such as housing and social services]. [Dominican activists were worried] that these were things set up with interlocking boards and that these agencies were gatekeepers . . . with interlocking boards [of directors]. It was amazing the same people were on the boards . . . so we [Dominicans] ended up organizing [our own organizations].

When Dominicans attempted to secure space for their fledgling organizations, they experienced a level of hostility from the local white leadership who led the existing institutions. Ocampo explained how the local Washington Heights community board of the late 1980s—composed of the old white leadership of the neighborhood—attempted to stall the progress of Quisqueya United as they requested office space:

[In order to get the space] the Housing Authority had asked, because that was community space, . . . they asked for some show of support. We had to go before the community board and ask them for, "Would you give us a letter of support, or a resolution of support or what have you?" . . . [The] Housing Authority said what they wanted was more or less a formality and it was a very small space. . . . a chunk of it someone had already committed to the Heisman Foundation, and they were going to do childcare and this little space was going to be [Quisqueya United]. From where these people [the Heisman Foundation] came is a mystery. It turns out they were never able to do stuff there. . . . They didn't do it. They didn't even know how to run a childcare center. And [Quisqueya United] couldn't get that space because it had already been committed.

Anyway, when we go that night to the community board meeting, to get support . . . as we were making our case in the public session . . . in comes this person who . . . created massive confusion by asking for this same space.

I asked Ocampo why this person, someone he recognized as non-Dominican, wanted this space.

They wanted it, [because] they heard we wanted it. . . . I ended up on [the] community board floor making some quick alliances with the non-Dominicans. And managed to get the support . . . it was quite a scene. . . . It was a good indication that people just did not want this to happen. Not letting it happen. So we navigated that struggle [and got some space]. . . . But it was a given we were gonna get it [from the Housing Authority], but it shows you a lot about the process, [about] what happens with racism.

One of Quisqueya United's founders continued, "We didn't understand how they could stop us, or why they tried. We finally got space in a church. . . . It was difficult to start something when all [the] established political leadership wanted to see you fail." Still, despite the resistance, in a proactive manner, local leaders of the Dominican community began to map out political routes in New York City.

In the early 1980s a twenty-year-old Dominican man, Miguel Amaro, approached the leaders of the old guard of Dominican activists—those who were part of Línea Roja—with the idea of organizing an annual Dominican parade. One activist who was present recalled, "He said 'I want to talk to you in secrecy but I have a plan to organize here and I want you to be the guiding force.'" The old guard agreed to meet, explaining, "We did it because he was a young leftist militant." One activist present during one of the initial meetings stated that when this young man left the room, everyone present thought he was misdirecting his efforts:

We really believed he was crazy. [We believed] the Dominican community wasn't about that. The Dominican community was into organizing itself to go back. But Miguel [Amaro] was able to understand the feelings of the community before us, the famous leftist leaders. He understood where the community was going and saw that one thing that brought a sense of pride and a sense of patriotism was organizing a parade. And he did it.

In 1981, this twenty-year-old Dominican founded the Dominican Day Parade, then known as El Festival Dominicano, with a march down Audubon Avenue in the month of August. Hundreds of people arrived to celebrate Dominicanidad in the streets of Washington Heights.

The effort to build a force in the United States would also need the support and political savvy of the older guard of first-generation activists, however. The turning point for those old-guard activists who believed they would return to the Dominican Republic was the 1984 Dominican elections. As one activist explained,

> The turning point for the mentality of the community was in 1984. [It occurred after] the disaster of the government of the PRD. Because with the government of 1978, we didn't have much hope . . . because the most conservative of the PRD rose to power. But in 1982 the number of people that came from the militant left [in the Dominican Republic] . . . there were dozens of compañeros and compañeras that went back because Salvador Jorge Blanco represented the intellectual side of the party. With him there were people with berets with stars on the front demonstrating their respect for Ernesto "Che" Guevara and what he symbolized. And so all these young intellectuals from 1982 rise to power [in 1984] and this was the government, probably the most corrupt that has been seen in the history of the Dominican Republic. . . . The external debt shot up, the [Dominican] peso lost so much value and approximately eleven or twelve ministers in the government divided amongst themselves what [former president and Trujillo cabinet member Joaquín] Balaguer typically divided between five hundred generals or wealthy families in the country. So during the government of Salvador Jorge Blanco, ten or eleven people were able to gather thousands of millions of pesos. Some of the young poor people that we used to see and organize with in the university were among those in the government . . . traveling to buy Arabian horses and with a Dominican plane at their disposal. . . . Those were our compañeros. . . The hope we Dominicans had that there would be a positive change in the country and that we would return, well that diminished.

At this point, many activists began to foresee the permanence of the Dominican community here. This perspective was advanced by the rising second generation coming of age in New York.

The Second Generation and CUNY Enter Local Organizing

In the 1980s a new generation of young Dominican émigrés and children of immigrants attended public schools in the city. Many went on to public universities in the CUNY system, primarily CCNY, a CUNY campus located on 139th Street. The public education experience afforded this generation a unique experience. In addition to fostering friendships with non-Dominican people of color, Dominican-Americans became student-activists and began to organize with other students of color and progressive white students around common causes, primarily public education funding, or more precisely government disinvestment in public education. Osiris Robles, a Dominican Nation organizer, attended CCNY in the late 1980s and early 1990s. During his tenure at the university he was one of the most active student leaders organizing against budget cuts. He worked alongside other students of color. One of the fruits of their struggle was the establishment of student office space in 1989, which they named the Assata Shakur–Guillermo Morales Student Center, after Black and Puerto Rican militant revolutionaries. Osiris Robles played a key role in securing this space, a center for the Dominican Nation as well as other student-centered activities.

The young Dominicans raised and educated in New York who were at the forefront of much of the new activism extended the reach of established community-based organizations. They served as cultural and financial brokers, connecting Dominican associations to established Puerto Rican leaders, many of whom they had met in the CUNY system. It was at this moment that the Dominican community began to appear as a local political force. Although a number of Dominican individuals were by this time in positions of leadership in city government, local Dominican activists felt that the general population of Dominicans was still disproportionately disenfranchised.

The second generation, along with those of the first generation who were now focusing more on New York issues, began to make connections to other Latino and Black activists in New York schools in their attempts to gain access to power and resources and to challenge racialized class and power structures. Mariana Bidó, one of the activists involved in Línea Roja and the early years of the ACDP, became involved with La Liga por la Lucha Revolucionaria, or the Revolutionary League, in which Amiri Baraka was one of the principal figures. The league was involved in a movement to liberate political prisoners in the United States.

Simultaneously, a series of young organizers, all younger than thirty—feeling frustrated at the poor education and police brutality young Dominicans are subjected to in New York—established local grassroots activist organizations in Washington Heights. As outlined in the introduction, the two organizations at the center of my fieldwork were established by this population of youth, who were between thirteen and thirty years of age when they became active organizers. These individuals hailed from the first, second, and 1.5 generations.

During the 1980s and early 1990s, Dominicans of all three generations came together to establish some of the best known and influential community organizations in Washington Heights. From the time of their incorporation as nonprofit agencies, they have focused on confronting issues in New York. Although it may appear that organizing focused on the Dominican co-ethnic community, the organizers were clear that they needed to reach out to other community leaders of color more consistently in order to build stronger institutions, political capital in the city, and for some, a stronger grassroots movement for social justice. Dominican and non-Dominican people of color faced similar processes of racialization, deindustrialization, and government disinvestment in public education.

Building Bridges: Working with Other People of Color

In the mid- to late 1980s, Dominican-American grassroots organizers, particularly those organizing Quisqueya United, began the search for funds to develop their organizations. Their networks with other people of color would become especially important at this time. For example, some Dominican-American organizers were educators and formed part of the Puerto Rican–Latino Educational Roundtable. Their efforts to this end were deliberate and strategic.

Mariana Bidó was in her early twenties at this time. Upon graduating from CUNY, she worked as part of the volunteer staff of ACDP, an agency established by Línea Roja members to address local issues. Soon after obtaining funding for that agency, Mariana left to work with El Puente, a public school in Brooklyn. El Puente began as a community-based organization. Puerto Rican organizers in the area were working on a number of community empowerment programs at the grassroots level. One of the areas of focus was education for Puerto Rican and Latino youth and the development of a local school. El Puente was a fruit of this effort. Mariana stated that she left ACDP to work with El Puente because she believed that the Brooklyn organization was working on social justice and empowerment issues more directly at the time. She believed she could contribute, learn from, and advance grassroots justice better via this institution.

Ties to Puerto Rican and Black organizers and organizations—such as Bidó's tie to El Puente and, earlier, to Amiri Baraka—were important. In fact, Puerto Ricans signed the incorporation papers of ACDP because the first-generation Dominican leaders of the organization were not yet U.S. citizens and could not sign the paperwork that would grant them 501C3 (nonprofit) status. Obtaining 501C3 status was crucial given that this organization, along with many others, hoped to secure funding from external agencies.

Securing Resources and Political Capital: Elected Officials, Institutions, and Philanthropy

In their efforts to more directly and consistently target local politics, Dominican activists began to chart a route toward empowerment that included electoral politics and obtaining funding for institution-building projects. Through efforts at the school board level and in other grassroots organizing, Dominicans began to gain recognition in local politics. They did not achieve (and still have not achieved) control over the boards and institutions that dictate policy and resource distribution to the community, but they began to gain a presence in local political spheres. In 1982, the mayor of New York City and the governor of New York state recognized Dominican Day, and now the Dominican Day Parade takes place up Manhattan's Sixth Avenue every August. For many, this recognition marked a new era. With the New York political machinery acknowledging their arrival as a vibrant community and with all institutions coming together to help organize or participate in this major event, people began to feel the permanence of the Dominican presence in New York. This recognition would also extend into official appointments of Dominicans in city government.

In 1983 Governor Cuomo appointed a Dominican to the Advisory Council on Hispanic Affairs, and seven Dominicans were elected to the Area Policy Board 12, which distributed anti-poverty funds to local organizations. This gave rise to a new activism and new kinds of organizations focused on obtaining resources for the Dominican community.

Funding and service provision in Dominican community-based organizations came into their own in the late 1980s and early 1990s. The degree to

which Dominican organizers were able to obtain and maintain funding depended in large part on the networks they had established beyond the community earlier in the decade.

Dominican-American organizers began envisioning new methods of organizing movements in New York. Having established community organizations, some leaders focused their energies on funding. Concerns about funding were a major reason why the founding board of directors of Quisqueya
United hired Abraham Pierino as executive director. Marcos Villegos, one of
the founding board members, explained:

> [Abraham] was one of those people that was found to help us. [Abra-
> ham] was the person with more experience with [getting funds]. But at
> the beginning [Abraham] never demonstrated any intention or interest
> in directing [becoming director of Quisqueya United]. The director of
> [Quisqueya United] and the one that everyone saw as the head of [it]
> was [Michael Ocampo]. What happened with [Michael] was that he has
> a different temperament than [Abraham]. You have to give him the mil-
> lions in his hands for [Michael] to function. [Abraham] is the kind of
> person to whom you give the idea and he goes out in search of the mil-
> lions. . . . When someone said, "Here's the money," the $80,000, $88,000
> to be exact, actually $89,000, that HAICA gave us . . . that's an organiza-
> tion that works to prevent pregnancy, a consortium of organizations.
> That was the first project that [Quisqueya United] got. [Abraham] en-
> tered into an agreement that I found out about years later. It was be-
> tween him and [Rodolfo Riomar, a founding board member] that he
> would accept coming here, accepting a salary cut, but only if [Riomar]
> would guarantee him that with any subsequent grants that he would get
> he could raise his salary to the level at which he was before and the two
> of them agreed. Then that's how [Abraham] wound up being the direc-
> tor, the executive director of [Quisqueya United] and I the director of
> programs, because I was the one that had the base in the community.
> [Abraham] deserves credit for having organized to get the funding. But
> I established all the workshops for [Quisqueya United], all of them, be-
> cause I was the one that knew this community. I lived in this community.
> I've always lived in this community. And so, [Abraham] no, he lived in
> Brooklyn and didn't have much interaction with people here, but he did
> have a vast relationship with people down there [with other organizers,
> politicians, and funding agencies] and he and I, that combination was
> perfect for the start of [Quisqueya United].

Grassroots activism continued through the end of this decade: anti-drug marches, protests against sexual harassment in a local school, rallies against police brutality, and mobilization around education reform. Dominicans wanted to have more control on the local community board and on the school board (Lescaille 1992; Ricourt 2002). Education was the issue that raised the most concern and rallied the most community support during the 1980s. Disenchanted with the overcrowding in local schools and with the lack of a Dominican presence in decision making, residents struggled to get their voices heard and their community represented on the local school board for District 6. In 1986 local Dominican teachers and parents registered 10,000 parents to vote in the 1986 elections. Their efforts paid off when Sixto Medina was elected to the board by a predominantly Dominican voting constituency. Medina became the first Dominican elected to this board. His election was possible because in New York City, noncitizens can vote in local school board elections, allowing many Dominican parents to cast their votes. Particularly in School District 6, where Dominican students formed the majority of the public school attendees, parents expressed the sentiment that Dominicans needed to have a voice in decisions made about their children and their education. As one mother and former school board member recounted, "It wasn't easy to get there. But we had to do it. Who else was going to just give us a seat? No, we had to work to get that. We do it not just for our kids, but for our community. Where would we be if we didn't try to create vehicles for power?"

During the 1990s, the New York Dominican community deepened their roots in the city and broadened their routes into national politics. The early 1990s saw the election of one Dominican to the city council and another to the New York State Assembly, as well as a dramatic proliferation in and financial growth of local organizations, many of which focused on direct service provision and youth programming.

In the early 1990s, when the issue of redistricting reached Washington Heights, local organizers started thinking of ways to run a successful campaign to elect a Dominican leader. For grassroots organizers, such as those involved with Línea Roja and the PTD, building this local leadership was becoming a primary focus. After having successfully worked to establish two key organizations in the neighborhood, Quisqueya United and ACDP, they focused their attention on electoral politics. For them, "[Guillermo] Linares was a clear candidate. He knew people in the community, he was from the community at that time, and we had to get behind him to win this election." Osiris Robles, one of the organizers in this campaign, stated, "Era un deber de nosotros tener un tipo de representación y trabajar para lograr esa meta" [It was our duty to have some kind of representation and to work to reach that goal.]

Linares was among the new generation of Dominican-American organizers who had attended and graduated from CCNY before he became a public school teacher. He also became involved with ACDP, eventually becoming the organization's executive director. Linares believed he could win the support of the local voting community—Dominicans and Puerto Ricans—and obtain a seat on the city council. Members of the old left guard, particularly those from the Línea Roja and the PTD, and the younger organizers from Dominican Nation joined local Puerto Rican leaders and Linares in building a grassroots campaign. Central to his campaign was establishing an individual connection with local residents through, for example, arranging meetings in the homes of local residents (Ricourt 2002). These meetings, which also served as fundraisers, were organized by the residents themselves, including Puerto Ricans and African-Americans. Linares also received the support and active endorsement of the city's Black leaders, including David Dinkins. These efforts culminated in 1991 with the election of Linares to the newly created District 10 seat on the city council.

In addition to organizing Dominican candidates' campaigns—namely those of Guillermo Linares and Adriano Espaillat—Dominican organizers also began to work for the campaigns of non-Dominican candidates. Perhaps one of the most significant campaigns of support, the one that significantly benefited local organizing, was for David Dinkins, an African-American who had served as assemblyman and president of the New York City Board of Elections. Dinkins' campaign and his subsequent mayoral administration was a unique and significant point in history for people of color in New York and for the city of New York in general.

In 1989, after serving as Manhattan borough president for four years, David Dinkins launched a campaign for the mayor's seat. In his successful campaigns against Mayor Ed Koch in the Democratic primary and against Republican candidate Rudolph Giuliani in the mayoral election, Dinkins sought the support of the city's Black, Latino, and white populations. Among those who answered his call were Abraham Pierino, director of Quisqueya United; Rodolfo Riomar, founding Quisqueya United board member; and Guillermo Linares. Dinkins ran a successful campaign, becoming the city's first Black mayor. Dinkins' election as mayor came at a time when New Yorkers—Black, Latino, immigrant, and liberal white alike—had grown disenchanted with Mayor Ed

Koch's divisive and corrupt government. Koch made few attempts to resolve the fiscal crises and racial tensions plaguing New York. In fact, his business and political entanglements implicated him in massive corruption schemes.[4] And his comments in the days following incidents of racial violence—including the murders of Michael Griffith in Howard Beach, Queens (in 1986), and of Yusuf Hawkins in Bensonhurst, Brooklyn (in 1989) by a group of thirty white males —fueled racial tensions. In 1988, Koch further crippled his chances for reelection with comments on Jesse Jackson's presidential primary campaign. He attempted to dissuade white voters from supporting Jesse Jackson's run for president in 1988, saying that Jews "would have to be crazy to vote for Jackson." Tired of Koch's actions and divisive politics, New Yorkers—including the hundreds of new voters of color the Jackson campaign had registered and those who believed in Jackson's Rainbow Coalition—were ready for a change in city leadership (see Day 1990: 166; Sanjek 1998). Dinkins garnered endorsements from Blacks, Latinos, and whites; more than 10,000 people volunteered to campaign on his behalf (Day 1990: 160). He also had the support of political heavyweights such as Jesse Jackson and Governor Mario Cuomo during his campaign.

Perhaps more than any New York political figure before him, David Dinkins was able to create an interethnic/interracial network in mainstream city politics. And, as Barbara Day (1990) said, "Dinkins's victory was earned by an alliance of organized labor, African-Americans, Latinos, prochoice women, lesbians, and gays" (174). Kasinitz (1992) also notes that the Dinkins campaign's outreach to the West Indian communities resulted in overwhelming support from these voters in both the primary and in the general elections. These communities celebrated the end of Koch's New York, believing in the "mosaic" and innovations Dinkins promised.

Dinkins' success was also a success for local Dominican organizing. Dinkins selected Rodolfo Riomar, a Dominican doctor, organizer, and cofounder of Quisqueya United, to lead his transition team. Guillermo Linares also served on that team. In his reading of the city as a "mosaic" of peoples, Dinkins sought to create an administration that included people of color in a way very different from that of his predecessor. Dinkins appointed a number of Dominicans to different high-level offices, including Zenaida Mendez as head of the Office of Hispanic Affairs, Michael Ocampo as assistant commissioner for the city's Department of Employment, and Rolando Acosta as deputy commissioner, making him the highest-ranking Dominican in city government at that time.

Acosta, Riomar, and Ocampo had formed part of the group that founded Quisqueya United. Their connections to the Dominican community of Washington Heights remained important as they served under Dinkins.

In 1991 David Dinkins established the Beacons Initiative. Conceived as a partnership between community-based organizations and local schools, Beacons sites were designed to establish programs and provide services to communities throughout the city. In the first year, eight organizations were selected to lead Beacons sites, each receiving half a million dollars from the city. Quisqueya United was among them. Michael Ocampo stated, "In the Dinkins administration those of us that were on the inside worked very much to strengthen what was on the outside." The growth of Quisqueya United and other programs throughout the city could not have occurred had Dominicans not established a working partnership with David Dinkins and other Black politicians. This conclusion is supported by Rudolph Giuliani's actions after he defeated Dinkins in 1993. Giuliani slashed the budgets for youth programs, including the Beacons Initiative, drastically reduced city funds going into communities such as Washington Heights, and initiated a frivolous investigation of Quisqueya United's accounts (no wrongdoing found), while simultaneously slashing its city funding by half.

Grassroots community activism has continued since that era of massive growth under Dinkins, but with a revised concept of community empowerment that includes making inroads in established electoral politics and congressional lobbying. Linares' position on the city council and Espaillat's successful campaigns for state assembly are indicative of the community's growing strength and political aspirations. In the late 1990s Dominican organizations began to envision organizing at the national level for the purpose of influencing national policy. Among the organizations taking the lead in this direction are the newly established Dominican-American National Roundtable and Dominican Nation.

As highlighted earlier in this text, Dominican Nation organized a national conference in 2000. Though not the first national Dominican conference in the United States, this particular conference—led by the second generation with the first generation serving as advisors—was an important and telling event for Dominican-Americans. Conference organizers brought together numerous sectors—local residents, local politicians, national politicians and Dominican representation, other Latinos, and other blacks, including Haitians—to map an agenda for Dominican empowerment in the United States. Leticia Reyna explained, "It wasn't about people in the ivory tower coming down to us with solutions. We were doing it ourselves. . . . Now I want us to get to work, let's see what we're really going to do. That's the point of the whole thing, let's get people mobilized."

The leadership of Dominican Nation began their conference planning process in early 1997. They assessed their network and established that they had close working relationships with other local organizations, with local activists, and with politicians from the PTD. At that time, four of the key leaders, having graduated from CUNY and from universities outside of the New York metropolitan area, recognized the potential significance of their college networks in planning for the conference. The leadership also realized the important role CCNY would play in their conference as well. The explicit goal was to join Dominicans living throughout the Dominican diaspora—but particularly those residing in the United States—to discuss and draft an agenda aimed at charting a new route—political, economic, social, and cultural—for the future of the diaspora in this country. The idea, according to one organizer was to "listen to what people who live through all of this have to say. It's the housewife and the sixth grader and the taxi driver that has to direct the new politics."

Leaders of Dominican Nation met with their conference advisory board, which included first-generation activists. Upon their recommendation, they met with city council member Guillermo Linares to see if he might be able to offer support. Linares was eager to be affiliated with this conference; in the fall of 1999, he began sharing his network with Dominican Nation, which extended into the Mexican-American and Puerto Rican communities, as well as to the White House. One of Linares' first contacts was with the National Council of La Raza (NCLR), a nonprofit organization located in Washington, D.C. With roots in the Mexican-American community, NCLR's stated mission is to "reduce poverty and discrimination, and improve life opportunities for Hispanic Americans." NCLR works as an umbrella organization and, in the United States, is the organization with the largest Latino constituency base. Guillermo Linares had worked with them in the past and introduced Dominican Nation members to Raul Yzaguirre, NCLR president. Members of Dominican Nation traveled to Washington, D.C., to meet with Yzaguirre. The goal was to help structure the organizational agenda—in logistical and ideological terms. Yzaguirre's help was invaluable to Dominican Nation, providing a clear glimpse into the successes and difficulties of past conferences. Dominican Nation members returned from this meeting charged with a hopeful energy: "He's done so much. It was really important to learn what's worked in the past. . . . And it was so great to hear him say that he was sure this would be a great conference. . . . He believed in this when all we'd been hearing from other people so far is that we're *muchachitos*. He took us seriously."

Once in New York, faced with the task of securing funds for a large conference that was free to the public, Dominican Nation took another of Linares' suggestions and initiated dialogue with Antonio Mir, a Puerto Rican organizer and former president of the Hispanic Federation. Mir, a key player in Latino politics in the 1980s and 1990s, brought his network to the organizers. He also brought a bill as a consultant, which was picked up by United Way of New York. United Way-NYC is an umbrella organization serving advocacy and community-based organizations in New York City. United Way-NYC agreed to offer Mir a stipend for his role in developing this grassroots conference. Having successfully brokered an agreement, Mir began to expand the reach of Dominican Nation, helping to attract a wider pool of funding agencies and guest speakers. Dominican Nation also received the support of the Hispanic Federation and *El Diario La Prensa*, a city-wide newspaper with a large Spanish-speaking readership.

The conference was held, as planned, from February 25 to February 27, 2000. Speakers came from numerous Dominican organizations, NCLR, the Puerto Rican Legal Defense and Education Fund, the National Coalition for Haitian Rights, and the New York Immigration Coalition. Elected officials and representatives from public offices such as the New York Civil Liberties Union, Congressman Charles Rangel's office, the district attorney's office, and the New York Board of Regents also spoke. One of the keynote speakers, Honorable José M. López, judge for Superior Court of the District of Columbia, congratulated the organizers as "heroes to this community," praising them for a successful conference and for convening so many Dominicans to discuss complex and critical issues born in the United States:

> I never forget one of my college professors. He was from Haiti. When asked by the students about the problems back home, he said home is where my problems are. And I live here so my problems are here. Ladies and gentlemen, here is where we have the housing problems. Here is where we need better schools. And it is here where the political powers decide the issue of our every living day. Here are the problems and here we must focus on them.

His comments clearly forecast the direction in which many Dominican-American activists, particularly with key organizations in Washington Heights (and especially so in Dominican Nation), have taken their efforts. One might say that Judge Lopez' perspective is biased by his role in the judicial system of the United States. However, more Dominicans like him are aspiring to elected and appointed positions in government. But more importantly, greater numbers of immigrant and native-born Dominicans involved in organizational activities in New York and elsewhere are attempting to affect policies and programs that impact the day-to-day living conditions of Dominicans living in the United States; if one can gauge anything from the workshops and the high attendance at this conference, it is that young and old, U.S.-born and immigrant, Dominicans are routing a new path toward civic engagement in U.S. politics.[5]

On Sunday, February 27, 2000, before delivering a speech to conference attendees, First Lady Hillary Rodham Clinton met with Osiris Robles, Joaquin Alexander Robles, and Leticia Reyna, all organizers of Dominican Nation. They spoke about the drive and goals behind this new project. In the brief period they spent with the first lady, they reiterated the national direction growing activism was now taking.

Later, the first lady took the stage, joining Alicia Silva, a graduate of Dominican Nation's pre-university program; Dinorah Rosa, fundraising coordinator for the conference; Osiris Robles, general coordinator of Dominican Nation; Guillermo Linares, Washington Heights city council member; Johnny Ventura, mayor of Santo Domingo; Lorraine Cortes-Vazquez, president of the Hispanic Federation; and Thomás Morales, vice president for student affairs at CCNY. The choice of speakers for the day represented key political targets for Dominican Nation, as well as for the Dominican-American population: U.S. federal government, local government, politicians from the Dominican Republic, large Latino organizations, and the growing sector of local youth and young leadership engaged in the grassroots political process. Dominican Nation, and other groups emanating from Dominican-American organizers elsewhere, seeks to impact the political process from the local to the federal levels through the work of a young, local, rising leadership and its pan-Latino and interethnic/interracial network. Politicians from the Dominican Republic were included in the new agenda in hopes that they might lend support to the project of empowerment.[6] This reading of the new relationship to "home" was evident in speeches: Guillermo Linares, city councilman, introduced Hillary Rodham Clinton by first saying, "It is a great honor for me, as the first Dominican-American elected to government in the United States, to welcome you, to address our leadership as a Dominican community, our future, our Dominican future, and the future of this United States." Proclaiming the significant role of youth in the new Dominican-American agenda, Hillary Clinton explained,

> because Dominican Nation serves as a powerful voice for inclusion, for tolerance and diversity, for economic and educational opportunity . . . I want to thank you for your dedication to your community. This conference would certainly not have been possible without young people who have come of age here in America saying to themselves we now want to be a voice for a better future.

The event brought to the fore the direction Dominican-American organizing had been taking for some time, that of creating dialogue and fostering power in national debates and locally based issues, with the home country called upon to support the new national politics.

In perhaps the most poignant speech, Dinorah Rosa highlighted the heterogeneity of the group that had come together to plan the national agenda and the historical and political significance of this conference.

> Over the last four days, we have brought together individuals of Dominican and non-Dominican descent, the young and the "not so young," our laborers, our educators, our elected officials, our professionals of various fields and our students to find solutions to our shared problems collectively. What we have begun in the past few days is a fundamental rethinking of the Dominican reality. What we have witnessed is a synergy of thoughts and action plans that have and will continue to mobilize and commit people to resolve the issues and concerns that affect our communities.
>
> The sixteen workshops we held yesterday have helped us weave together grand ideas and pragmatic solutions. We have celebrated the great accomplishments of our community as well as discussed at large the challenges that we continue to face. We have contemplated issues of civic responsibility; and importantly how public service by our young people can foster social change within our disenfranchised communities.
>
> The people have spoken! It is now our responsibility—that of our elected officials, our young activists, private and public entities, and all our community members—to create the critical connection between thinking and doing. We must walk away not only thinking this was a fabulous conference, and indeed it was, but asking ourselves "how can I contribute to our National Agenda?"
>
> I rejoice in what we have accomplished in the past three years, and

more importantly, in the past four days. This has been a labor of love of hundreds of young people. The members of the [Dominican Nation] have worked diligently to organize this conference for our people. Let this conference be the historic marker that defines the Dominican community in the early part of this century. Let this be the reference point that people recall when they think of a time when the Dominican community, organized by its youth, stood together to demand their rightful place in American society.

Though some would argue that this new generation lives "betwixt and between," not knowing exactly where "home" is located—either in their parents' country of origin or in the United States—it is clear that some have begun to call upon those in their Dominican network and those in their ever-expanding interethnic/interracial network to help build on the projects run by and for Dominican-Americans. Far from disengaging in the political process in the United States, this group of second-generation Dominican organizers has attempted to enlist others in this endeavor. And we can rest assured that this new generation of local leadership will work to have an even greater effect on political matters in the United States in the years to come. In a closing speech, one keynote speaker summed up the work that lies ahead:

> Back then [in 1961] being Dominican was *exotic*. There were few of us if any. But it was also frightening, there were no resources, there was nowhere to turn, it was very lonely. It heartens me to see that we have grown so beautifully. I am very excited about the proposition about a national Dominican agenda because I believe there is greatness in our people that can make great contributions to the progress of this great nation.... I am encouraged by this well-attended event that there is a great interest in the development of the Dominican-American community. And that, ladies and gentlemen, is half the battle. The other half is going to be time and cooperative effort. And as I look around I am pleased to see the inclusiveness of your effort. You have opened the door to the greater community. . . . We must continue to build the skills of making coalitions.

It is clear at the start of the new millennium that these kinds of national-level efforts led by second-generation activists have established permanent themes in the political repertoire of Dominican-Americans. What is equally clear is the significant way such efforts involve other people of color. Since the 1980s, when grassroots organizers laid the foundation, Dominican leaders and

organizations have reached a level of political maturity and power that demands recognition. Numerous non-Dominican politicians running for offices
throughout New York state recognize the power of this community. Politicians
such as Governor George Pataki, Mayor Michael Bloomberg, Senator Hillary
Rodham Clinton, and Manhattan Borough President C. Virginia Fields have
all worked with Dominicans and traveled to the Dominican Republic during
their campaigns for office. Hillary Clinton's 2000 speech at Dominican Nation's conference was the first time a first lady had met with Dominicans in
Washington Heights or in the United States as a whole. It suggested not only
that Clinton understood the rising importance of Dominicans in New York
politics, but that Dominicans had begun to realize their potential for political
leverage in politics outside the immediate neighborhood.

A twenty-seven-year-old organizer, Gabriel Aponte, has been a part of
Quisqueya United since its inception. He began as a participant and is now the
assistant director of the organization's Beacons center. His rise in the organization has paralleled the growth of Dominican-American power in Washington
Heights. He recognizes the important trajectory local politics has taken:

> Since I've been with the agency [a lot has changed]. Definitely. Number
> one is we got our Dominican councilman. We got our Dominican as-
> semblyman. Our people have started to get into positions of power
> where in the eighties [and] way before that . . we were nowhere near
> there. Okay, you had a couple of Puerto Rican brothers . . . but as far as
> Dominicans seeing Dominicans up there, Dominican faces and espe-
> cially in this community where it was mostly white men running this
> and saying where the money goes and where this goes and where that
> goes . . . to see Dominicans there, I mean, I think that was the major step
> . . . to see Dominicans on the school board and even being president of
> the board. That's important for the community, very important. . . . The
> fact that the community is more involved as far as things happening in
> the community, the way they come out and speak, the way to let their
> voice be heard. But before things were happening, it was like who's going
> to listen to you? The community members are actually more involved
> politically in the community, they're more involved in the schools,
> they're . . . trying to join PTAs and stuff. . . . Even though it could be
> better, it's starting to move along, little by little. So as far as changes in the
> community, it has been better. There are more Spanish-speaking and
> Dominican-focused offices in the community and before there were

white, Italian, Irish. We still have some here, but you have a lot more of our offices now.

Though new organizers may not recognize the role that interethnic/interracial collaborations played in developing Dominican power, all local residents witness the fruits of that labor. Today, Dominican-American organizers are trying to use all the skills and networks established during the 1980s and 1990s to secure a place on the national political scene. In 2002 Guillermo Linares ran for the New York State Senate. The Dominican-American National Roundtable has secured offices in Washington, D.C., and organizations such as Dominican Nation continue to provide a local voice in these developments. Regarding these national efforts, Abraham Pierino explained:

> We have a yearning and a need to be in Dominican communities throughout the United States that don't have the level of support that is required. So we're looking a lot now toward organizing nationally, organizing . . . as a community. We may surge now as the third largest Latino community in the nation, [which] I think we will actually [be] after the census. So that means we have to really begin to organize from a national perspective.

Conclusion: Mobilization, Political Empowerment, and Institution Building across the Generations

Tracing the histories of Dominican-American organizing trends and leadership, we can see the ways that changes in the local and national political climates altered the strategies and foci of these activists' efforts. Also evident is the important role of the second generation in relocating Dominican politics in New York. That this shift occurred in consultation with and with the support of other organizers of color is another crucial element of Dominican-American politics. What began as grassroots mobilizing exclusively aimed at solidarity with home country politics was significantly altered when Dominicans residing in New York began to deal with another series of concerns centered on their lives in Washington Heights. Their development into one of the more vocal communities in New York began with grassroots rallies and gatherings and led to educational and political organizing, institution building, and entry into local and national (U.S.) electoral politics and civic participation.

The individual and community histories I have outlined thus far present an interpretation of the expanded participation of Dominicans in New York political discourse. Although there are other paths—including the transnational—and other political trends in the community, the organizations and activists I have highlighted represent the most significant contemporary organizing trends among Dominican-American activists in Washington Heights. They represent some of the largest organizations in Washington Heights and are among the best known.

The matter at hand is the way we come to understand the causes and development of organizing. This history suggests that as political mobilization throughout Latin America declined in urgency for Dominican activists residing in New York, they began to focus on what was happening to their local community of Washington Heights. Underlying all this work was an awareness of and engagement with the political, economic, and racial context by which their lives were circumscribed. As the anti-poverty programs of the 1960s and 1970s were implemented in New York, it was no surprise that local activists would begin to tackle policy and funding, trying to redirect federal and state resources into their neighborhoods. But acquiring these resources took some time and involved networking with established communities of color in New York. And this community-building agenda required a network of organizers to focus their attention on local issues.

It was in the 1980s, within the context of Reagan's war on drugs and the ensuing mass-media focus on drugs in the Dominican community, that grass-roots activism increased in Quisqueya Heights. The 1980s were also marked by a new trend in philanthropy where Dominican-American activists worked to secure much-needed funding. Sprouting organizations were able to use the language of mainstream media and philanthropy to their advantage. If society wanted to see a change in what was perceived to be the Dominican, youth, or immigrant problem, then community-based organizations were best equipped to accomplish this task, because their staff shared the background of the target client base. Thus, Dominicans were strategic as they worked to develop local organizations. Recognizing their status as a racialized, ethnic, immigrant, disposable labor force, they sought ways to redirect power to themselves.

Dominican-American organizers learned from and worked with other organizers of color to develop the Dominican entry into local politics. Far from automatically pushing Dominicans into a path of "downward assimilation," as Portes would suggest, collaborations with other people of color—particularly

Puerto Ricans and African-Americans—was an essential element of early Dominican political developments in New York City. As a result, Dominican-American youth and educational organizations grew in number, scope, and funding in the 1980s and 1990s.

By the 1990s, many organizers and academics began to speak of the "Dominican-American" and what needed to be done to gain some real power in the United States. Unlike earlier waves of white immigrant groups, Dominicans' status and prospects would continue to be delineated by racial codes and racialization processes operating in concert with contemporary socioeconomic shifts in the United States. It would no longer be enough to obtain resources from supralocal institutions. It would also be necessary to find a way to influence policy that affects the Dominican community nationwide. As I will demonstrate in the following chapter, in their attempts to achieve this goal, Dominican-American leaders have taken two different, though not mutually exclusive, paths.

To simply assume that these developments constitute a natural political maturing of an immigrant community does not give sufficient attention to the historical specificity of the local and national political contexts at different times in the United States, the Dominican Republic, and New York, nor to the ways in which larger processes affect community organizing in general, and immigrant community organizing in particular. As scholars of contemporary immigration indicate, not only is straight-line assimilation nearly impossible and improbable for immigrants of color, this has never actually been a useful model for describing immigrant "incorporation" (see Sacks 1999). Numerous variables, namely racialization processes and politics, determine the extent to which immigrants can attain economic and social mobility in the United States. The Dominican-American organizers with whom I worked are continuing to develop their networks with other people of color in efforts to confront (and change) local politics and policies. That they use identities—such as Black, Dominican, and immigrant—that are continuously thrust upon them should be no surprise.

To summarize, during their early years of large-scale participation in local politics, the young Dominican population reached out to other, more established communities of color for support. Leaders of these various populations had met in New York City's public schools, including CUNY. By creating alliances with Puerto Ricans and African-Americans in the early years, the Dominican leadership was able to gain a degree of political mobility. The older white groups still residing in the neighborhood of Washington Heights—

Greeks, Jews, and Irish—fearing displacement by this growing population of immigrants, united in opposition to Latinos and Blacks (Katznelson 1981). However, Dominicans' long history of activism and their association with Puerto Rican and African-American elected officials and institutions allowed the early entry of Dominicans into the city's political machinery.

I am suggesting that relationships and ties to native minority groups were an important and empowering option for the Dominican community in their early years of political growth in Washington Heights. Alliances with Puerto Ricans and key leaders in the African-American community continued after the 1980s. These relationships continue to be activated for major events such as rallies and conferences, for fundraising, and for political support.[7] I am not suggesting that all Dominican-American organizers should follow this path, but for some activists this interracial/interethnic organizing is an important, necessary, and empowering component of organizing. Dominican-Americans' history of activism, particularly their strategic use of networks of people of color, directly challenges the assumptions central to Portes and colleagues' segmented assimilation model. That is, not only are second-generation Dominicans moving beyond strictly defined ethnic group boundaries, but their work with native minorities is proving crucial for their political mobility in the United States.

Dominicans who established and developed organizations in Washington Heights have long witnessed the emergence of the second generation—that is, U.S.-born and U.S.-educated individuals—in local institutions. This generation sees itself and its future rooted in the United States; they constantly organize to confront issues such as underemployment, government disinvestment in public education, police brutality, and Dominican-Americans' lack of political power. Their activities center on educational, economic, and political empowerment in the United States, with home country issues being raised by the older leaders of established community-based organizations only occasionally and at key moments (such as Dominican presidential elections). People are most concerned with issues they face in the United States and continue to work to develop political empowerment in this country. The first generation may discuss and organize for politics in the Dominican Republic, but their attention is also directed to the issues they confront in New York. As one organizer revealed, Dominican activists work with the hope that some day their political power will be such that they can tackle any issue and be heard.

There has been some difference in the degree of participation in island politics between the generations, although they have come together over the past two decades. Their dedication to establishing political routes in the United States continues to flourish, as the growing youth population takes up the reins. As the director of one local Dominican organization stated, "There's always been some organizing in the community. [However,] activism in and of itself is not enough. There's a role and a purpose for activism. But I've always been clear that activism has to lead toward infrastructure. And the role of activism is to create conditions to increase resources to deal with issues." Dominicans in New York have been doing this, particularly in Washington Heights, sometimes through social-service delivery and other times through grassroots or electoral politics in the city of New York.

It is important that we reexamine and reconsider the very powerful and dynamic way that generations of racialized immigrants participate in U.S. politics. We should also document the extent to which collaborations between people of color exist and analyze what these collaborations mean for the different communities under investigation. To demarcate the boundaries of political mobilization and citizenship, primarily in the realm of the transnational or the co-ethnic, and to eliminate consideration of the national and the interethnic/interracial relations fostered in the United States misses a significant understanding of the powerful and multiple ways in which immigrant populations are reconstructing their communities throughout the United States. Dominicans have been marginalized in this society's social and economic hierarchy. In a city like New York, where unemployment, racism, gentrification, and police brutality touch the lives of people of color in specific ways, Dominicans do not remain unaffected.

In attempts to discuss and confront these issues, Dominicans have responded in various ways, one being the creation of a series of community-based organizations. It is clear that they are concerned over issues such as police brutality in Black and Latino communities, welfare reform, and exploitation of Latino immigrants in the U.S. economic and political system. In 2000 Dominicans marched in Washington for Latino rights, and over the years they have organized around city hall to protest cases of police brutality in their communities; in their protests, they raise issues of race, class, and immigration. Dominican Nation youth talk about why this is important to them as a group:

> If I don't get up and say something, they could get me tomorrow. No, we need to stand up and do something. Things in this country aren't good for Latinos. The government isn't going to do anything until they know

we mean business. They think we immigrants from Latin America come here and don't do anything. We just take from them. We take their money . . . [or] we take their jobs. And they see us as lazy, only making problems. But they cause the problems for us. Most of us wouldn't be here if they didn't cause problems.

5

The Leadership

Most Dominican-American leaders I interviewed in Washington Heights shared a number of beliefs. First, that organizers must work to empower Dominicans. Second, that Dominicans must focus their energies on issues they face in New York. And, finally, that in order to build a stronger political and financial base, Dominican organizers and leaders should collaborate with those outside the Dominican community. Nonetheless, as Dominican-American leaders have moved from being solely transnational organizers to acting in local politics, they have developed different ideologies and practices around this new form of politics. They have begun to change their perspectives on community empowerment and development. These ideologies—all of which center on obtaining resources and power for Dominicans—ultimately inform the ways organizers envision the community, as well as how they build bridges and identify with other people of color in New York and in the United States.

This chapter explores two facets of the Dominican leaders of Washington Heights: (1) how these leaders have worked with or imagined themselves allied to other people of color; and (2) the different ideologies around community development and the ways leaders used their networks and ideologies in Dominican-American organizing. This analysis includes descriptions of both the "old guard" and the "new guard" of leadership.[1] I analyze the manner in which local organizing began to develop in two contrasting directions. Although most organizers work on behalf of the community and all believe they are working in the best interests of the community, they do so with distinct ideologies. I argue that these different modes of organizing have led to different views of what constitutes community development and, consequently, different kinds of collaborations in organizing and politics.

Leaders in this community have developed their activities with reference to one of two tendencies. Organizers in both categories act as political (and, at times, social-service) brokers between the Dominican community and supralocal institutions and politicians outside the community. However, one set of organizers focuses on harnessing this relationship for the purpose of obtaining resources and social capital for organizations and programs whereas the other seeks to broaden its base of power.

Ethnic entrepreneurs make up the first category of organizers in Washington Heights. They are involved in the effort to secure resources and provide social services in the community. Their alliances with other people of color are created, in part, in the attempt to secure grants and political favors for the community. The second category privileges a grassroots base and aims at mobilizing community members. I call this category of activists the *community mobilizers.* They reach out to other people of color in grassroots efforts, often to challenge state policies and practices. Many of the activists who helped to establish prominent organizations in the neighborhood—including those with which I worked—also participated in leftist movements in the post-Trujillo era in the Dominican Republic. These actors and their ideologies can still be found operating among those who work at the grassroots level.

This analytical distinction is not meant to imply a zero-sum game in which organizers are either one type of leader or the other, but rather that two tendencies exist among Dominican-American organizers. People may identify with one ideology or use one type of strategy more than the other, but they can and do use both modes of organizing. In addition to biographical accounts of the individuals and organizations that make up these different camps, I offer examples of events in which the two trends of organizing became evident.

Two New York Activists

Abraham Pierino arrived in New York City when he was ten years old. His mother had left the Dominican Republic for New York two years prior. Upon being reunited, the family lived in the area of Washington Heights known as Hamilton Heights, where Pierino attended public schools. In the early 1970s, however, fearing gang activity and violence, his mother moved the family to Brooklyn. It was as a teenager in Brooklyn that Pierino began to develop his network of contacts in community-based organizations. At the age of seventeen he participated in the New York City program called City As School. He spent his senior year of high school not in classrooms but in organizations throughout the city, learning about the work they carried out at the community level. Inspired by much of what he saw in these organizations, he enrolled at CUNY's Brooklyn Campus, entering the School of Contemporary Studies. Community-based organizations throughout the city became his focus of study. During this time at CUNY, he got involved with two new organizations, an involvement that would catapult him in new directions of community development. He helped in the early years of The Door, a multiservice youth development program located in Lower Manhattan, and El Puente, a Puerto Rican community and school program in Williamsburg, Brooklyn. Armed with these experiences, he took a job with the New York Urban League, where he said he was "learning about the African-American community and how it organizes itself from a national perspective." He then spent five years providing technical assistance to community organizations through two city agencies: Progress and the Community Service Society.

Pierino is now executive director of Quisqueya United. As noted in chapter 4, he was hired by the founding board of directors after the agency began to receive major grants.[2] The board recognized the social and political capital he had acquired throughout his years in community-based organizations and institutions across the city. Sitting in his office one afternoon I asked him why, given all the experience he had in so many organizations, he decided to work with Quisqueya United, a position in which he has remained for nearly years. He responded:

> It's a Dominican Mecca. The Dominican Mecca. This is it. This is the most important Dominican community in the United States. It's the largest—historically, spiritually, emotionally. It's a community that I have deep roots in. . . . And if you want to be relevant to the Dominican community in the United States, this is the place to be. And I came to the point in time when I realized [that], and it became increasingly important for me to focus all the knowledge and skills that I have developed over the years, to focus it on the Dominican community. I worked in the Puerto Rican community. And they have national organizations. The Black community has everything. They have nothing and they have everything. It's all relative, of course. But we didn't have anything. And still the Dominican community is huge and growing by leaps and bounds,

and we only have four organizations that deliver services in our community, or Dominican organizations. That's obviously not enough organizational infrastructure to make a change and sustain an impact.

Pierino's history in community-based organizing granted him a unique experience in grassroots politics with people of color. He transformed this political capital into a perspective on community development that focuses on infrastructure, funding, and service provision. He believes that it is through these channels that one will "make a change and sustain an impact." This, Pierino believes, is what community organizing and empowerment entail, and he implements this belief in Washington Heights. His work with other communities of color is designed to move this agenda forward. Pierino typifies the ethnic entrepreneur.

Joaquín Alexander Robles has had a somewhat parallel though slightly different trajectory than Pierino. Born and raised in Washington Heights, Robles was still a young teenager when he helped to found Dominican Nation. He remains an active member and leader of this organization. Upon graduating from college (where he organized a Latino club) he worked on developing Dominican Nation's community empowerment campaign as well as its new national focus.

Because Dominican Nation is still primarily a volunteer-led effort, Robles has consistently maintained both a job and his role as a leader in the organization. His first job after graduation was with Aer Lingus, an airline. But his interest was in urban planning—he received a bachelor's of science degree in professional studies with a focus on urban planning and community organizing. He then worked with the Community League of New York as a community liaison and organizer. During his tenure in this position, he provided technical assistance and advocacy services for different communities throughout New York City. In 2000, he made the transition from organizer to legislative associate at the New York Immigration Coalition (NYIC). During his time in college and through his work with the Community League and the NYIC, Robles worked with and for Latinos, immigrants, people of color, and the working poor. He established a background in community work and advocacy that recently was the basis for his selection as a community liaison for the office of Manhattan Borough President C. Virginia Fields. Throughout his academic and employment careers, Robles has remained an active organizer of Dominican Nation, serving as one of three outreach coordinators for the organization's 2000 national conference.

His work in Dominican Nation has focused on creating a space where community members, including youth, can come together, share collective political space, and create and foster their own plans for social change. He explained why maintaining this kind of (volunteer) role in the Dominican community is important:

> You go from the community—stating the issues, stating the needs—to a more powerful political machine, or force, saying that we're here, we're going to stay, these are the issues, we are going to change those things. But we need the community to get involved in order for these changes to happen. . . . I think that it's okay to provide public service, but it has to go beyond that. It has to be going beyond offering someone twenty dollars to buy [groceries]. . . . It's kind of like the saying that when someone's hungry, teach them how to fish. People are our greatest asset in this community. We just need to come together collectively to make change happen.

Robles' perspective is one that privileges grassroots mobilizing for community participation. He advocates a grassroots approach to achieving social and political transformation. His example of giving someone twenty dollars for groceries was a direct indictment of service providers, a suggestion that by emphasizing service provision, they are maintaining the status quo in this society. Robles believes that although services are needed and service-delivery organizations have an important role, real change in the conditions that affect Dominicans and others will come about only if local residents are provided the tools that allow them to take the reins of local politics. Robles typifies the category of community mobilizer.

The distinct perspectives to which leaders such as Pierino and Robles subscribe influence local organizers to pursue different visions of community development. I am not suggesting that the two kinds of local organizers and their modes of action are mutually exclusive. Although activists generally follow one or the other ideology, they usually recognize the importance of the other perspective in the life of Dominican politics. Neither am I implying that one perspective or form of organizing is necessarily better than the other, nor that one group of actors is necessarily more "wholesome" than the other. Rather, in the Dominican-American community of Washington Heights, these two ideologies have led organizers to envision different paths to community empowerment. It has led them to identify with or identify themselves as people of color in different manners and for somewhat different goals. While the ethnic entrepreneur is most interested in obtaining economic resources and political favors for the community and reaches out to people—including people of color in leadership roles—who can help them obtain these, the community mobilizer seeks to bring local residents together with those whose circumstances they share—including people of color—to demand changes in policy and practice from the state. While ethnic entrepreneurs create a vertical network of solidarity—that is, one that extends upward to people with some degree of power—community mobilizers create a horizontal network of collaborators.

These distinct patterns of organizing and political ideology are not unique to Dominican-Americans. Much has been written about the political heterogeneity of other groups as well. Manning Marable and Leith Mullings (1995, 2000) have analyzed the ways in which African-Americans developed three different political ideologies during the periods of slavery and emancipation. They identify an integrationist trend, a Black-nationalist tradition, and an ideology based on radical transformation of the society. The integrationists' goal "was to bring Negroes into every profession and to ensure their full participation in voting, serving on juries, and running for elective office" (2000: xix). The Black nationalists believed that in order to achieve any degree of economic and social security or integrity, Black Americans had to develop autonomous institutions and communities. The third group "advocated a radical transformation of the United States based on a fundamental redistribution of resources" (2000: xx). Although these three modes of thought were quite different, Marable and Mullings note that they were not mutually exclusive but "broad, overlapping traditions." And "organizations and individuals may have exemplified one tendency or the other, [but] organizations and movements usually displayed a spectrum of views" (xxi). It is therefore difficult and impractical to categorize one organization or institution as adhering entirely to one political ideology. It is also counterproductive to pigeonhole individual actors into a single mode of thought. That is, individuals, like organizations, change their political perspectives and positions over time. And in the case of the three modes of thought Marable and Mullings lay out, all addressed the same concern, that of "the possibility of black Americans achieving equality within America's racialized social body" (Marable and Mullings 2000: xviii). These arguments are germane to the study of Dominican-American organizing as well.

Scholars examining contemporary immigrant populations and immigrant political participation have also recognized community heterogeneity (see

Kwong 1979; Guest and Kwong 2000; Schiller et al. 1987; Kasinitz 1992). Kenneth Guest and Peter Kwong (2000) have argued against essentializing immigrant communities. They critique Portes and Bach (1985) for suggesting that immigrant enclaves are homogeneous communities whose members work with a shared sense of ethnic solidarity and camaraderie. Schiller et al. (1987) note that class and regional identities significantly affected Haitian immigrant organizing in the period they studied, from the 1960s through the 1980s. The development of Haitian organizations and politics was marked by class tensions and rivalries, making it impossible to describe Haitian-American organizing with one single broad stroke. Kasinitz (1992) offers a similar analysis for the West Indian community of Brooklyn, New York. Describing New York's Chinatown, Kwong (1979, 1996) and Guest and Kwong (2000) document the political tensions that exist between the elite Chinese business owners and the Chinese immigrant workforce. The distinct interests of each group lead it to develop a different view of community development and social mobility. Kwong and Guest state it is erroneous to overestimate ethnic solidarity and homogeneity when discussing immigrant groups.

It is imperative to recognize and understand the heterogeneity and complexity of any group's political development. In the discussion that follows, I will address the manner in which the ethnic entrepreneur and community mobilizer ideologies have created differing forms of Dominican-American organizing and interethnic/interracial collaboration.

Claiming the Neighborhood through Service Provision: Quisqueya United

From Grassroots Action to Institutional Development

As noted in chapter 2, Quisqueya United was established in the late 1980s, when some of the old guard progressive leaders began discussing the need for organizations that would work for the Dominican population that intended to remain in the United States. From these conversations developed organizations such as ACDP and Quisqueya United. Michael Ocampo, a founding member of Quisqueya United explains,

> There was an obvious community presence created in the Heights. Needs coming up, young people coming out of college looking to make their mark on the day, the seventies, you know, the radical seventies. People were fighting [over] how to change the system. Of course, some

of [the] others were not swept away by the political developments. The fact that our community was being squeezed out from the Upper West Side, there was this problem of settlement up here, being that there were very little efforts available to help folks with that. We knew that the agencies around us were not addressing those needs. So, we're talking about organizing, right? We're talking about organizing Dominicans here.

In the early years the organization took part in community rallies, such as those protesting the murder of José "Kiko" García and the abuse of a little girl in a local school. Marcos Villegos, a member of Línea Roja and the PTD and founding member of Quisqueya United, worked to attract and mobilize community members during these years.

The staff was fully volunteer until the organization obtained a pregnancy prevention grant. Michael Ocampo, the founding director of Quisqueya United, recalled that in the 1980s, with respect to social services for Dominicans "there was nothing happening. Nothing." In attempts to address this problem, founding members "gravitated towards a social-service, a community-service society." When they began to obtain some funds for other programs, the new executive director, Abraham Pierino, along with Rodolfo Riomar, a founding member, restructured staffing arrangements as well as the organization's work to revolve around service provision. As the organization began to move drastically in this direction, community mobilizers such as founding member Marcos Villegos left to pursue other projects. The ethnic entrepreneurs who remained, particularly Abraham Pierino, turned this organization into one of the largest service-provision organizations in the city. It has secured many grants, developed a budget in the millions, and established collaborations with city institutions such as the Agency for Children's Development, the Legal Aid Society, and the Human Resources Administration. These developments are deliberate attempts to secure resources to provide services to area residents, particularly Dominicans. Quisqueya United leaders were able to accomplish these goals through working with people in positions of power.

Reaching Outside the Community for Funding

A sense of urgency permeated all actions of Quisqueya United and of many other agencies that developed in the 1980s. Abraham Pierino stated, "We have always been an activist organization. In fact, the very first thing that we ever did ever was organize a march against drugs in our community at a time when people were really afraid to come out. . . . We had to organize the community."

Given their perspective on community organizing, Quisqueya United took an interesting step after initiating local mobilizations. After leaders organized to confront the issue of drugs in the community, the director sought and secured city funding to further this work by targeting drug prevention among youth. Pierino explained,

> After we finished organizing around drugs, I immediately, it was so successful, it involved so many people, the community spoke out. I took that and I went to the city and I said, "Look, we have a drug problem and we don't have a single drug program in our community, and people are acting on that. That has to be addressed." And that developed into the only drug treatment program in the community targeting one of the neediest populations, which is women with small children. So it wasn't just enough; the activism for me has to lead to somewhere.

The "somewhere" to which Pierino refers is funding and service provision. Much of what Pierino and other Quisqueya United organizers were able to obtain in the early years came through previously established networks. As noted previously, Pierino's network extended into the Puerto Rican community and city institutions. In 1989 he made a decisive move to collaborate with African-American politician David Dinkins, as did other leaders in Quisqueya United. Quisqueya United staff had also worked for Congressman Charles Rangel, another African-American politician representing Washington Heights.

These working relationships benefited Quisqueya United when it applied for funding in the early 1990s. The most important source of funding came through Mayor Dinkins' office via his newly established Beacons Initiative (see chapter 4). Michael Ocampo, who headed the Department of Employment under Dinkins, explains,

> I went into an agency that contracts money. And, boy, did we contract a lot of money. And we contracted a lot of money. . . . We went from $700,000 for a youth program. Under the Dinkins administration it was $7 million for all kinds of programs for youth up here. That coincided with the stimulus package, summer jobs . . . a lot of resources [were] coming into the community [at that time].

Definitions of and everyday forms of activism began to change in Quisqueya United as the organization's funding and professional networks expanded. Abraham Pierino stated,

The activism has to lead to somewhere. I'm not an activist for [activism's] sake, I'm not a rebel for rebellion's sake, so to speak. It's a very targeted way to put pressure on the system, to organize people so that their point of view has a vehicle to express itself and to articulate its own agenda and move that forward. That's what it's always been leading to. In all the activism we have done, we've tried in some shape or form to channel that information towards resources to the community.

Leaders of the organization believed they shared this goal with other key leaders of color:

Well, we have the same agendas. As Latinos [our] variations don't even come close to the similarities in terms of what we have to do and the barriers that we have to deal with. In education, for example, all Latinos have major issues to deal with. So I think that's why. And the same thing, the African-American community is a torchbearer for so many things. They led the civil rights movement in this country. So we have a lot to learn from them. And we have similar agendas. We really do. . . . In every area we find ourselves in the same statistical pool that's usually not fantastic, great news. Which means we have to climb out of the same hole in many ways. Even with a few variations here and there. But whether it's health, whether it's education, economic development, we're trying, we're living in communities that have similar problems that require similar solutions. And so it makes more than enough sense for us to pool our resources together. And work together. And now, today, for example [Quisqueya United] works very closely with a lot of organizations in central Harlem. We're responsible now, believe it or not, for example, we have the contract from the state to register all children in Federal Child Health Plus Program, including central Harlem. There's a Latino organization that's been accepted in Harlem by groups there and can play that role and can play leadership in that area of reaching out to the community around health issues in central Harlem. So working with other people and getting the resources under our control has always been a theme.

Modeling Community Development from the Top Down

The current overarching strategy of the organization is threefold, as Abraham Pierino explains:

1. We've got problems in the community that need to be addressed, resolved. And that [*sic*] people who are plagued by those problems can't move forward without it. . . . A lot of the things we do are geared towards resolving some of those issues. There are social services. Support services, and without that kind of support [people] won't go forward.

2. We gotta find a way to promote development . . . and that's why we have a lot of development things going on . . . the most important [being] youth development. That's what youth development is all about, these are services that are provided, activities that engage young people in a way that does not bind them or is not defined by their deficiency.

3. Where activism comes into play is that we also, unfortunately, have to defend the community because this community is constantly under attack. In all sorts of ways, for example, I found out when I first developed [Quisqueya United] that the Department of Youth Services [now the Department of Youth and Community Development] in the city registered Washington Heights as having the highest number of young people in the city of New York and gave us the smallest allocation of funds. So I took that piece of information, I ran to the city and made a big stink of it, and slowly we increased the amount of youth dollars coming in. So the third major function becomes defense. . . . And somebody had to stand up for the dignity of the community and defend it.

. . . All of the programs and events fall under those three categories.

Guiding much of the work of this organization are issues of entitlement and belonging; that is, that the resources allocated to Dominicans in Washington Heights are still less than what activists believe they should be. The disrespect and racism organizers felt in the early days of institution building, the feeling of being shut out of funding and policymaking, prompted them to create their own organizations. In this effort, they have established impressive nonprofits that work primarily with the predominantly Dominican community of Washington Heights. Over the years Quisqueya United has developed a multimillion-dollar service-provision focus. Its programs receive funding from major sources such as the W. K. Kellogg Foundation, the Fund for the City of New York, the Annie E. Casey Foundation, the National Institutes of Health, and the City of New York. One of Quisqueya United's major programs is an after-school program run out of a local public school, a part of the city's Beacons Initiative.

Quisqueya United's Beacons sites revolve around three clusters: education, culture, and recreation, with a strong emphasis on family participation. In 1994 the staff implemented a service integration model (SIM). The site director, Martín Guevara, supervises the ten family programs that fall within this model. The principal components of these SIM programs follow:

1. Attendance Improvement and Dropout Prevention (AIDP).
2. General Youth Council, a component of the AIDP project that meets daily as an educational and social-support mechanism and where new youth programs are also discussed.
3. HOPE, which focuses on AIDS and HIV prevention by providing gay men's volleyball training, ESL classes, leadership training for all participants, a support group for men living with AIDS and for drug addicts, and a support group for family members of people with AIDS.
4. Family Center, offering a mental health referral clinic (Monday through Thursday), parents' support group, men's support group (for ex-batterers), teen-parent support group, and literacy class.
5. Immunization, where a staff member provides immunizations and lead abatement screenings once a week.
6. Family Preservation Project, with case managers offering entitlement and economic development counseling, as well as weekly ceramics and artesania classes for adults (some staff say this serves as a release for participants) and domestic violence group workshops (for people who have been mandated by the courts to take them. Workshops generally average fifteen couples per session).
7. Day care.
8. Center for Rehabilitation, Education, and Orientation (CREO) and Family Assistance Program (FAP), which primarily work with Latino and African-American women addicts and families who have cases with the city's Agency for Children Services or have had children taken away by courts. These programs provide domestic violence workshops and run support groups for children who come from homes where domestic violence is present.
9. START, within which a caseload of twenty young adults receive case management support, home visits, a support group, and one-on-one counseling.

10. VISTA volunteers, who provide volunteer services such as college preparation services, citizenship training, environmental awareness, and smoking cessation classes. The volunteers receive a federal stipend, and Quisqueya United's central offices manage their time.

It is clear to even the casual observer that this organization is involved in a great deal of program development benefiting local residents. What I wish to point out with this long description of the programs, however, is the ideology behind this kind of community organizing. Clearly, the organization is involved primarily in service provision. Staff members' main role is to provide services and support for local residents. There is no question that this work is important, but the degree to which this organization has developed a top-down approach toward community development and empowerment is the issue at hand. As Quisqueya United's former site director explained,

> We assess our community by what our community brings to us. We work with their concerns, issues, and needs. We provide for their concerns, issues, and needs. You need a lawyer? We give referrals. You need action for youth support? We provide it. If anyone comes with a problem, we accommodate them, respect them, and deal with it. We respect who they [community members and Beacons Initiative participants] are, offer them confidentiality, don't judge, and have empathy. We don't just relate, we relate and provide services. When providing resources, we're keeping in mind all the resources we can provide.

As one staff member stated, in "all the activism we have done, we have tried to channel resources into the community." The goal is to "provide services that empower people." As I illustrate in the next section, this ideology of power through service provision is very different from the way in which community mobilizers envision Dominican political empowerment.

Enacting Leadership from the Grassroots: Dominican Nation

From Youth Programming to Community Activism

A group of very young Dominicans, ages thirteen through twenty-one, founded Dominican Nation in the late 1980s, around the same time that Quisqueya United emerged. The organization was inspired by a conversation among student organizers in 1987 at the Universidad Autónoma de Santo Domingo (La UASD), a major university in the Dominican Republic. The conversation held at La UASD revolved around military and police abuse of young students in the Dominican Republic. Osiris Robles and other youth from New York felt that police abuse was also a concern for youth living in Washington Heights and that no organization was addressing this issue. Robles remarked that something had to be done about the way young people living in Washington Heights were treated. Following up on this conversation, he joined other young 1.5- and second-generation Dominicans in New York City to create an organization that would focus on youth issues, with youth serving as the principal organizers.

When the organization was first founded, youth met weekly to discuss a specific issue or concern. It was a social space for the youth, but also a very political one. From many of these discussions emerged plans for action. After discussion and reflection, Dominican Nation members often became involved in grassroots action: working for Guillermo Linares' campaign by doing outreach to local residents; organizing rallies to protest the killing of José "Kiko" García by New York City police; and protesting a local teacher's abuse of a young Dominican student (and the school board's failure to take action). Lenora Ríos, one of Dominican Nation's youngest members in its earlier years, spoke about why she participated in the organization and in its activities:

> There really wasn't any place I could go where I'd be able to say something. We had, we faced a lot of things. For example, in my school we didn't even have enough desks in the class for all of us. I think parents were trying to do something about this, but why shouldn't we say how we feel also? I don't know who else was out there, but we were a youth movement. We did what we wanted and we said what we wanted. And we did a lot. It made me feel really good about all of us [young people].

Dominican Nation has continued to privilege a community-forum style of planning and grassroots organizing. Community participation and street action are not only embraced, but are also seen as necessary tactics in their vision of community empowerment.

In 2000, Dominican Nation transported this ideology into a national effort, organizing the 2000 conference (see chapter 4). Although their constant and strongest programs were still with Dominican youth, they developed this national agenda to address Dominican-American concerns nationally. Given their grassroots, community-mobilizer perspective, they worked to ensure local residents' participation during all phases of planning for the conference. They held monthly community forums and annual community conferences to gauge what community members felt were the most important issues to be addressed and why and from this feedback drafted the skeleton of a national agenda.

Reaching Outside the Community for Action and Justice

In their efforts to develop grassroots action, Dominican Nation organizers have reached out to other people of color. Because of the relatively young age of this cohort of local Dominican-American activists, their work with other people of color has primarily been in movements in CUNY and around issues of police brutality.

Osiris Robles, a key founding member of the organization, attended CCNY in the late 1980s and early 1990s. He was one of the leaders of 1989 student protests against Mayor Ed Koch and Governor George Pataki's assaults on public education. He explained,

> El trabajo era eso con otros grupos Latinos, Afro-Americanos, Asiáticos. . . . Creo también que me dio una oportunidad de trabajar con grupos de otras preferencias sexuales. Y eso no se ve en los países de uno. . . . Los diferentes frentes de trabajo en los cuales yo he estado participando me ha permitido a mí valorar el trabajo con todos los grupos étnicos y tener en cuenta que lo fundamental es identificar el objetivo que uno piense alcanzar, y no somos tan diferentes.

> [The work was with other Latinos, African-Americans, Asians. . . . I also think that this gave me an opportunity to work with people with different sexual preferences. And you don't see this happening in our countries of origin. . . . The different organizing I've participated in has allowed me to value the work done with other ethnic groups and to keep in mind that the fundamental thing is to identify the goal one wants to attain, and we aren't really all that different.] (Translation by author)

Although ethnic entrepreneurs share this understanding of a common plight with other people of color, community mobilizers address it differently. That is, while ethnic entrepreneurs form networks with people of color in positions of power to obtain resources for service provision, community mobilizers from Dominican Nation believe that Dominicans must work in solidarity with other communities of color to alter the system that distributes resources and power.

Dominican Nation has maintained its street activism with other people of color. During my fieldwork, they participated in rallies supporting Mumia Abu-Jamal, a Black journalist in federal prison, protesting the New York Police Department, and protesting the city government's financial disinvestment in impoverished communities of color. One leader explained why this kind of work is important:

> Hoy yo he llegado a la conclusión de que se tiene que trabajar en net-working. Hay que trabajar en conjunto con los demás grupos étnicos. O sea, la superación de nosotros como comunidad dominicana no se va lograr separada de la superación de la comunidad puertorriqueña. La superación de la comunidad Latina no se va a lograr separada de la comunidad afro-americana. Y yo creo de que en este momento eso requiere, tiene mucho más valor, hacer un esfuerzo de eso, de que tene-mos que trabajar en networks requiere hoy, o tiene mucho más valor por la tendencia del crecimiento demográfico en los Estados Unidos. O sea, todas las proyecciones te dicen que la llamada minoría será la ma-yoría. Y si no hay grupos de personas que tengan la visión de entender que nosotros no podemos permitir caer en actitud de divisiones, vamos seguir en lo mismo, o quizás peor, como comunidades. . . . Si no hay un entendimiento claro y hacer un esfuerzo de compartir nuestras exper-iencias, trabajar en conjunto, permitimos ser divididos por un tercer grupo. Entonces yo creo, el trabajar con diferentes grupos étnicos le facilita a uno abrir una mesa de intercambio, una mesa de conver-sación, donde podamos buscar las cosas en comunes que tenemos nosotros como la llamada minoría. . . . Tenemos que planificar al largo plazo.

> [Today I have reached the conclusion that we must work on networking. We have to work in collaboration with other ethnic groups. That is, our advancement as a Dominican community will not happen separately from the advancement of the Puerto Rican community. The advance-ment of the Latino community will not happen separately from the ad-vancement of the African-American community. And I think that in this moment this requires, it has much more value, to make a strong effort toward that end, that we have to work in networks. This has much more importance given the demographic trends in the United States. That is, all the projections indicate that the so-called minority will be the major-ity. And if there aren't groups of people with the vision to understand that we cannot allow ourselves to fall into an attitude that divides us, we're going to continue in the same situation, or perhaps worse, as com-

munities. If there is not a clear understanding and an effort to share our experiences, to work together, we allow ourselves to be divided by a third group. So I believe that the work with other ethnic groups allows one to open the door to a table of exchange, a table of conversation, where we can look for the things that we, the so-called minorities, have in common. . . . We have to plan for the long-term.] (Translation by author)

The plight and mobility of Dominicans is, in this perspective, intricately linked to those of other communities of color. It is not enough to obtain funding for services. In fact, this perspective suggests that undue emphasis on the goal of financial growth can divide people. Dominican Nation has only recently begun to apply for long-term funding. On one occasion of brainstorming a proposal for youth programming, key leaders were concerned that they might be overlooked in light of the funding track already established by Quisqueya United. Osiris Robles said that on one occasion Abraham Pierino pulled him aside for a conversation about funding wars. He recounted that Pierino congratulated Dominican Nation for the work they were doing but said that Dominican Nation became Quisqueya United's competitor for much-needed grants as soon as they were established in Washington Heights. This necessity of competition engendered by the scant supply of funding for services and programs poses problems for the flexible kind of camaraderie and solidarity that Dominican Nation organizers seek.

Dinorah Rosa joined Dominican Nation in 1998. She had previously worked with various Dominican and Puerto Rican organizations: the Puerto Rican Legal Defense and Education Fund (PRLDEF), the Puerto Rican Policy Institute (under Angelo Falcón), and Aspira of New York, an organization founded by pioneering Puerto Rican activist Antonia Pantoja. Rosa's experiences, ideas, and understanding of the work of Dominican Nation are shared by many community mobilizers. In 1998 Rosa worked with the political empowerment group of Dominican Nation. She explained what skills she felt she brought to this project:

Rosa: What we talked about was working with other groups of color,
         not for political benefit of it for us, but just because, and this was
         like me and [Nocena] who, because we worked with Haitian
         immigrant groups and we felt that the needs that they're talking
         about are not that different from the needs we're talking about so
         it behooves us to kind of just try and connect. . . . We were saying
         these things. People were really connecting to that.

Aparicio: What sorts of issues are you seeing similar with these communities, and how does that lead you to want to work together?

Rosa: The need for more educational services. The need, the safety
issues in your community. Health services in your community.
Immigrant services and issues and anything [like] that, you
know, police brutality. I mean, everything that I have ever
heard in a meeting in Washington Heights about what's wrong
in the Dominican community, I have heard it in other communities. Perhaps, you know, the names might be different, the
language might be different, but it's the same issues. And
although we're sort of the community en vogue right now
because of our numbers, it still seems to me like a repeating
story. . . . Whenever I would hear the issues of the Dominicans,
I would say, yes, you know. You're right. We need to do this,
and I keep on thinking, well, how do we link this to other
groups? Because other groups are making the same calls. We'd
have more power together, and maybe we could change things.

Modeling Community Empowerment from the Grassroots

Local Dominican activism falls within the context of a longer political and
economic trajectory that reaches back to revolutionary movements in the
post-Trujillo republic. And perhaps more important, local activists acting as
community mobilizers still place themselves and their organizing within this
larger context of global history and politics. Such is the case with Dominican
Nation leaders. In fact, at the closing of the Dominican Nation conference in
2000, Osiris Robles identified the success of the conference as being a direct
result of the strong political lineage that stretched back to revolutionary politics in the Dominican Republic:

Creo que si Duarte estuviera vivo hoy estuviera muy orgulloso de los
jóvenes, de la creación aquí presente . . . que las hermanas Mirabal,
Manolo Tavárez también estuvieran aquí presente. . . . Las mujeres, los
hombres aquí presente, realmente hoy creo que presentamos un movimiento progresista con capacidad de desarrollarse en los Estados Unidos.

[I think that if [Juan Pablo] Duarte [father of the Dominican Republic]
were here, he would be extremely proud of our young people, of what we
have created here . . . that the Mirabal sisters and Manolo Tavárez would

also be here.[3] . . . The women and men present here today, I truly believe that today we presented a progressive movement with the capability of developing in the United States.] (Conference closing plenary, February 2000; translation by author)

These organizers connect local organizing in the present to revolutionary leaders who demanded democracy in the Dominican Republic. They believe that in addition to establishing local organizations and expanding the network of people with whom they can work in solidarity, grassroots empowerment can be successful only if projects include local voices from the community. This ideology informed the earliest stages of Dominican Nation's new national agenda:

Había un acuerdo, un consenso de que hay problemas en la comunidad, de que somos tantos en numero y de que hemos tenido experiencia organizativa. . . . La segunda parte es ¿qué hacer? Y allí hicimos un planteamiento de realizar una conferencia. Desde el principio fue claro . . . de que la conferencia no era el objetivo final. Desde el inicio nosotros, la invitación fue que ese grupo de personas se convirtiera en promotor de un nuevo proyecto organizativo que se pudiera convertir en una alternativa en la comunidad nuestra. La meta era organizar para crear un lugar donde siempre se le presta valor a la comunidad. Juntos, podemos lograr lo que trabajando desde una oficina nunca puede.

[There was an understanding, a consensus, that the community had problems, that we are large in numbers and that we have had organizational experience. . . . The second part is, What do we do? And that's when we suggested doing a conference. From the beginning it was clear . . . that the conference was not the final goal. From the beginning, the invitation was that this group of people become the promoters for a new organized project that could become an alternative for our community. The goal was to organize to create a space where the community is always valued. Together, we can achieve what those working [only] from an office can never achieve.] (Translation by author)

Some community mobilizers recognize that their approach to community empowerment stems from their class status in society:

En Washington Heights la mayoría de las personas que se envuelven en lo que son las iniciativas de empoderamiento son de apellidos Rodrí-

guez, son apellidos García, Hernández. No son de los apellidos de la élite
de nuestro país. . . . Y somos las personas que se envuelven, tú vez, tu te
encuentra con Linares. Linares cuando llega aquí trabajaba en taxis.
Somos, coño, somos la representación de lo que es la comunidad de
nosotros, una comunidad pobre, pobre. Entonces hay que mirar en ese
contexto. . . . Como vivía mi familia cuando éramos siete [hermanos y
hermanas] y era solamente papi que trabajaba y mami recibiendo welfare. Tenemos que mirarlo de esa forma. Tenemos que mirar que la
comunidad no cuenta con buenos programas. O sea, programas que les
ayuden con ese empoderamiento de que nosotros hablamos.

[In Washington Heights the majority of the people involved in projects
of empowerment have surnames like Rodríguez, García, Hernández.
These are not surnames of the elite of our country. . . . And we're the
people that have gotten involved. You look at [Guillermo] Linares. When
Linares arrived here he worked as a taxi driver. We are, damn, we are
representative of our community, we are a poor community, poor. So we
have to look at it in that context. . . . Look at how my family lived when we
were seven [brothers and sisters] and only our father worked and our
mother received welfare. We have to look at it that way. We have to see
that the community doesn't have good programs. That is, programs that
help them with the kind of empowerment that we're talking about.]
(Translation by author)

Community mobilizers who shape Dominican Nation suggest that for a
successful movement to occur, power must emerge from the grassroots, rather
than rest with one or two main leaders. And they believe that this is also the
sentiment of local residents.

Estamos en un ghetto donde no se cuenta con buenos programas para
ayudar con ese empoderamiento comunitario de que nosotros hablamos. Yo creo de que si miramos lo poquito que hemos logrado en el poco
tiempo que hemos estado aquí, yo no me sentiría de pesimista con
nuestra comunidad. . . . La comunidad dominicana del 2000 tiene una
conciencia sobre lo que es el empoderamiento. . . . Tiene que haber un
movimiento colectivo de empoderamiento. . . . La gente que vinieron a la
conferencia no llegaron porque les atrae el nombre de [primera dama]
Hillary [Clinton] ó de [Representanté Charles] Rangel. Vinieron porque
están buscando un espacio donde ellos puedan contribuir a ese empo-

deramiento. Nosotros tenemos que tener un entendimiento de lo que es realmente empoderamiento. Porque si empoderamiento se limita a creer que es, que se limita a buscar uno ó otro representantes político, simplemente nos jodimos. Porque representante política tiene la comunidad puertorriqueña, tiene la comunidad afro-americana. Y, bueno, estarán mejor posicionado en lo que tiene que ver con los contactos que tienen en Washington [D.C.] . . . pero cuando tu miras las condiciones físicos de la comunidad, y cuando tu miras la cantidad de jóvenes Latinos que están terminando en las cárceles y están dejando las escuelas, no hay una gran diferencia. Somos pobres. Y juntos tenemos que hacer algo. Sí, se necesitan los líderes, los políticos, pero la comunidad es la que tiene que reconocerse como una fuerza.

[We are in a ghetto where there aren't good programs that help with the kind of empowerment we're talking about. I think that if we look at the little bit we've been able to accomplish in the little time we've been here, I wouldn't feel pessimistic about our community. . . . The Dominican community in 2000 has a consciousness of what empowerment is. . . . There has to be a collective movement for empowerment. . . . The people that came to the [Dominican Nation] conference [in February 2000] didn't come because they were drawn by the names of [First Lady] Hillary [Clinton] or [Representative Charles] Rangel. They came because they were looking for a space wherein they could contribute to that empowerment. We have to have an understanding of what constitutes real empowerment. Because if we limit empowerment to believing that it is, limit it to finding one or another political representative, quite frankly, we're screwed. Because the Puerto Rican community has political representation, the African-American community also. And, well, they're in a better position with respect to the contacts they have in Washington [D.C.] . . . but when you look at the physical conditions of those communities, and when you see the number of young Latinos that are winding up in prisons or dropping out of school, there isn't much of a difference. We're poor. And together, we have to do something. Yes, we need leaders, the politicians, but it is the community we must recognize as a powerful force.] (Translation by author)

Some community mobilizers do not believe that elected officials can be trusted to represent the true interests of the community. Joaquín Alexander Robles, indicating a degree of ideological kinship to Malcolm X, does not have complete faith or trust in recognized leadership in the community, particularly in elected officials:

> I think that some in our community, and this is something that Malcolm mentioned *en su tiempo de activismo* [during his time of activism], we have a lot of good people in our community and we have a lot of bad things in our community. And as a result of those bad things, you have a lot of targeted attempts that take advantage of that situation.

In a discussion of the way Riverbank State Park was built in Harlem and Washington Heights, Robles noted his strong dissatisfaction with elected officials and leadership in the community. This park, constructed atop a major waste disposal site located next to residential buildings, met with a lot of community criticism; yet local elected officials favored the city's plans for the park.[4] Robles suggested that they worked for their own personal interests and, having lost touch with the community on the ground, did not always work in the best interests of the community:

> Well, for me personally, it [elected officials' support of Riverbank State Park] kind of reinforced my belief that we need to have changes in our community and because of these other people that are supposed to look out for our community and they allow for this to happen. Definitely there is a need for changes in our community, and you do that by advocating, by organizing people, and that's basically how I felt about these issues. . . . These politicians were for it, without really caring what the impact will be on our community.

Members of Dominican Nation work to create mechanisms through which local leadership can continue to arise from the grassroots level. They have organized community forums where local residents meet to discuss issues such as redistricting and housing. From these forums, some community members have gone on to testify in city council hearings on such issues. Dinorah Rosa explains what she believes is the organization's major contribution to Dominican-American community development and empowerment:

> This is a group of just amazing intellectual capacity. It wows me all the time. Really, like good-willed towards others and that desire to, like, make social change not just because it's a pure or romantic idea or because it's going to eventually get me into office or whatever. . . . I think [what] will mark us as something amazing in this community would be the idea and the possibility of getting this emerging leadership going. So

it's not just about us being the leaders, but it's really about creating sort of this entire strata of leadership. And that I think is really *lo que podemos aportar a la comunidad* [what we can offer the community].

The models I have discussed in this chapter represent two differing ideologies and modes of action. I do not suggest that all actors working within these organizations are confined to one or the other model of action. Neither do organizers in either category negate the important role the other can play in community development. Although they may disagree in their primary emphasis, they do agree that they are working for similar goals of building Dominican-American power. Speaking about whether or not he agrees with the other mode of organizing, Osiris Robles explained that people must join in any movement that will work to advance the community in some way, claiming, "No se debe dejar de comer pescado por temor a las espinas." [You shouldn't stop eating fish for fear of the bones.] The different modes of organizing, however, have led organizations and community leaders to take opposite positions on major community issues. Such was the case in 2000 when the Federal Bureau of Prisons attempted to open a halfway house in Washington Heights, as I describe next.

Confounding Community, Confronting the State: Entrepreneurs and Mobilizers Address the Federal Bureau of Prisons

In the early part of 2000 the Federal Bureau of Prisons authorized the creation of a halfway house in Washington Heights. Set to open in late fall, the home was intended to house recently incarcerated young men originally from the New York region, though not necessarily from the Washington Heights area. The state selected a residential building located on 182nd Street between Audubon Avenue and Saint Nicholas Avenue (recently renamed Avenida Juan Pablo Duarte). This site selection was seemingly insensitive to the fact that the building was located one block from a public elementary school, two blocks from a public middle school (the one where Quisqueya United held its after-school program), in the vicinity of at least five other public schools, and in a neighborhood where affordable housing was becoming a thing of the past. The site was also three and a half blocks from Gregorio Luperón Preparatory School.

Activists and local advocates from Dominican Nation and Quisqueya United learned of the plans when the Correctional Services Corporation, the primary sponsors of the halfway house, put up building permit notices on the building in October 2000. The ways in which Dominican organizers and local policymakers participated in actions around these plans demonstrated the heterogeneous voices with which Dominican-American organizers understand and attempt to advance community development and power.

On October 18 and October 23, 2000, leaders of Dominican Nation co-sponsored community meetings with the principal of a local high school located on 181st Street.[5] With full support from this principal and with access to a meeting location in the heart of Washington Heights' Dominican neighborhood, the leadership was able to draw close to sixty neighborhood residents to the two evening meetings. Among attendees were leaders and members of Dominican Nation, youth who attended the local high school, local journalists and activists, and local residents. During one of the meetings, a local resident pointed out that *El Taxista*, a local newspaper, had published an interview with him regarding the impending halfway house in August 2000. During the course of the meeting he and others reiterated the issues he had raised in that interview: Over the summer 182 Realty, LLC, had purchased the residential building on 182nd Street and begun to forcibly evict tenants who did not accept "moving costs" to peacefully relocate to another building. The company then began plans to lease the building to the Correctional Services Corporation without notifying local residents or policymakers, and in early fall, began to renovate the building for the halfway house. Meeting attendees were adamantly opposed to having a halfway house in their neighborhood, and they opposed the manner in which authorities had approved the location without consulting local residents or considering the site's proximity to seven public schools. During the meetings, local residents decided to create and circulate documentation on the state plans, collect signatures for a petition, and organize a rally to voice community opposition to the construction of the halfway house.

Over the next two weeks the local city council member met with representatives of the Federal Bureau of Prisons and the Correctional Services Corporation. He also circulated a form letter via a memorandum to local "parents, educators, business and community leaders"; local residents signed the letter and mailed it to the director of the Federal Bureau of Prisons in Washington, D.C., and to their congressman, Charles Rangel. The local community board also raised the issue at their monthly general meeting on October 23, 2000. Although board members discussed concerns similar to those of local residents at the community meetings, they ultimately decided that this was not the appropriate time to discuss the matter and that the discussion was, in fact, out of order because the issue needed to be discussed in committee first. Someone suggested that the chairperson of the board draft a letter expressing concern over the matter, but some board members again stated that this was not how decisions were made and that the matter should first be discussed by the appropriate committee.

While policymakers tried to address the matter through these institutional mechanisms, attendees at the community meetings at the local high school initiated a petition campaign and reached out to other local residents through a phone bank. Their goal was to inform the community about the plans for the halfway house and to gain support for a rally they organized. On Saturday, November 4, 2000, between one hundred and two hundred local residents participated in an afternoon rally that headed north on Saint Nicholas Avenue/Avenida Juan Pablo Duarte and onto 182nd Street, ending in front of the building where construction was taking place in preparation for the halfway house. Local press—both citywide and from the Washington Heights area—covered the march and rally. Facing organized and determined residents and with opposition from elected officials, the Federal Bureau of Prisons eventually dropped their plans to open the halfway house.

In addition to the organizational effectiveness of local residents in this collaborative community effort to prevent the federal government from imposing a program on their neighborhood, what is equally striking is the nature of participation of different institutions in the community, particularly the role of young people and parents. Those who participated in the effort did so in different ways and invoked different definitions of and types of support from the community. And those local institutions that did not participate in the efforts invoked yet another working understanding of the community and goals for community improvement. But all made claims about what Dominicans, as a marginalized sector of people of color, should receive.

On October 18, 2000, I arrived at Quisqueya United long before the scheduled 5 p.m. youth committee meeting time. I had planned to speak with the director of the Quisqueya United Beacons site about the halfway house before going to the youth meeting. Because Quisqueya United's youth program was housed on 182nd Street, I knew I would still be able to attend the community meeting being held later at the school on 181st Street, though it would mean leaving the youth meeting early. The director indicated that although he was quite concerned about the developments, students from the program could not participate in community meetings because they needed to have written parental consent long before the event, and the executive director of Quisqueya United had suggested that the halfway house might not be such a negative development in the community. Pierino, the executive director, believed that the halfway house would bring more revenue to the community and offer employment to community residents, perhaps even empowering the community. At the start of the youth committee meeting, one of the staff facilitators raised the issue of the halfway house. Youth participants asked important questions: Who would be housed there? What types of crimes had they been convicted of? Who would determine the level of safety provided to local residents, particularly students in the area? Why were they building this unit without even talking to them? Though it is quite reasonable for local residents to be concerned about these matters, the staff member raised other issues that appeared to influence the tone of the discussion. He asked the youth if they thought people deserved a second chance at a "normal, productive life" and what kinds of opportunities they believed incarcerated people should be given to return to their communities. These issues, though equally significant and meritorious, were raised in a manner that redirected the youths' questions. After this discussion, in which the staff member's questions were addressed more directly than the initial concerns of the youth, the youths muted their arguments and the meeting proceeded to other matters on the agenda. Quisqueya United never took a public stand either for or against the halfway house, and its membership did not attend the community meetings or the march and rally.

Community activists who organized around the issue of the halfway house used their political capital and their human resources differently. Local policymakers worked through official, bureaucratic channels—the council member met with and addressed federal officials and the community board resorted to its own bureaucratic mechanisms to decide whether or not to draft a letter voicing its concerns. Another local organization had previously attempted to organize a rally in front of the building on 182nd Street. They distributed a flyer announcing a rally for Friday, October 20, 2000. The flyer directed people to "defend your rights" and "unite to fight for your community!" The flyer also listed sponsors of the event—all political and organizational allies of this one organization. Organizers from Dominican Nation said they believed that the organization listed its cosponsors in an effort to draw attention to the director of the lead organization. He had recently unofficially announced his candidacy for the local city council seat and was interested in demonstrating an active presence in community affairs. The October 20 rally did not attract many people.

Dominican Nation went about matters differently. That is, Dominican Nation utilized its network of local activists to plan the community meetings; they phoned people and sent a mass e-mail announcing the issue and upcoming meetings. They also gathered the volunteers who worked in the phone bank effort, which proved successful in getting people to participate in the march and rally. In ensuing developments over the matter, people credited the large community presence as pivotal in the eventual defeat of the halfway house. Though all organizations spoke on behalf of the community later on, Dominican Nation ensured that they made the call to local residents to participate; they are to be credited with gathering the largest number of community residents in this mobilization.

Conclusion

"Community" and defense of "the community" continue to mean various things to different organizations and political institutions in Washington Heights. Nonetheless, "the community" is always cited by all these actors in their efforts to raise financial support for programs or organize around a time- or issue-specific matter, when providing services, and when attempting to "empower" the community. Differences in ideology around what constitutes true community empowerment is not a phenomenon unique to Dominican-Americans. Numerous scholars have documented the heterogeneity of all political and community groups (see, for example, Kwong 1996; Jennings 1992; Marable 1994, 2002). And as Osiris Robles observed,

> Imagínese. Hasta en la propia familia, yo soy diferente a papi, tu eres diferente a tu madre, yo soy diferente a mis hermanos en algunas cosas. Entonces si eso se da en el núcleo familiar, ¿qué nosotros podemos pretender en los núcleos organizativo? Van a existir las diferencias. Hay que permitir que se desarrollen las diferencias, luego que se sepan trabajar las diferencias. . . . Y ojalá que todos los proyectos alcancen un desarrollo máximo porque solamente gana nuestra comunidad.

> [Imagine. Even in one's own family, I am different from my father, you're different from your mother, I'm different from my brothers in some ways. And so if that happens in the heart of the family, what do we expect in the heart of organizing? There are going to be differences. We have to

allow these differences to develop, as long as we know how to work with these differences. . . . And I hope all projects reach their full potential because our community stands to gain.] (Translation by author)

Those seeking empowerment for a racialized immigrant group such as Dominicans must embrace numerous strategies. The next two chapters will deal more directly with racial subjectivity and the ways in which racial discourse is interpolated into local projects.

6

Race, Identities, and the Second Generation

In this chapter I explore the identities and issues around which second-generation Dominicans organize, as well as the factors that have shaped their experiences of and perspectives on race. Many scholarly accounts of immigrant organizing end with questions regarding the second generation. How does the second generation see itself in the immigrant community and in the United States? What identities inform the ways in which they interact with other U.S. communities? What factors shape these identities? In this chapter I directly tackle these questions.

I begin with a review of the concepts raised in the literature on the new second generation. As outlined in earlier chapters, the ideas of ethnicity and identity choices are central to theories of segmented assimilation. An understanding of the new second generation and their identity choices requires an analysis of the way this generation encounters racialization. In the Dominican-American case, it also requires a reading of race in the Dominican Republic.

I argue that second-generation Dominican organizers living in Washington Heights, New York, confront race issues in both the Dominican Republic and in the United States. These processes inform the ways they see themselves in the United States and how they ally with other communities of color.

Second Generation and the Politics of Racial Discourse

During my fieldwork I worked with a community youth program at Quisqueya United. I arrived each summer morning to spend the day with these eleven young men and women. On many occasions these young people would hang out in the air-conditioned basement of the organization's Beacons Initiative site. While they planned events and programs, they also socialized. During these moments they would inadvertently raise issues and present their views around race and Blackness. One young man, Kenny, a dark-skinned Dominican, often arrived with half his hair braided and the other half still "fro'd out." In the late 1990s, it became very fashionable for young men in the hip-hop generation to braid their hair into intricate cornrows. Kenny's half-done hairstyle did not raise questions from the other youth. Instead, a couple of the young women would occasionally take turns trying to complete his braids. A couple of the young women (including those who had straight hair) would arrive with their hair braided or half-done in these hip-hop-inspired designs as well. On one occasion one of these young women, Wanda, a light-skinned Dominican, initiated a conversation about "Blackness" and men. While braiding Kenny's hair, she started to talk about how much effort it takes for people to maintain their braids in good condition and about how she likes guys with braids. This led into talk about what else she thought was attractive in boys her age. In her discussion with her peers, what struck me was the way she discussed features generally pejoratively associated with Blackness. She said, "But you know what I really like? Oh my God, you got them big, black . . . lips and it's, like . . . I love it. . . . If he ain't got those lips, it's just not right. I mean, it's okay, but it's just so much better when you got something to kiss for real." In her admiration of Kenny's hair and "big black . . . lips," this young light-skinned Dominican woman was embracing Blackness.

Although Wanda's reading of Blackness was also very sexualized, it is an important divergence from the way "Black features," such as "big lips" or *pelo malo* (bad hair) have been depicted in racist discourse in the Dominican Republic, an issue I will address later in this chapter (see Badillo 2001; Sagás 2000). The way second-generation youth embrace Blackness is very significant. They develop identities around Blackness within a context of racialization on two fronts. That is, many of their family members still subscribe to racial codes and racism enforced historically in the Dominican Republic (see Sagás 2000; Torres-Saillant 1999a). Thus, youths often hear terms such as *pelo malo* used to describe curly or kinky hair (see Badillo 2001; Candelario 2000; López 2003). And in the United States, they experience racialization as young Black kids on the streets of New York City, a process Nancy López has detailed in *Hopeful Girls, Troubled Boys* (2003). One afternoon at Quisqueya United a fourteen-year-old participant in the organization's summer youth program spoke with his peers about experiences of racism and harassment in public spaces in New York City:

Youth: Me and my friends we were sitting on a bench, right? And we were gonna play basketball but we were just sitting there. And it's like four blocks from my school. It was a public park and we were just sitting there. And the cop comes and they just park right behind us. They were standing there and my friend asks [me], "What are they doing here?" And they wait and they wait and then they go, "Hey, what are you guys doing here?" We're like, "We're gonna play basketball." And they go, "Well, hurry up, play or leave." But it's a public area. It's not, like, what do you call it, what do you call it? . . .

Peer: You're not loitering.

Youth: Yeah, there you go. It wasn't loitering. It wasn't in front of a private area. It was public and then we're telling them we're just there sitting. And they're telling us to leave. And then my friend starts talking in Spanish to one of the cops. He goes, "Look, we're just sitting here. Please, we're not trying to cause any trouble." And then the other guy he goes, "Hey, look, this is America. Talk English, English only." And then my friend goes, "No, Spanish is one of the most spoken languages." And my friend is like disputing with him, like, "Why can't I speak . . . ?" And he's like "just leave," blah, blah, blah. But the Latino cop, he kinda felt bad. He was like, "Just go, just leave, don't cause trouble." And then, when we're trying to cross the street, the cop purposely came right in front of us. And we would walk around to the side to try to leave, go around him, and he would keep on going so we'd have to take a longer way. For nothing.

Informants, especially young males, spoke often of this kind of harassment in the city.

Second-generation Dominican-Americans recognize race, racism, and marginalization in the United States. They state that they contend with these issues more forcefully than do their parents, the first generation. Perhaps it would be more accurate to say that they take on their Blackness and this society's racism more directly—in everyday life and in organizational settings. That they would embrace an identity that is subtly (or directly or violently) marginalized in the Dominican Republic and in the United States beckons us to reexamine the models set forth in the current literature on the second generation.

Another significant factor in the way second-generation Dominican-Americans understand issues of race and racism is that they use this understanding to organize contemporary Dominican politics. Leticia Reyna, a twenty-something second-generation Dominican lawyer and organizer of Dominican Nation, explained,

> I've never believed in "nation," in "race," in none of that. I have always believed that in helping people, you help yourself. I've always worked with poor people, with those that are screwed over. I always got involved in things that would work with poor people. And then I realized that I wanted to be part of that work to help poor people but always I had a little difficulty getting in [to help]. And then I realized that here [in the United States] I'm considered to be part of a group that's defined as poor, or screwed. So what I did was I infiltrated. Well, I didn't infiltrate. I claimed my Dominicanness and Latinoness as a way to help poor people. So if you're involved, well, you have legitimacy because you're born into that group. In this country you're racialized that way, so if you're part of a group, you have legitimacy in discussing issues around that group.

The manner in which Leticia saw herself racialized into particular identities is an experience with which other Dominican youth are also familiar. Many, including Leticia, have used the experiences behind their identity choices to organize, an issue I will demonstrate in the following chapter. Concerns regarding state violence, more specifically police brutality, have been central to much of the panethnic and Black-Latino coalitions in which Dominicans have been involved (Sales and Bush 2000).

Scholarship on Immigrants and Race

Alejandro Portes and others who set forth the segmented assimilation model agree that contemporary immigrants of color and their children are racialized. As discussed in chapter 1, according to Portes' model, in order to overcome the negative effects of a racialized society, immigrants must rely on their co-ethnic community's cultural capital. Yet there are a number of problems with this formulation. The racialization processes to which today's second generation

are subjected also delineate the extent to which ethnic options affect their social mobility. Implicit in these models, however, are racialized assumptions
that follow in the vein of much of the literature focusing on subcultures of
poverty or pathologies of the poor. In these formulations, which date back to
the ideas of Oscar Lewis (1965), researchers assume the existence of independent, identifiable urban subcultures and analyze their internal characteristics,
while negating the continuing significance of external institutions in the lives
of the urban poor. Lewis and his contemporaries posited a theory of urban
disorganization that identified the individuals in subcultures of poverty as responsible for their perpetual, intergenerational poverty (see also Moynihan
1965). Although Lewis noted the significance of advanced capitalism in creating conditions of poverty, he also claimed that many of the impoverished then
create a design for living, an adaptive function of culture, which they pass
unchanging through the generations. In his view, this culture of poverty, once
set in motion, is static, autonomous, and bound. It renders its members unable
to take advantage of changing social and economic conditions or of opportunities for improvement. Lewis offered a solution to overcoming these grim life
prospects: psychological counseling.[1]

Inherent in the concept of segmented assimilation is adherence to the ideas
of a culture of poverty and bound communities. Permeating the work on segmented assimilation are assumptions about race, poverty, and a self-deprecat-
ing culture of pathology among native-born people of color.

The authors suggest that given the vulnerabilities of many second-generation youth—that is, their lack of financial and social capital—if they begin to
identify with native minority groups, they will easily fall prey to these groups'
so-called maladaptive cultures. Thereby, these youth will develop an oppositional identity that will lead them on a path of downward assimilation in
which they can easily succumb to the purported ills of impoverished native
minority cultures: teen pregnancy, truancy, drug use, single-female-headed
households, and perpetual poverty.

The assumptions concerning the pathologies of native minorities are glar-
ingly obvious in this body of literature on the second generation (Pierre 2004).
The authors argue that second-generation youths' best chance for mobility
rests with the cultural and moral capital present in their own immigrant
groups. By implying that success or failure is based on the cultural components of immigrant versus native populations, this analysis clearly blames
native minority groups for their conditions of poverty and marginalization.
The authors argue that when poor immigrant groups live in places where na-

tive minorities also reside, it is the culture of the immigrant group that will save the second generation. Thus, the properties that guarantee either successful mobility or intergenerational poverty lie within the cultures of the groups under study, and inherent in the cultures of native minority groups are characteristics that limit their mobility in this country.

Other scholars have critiqued the assumptions underlying these arguments about the impoverished (see Leacock 1971). They have gone on to examine the ways in which government policies, economic developments, and capitalist exploitation continue to keep people around the world in poverty. Mass movements, particularly the civil rights movement, which incorporated "confrontational politics, which were often racial in form, resulted in public exposure to the deterioration of conditions in the inner city" (Mullings 1987). Anthropologists such as Delmos Jones (1993), Ida Susser (1982), Carol Stack (1974), and Roger Sanjek (1998), using a perspective similar to that found in the work of DuBois ([1899] 1961) and Drake and Cayton (1945), drew attention to the ways in which the urban poor were agents of change, constantly attempting to make choices and restructure elements of urban institutional life. This new work highlighted the constraints that left many of those struggling for change with few tenable options.

Jones (1993) reminds us that people living in poverty always struggle to achieve, to move beyond poverty, but that their success or failure must be analyzed in the context of their relationship to larger power structures. In fact, we could better understand the intergenerational nature of poverty if we understood the manner in which supralocal institutions created and maintained such conditions (see Piven and Cloward 1971; Mullings 1987; Jones 1993; Susser and Kreniske 1987; Sharff 1998). Despite these advances in the social science literature, proponents of the segmented assimilation model continue to invoke vestiges of Oscar Lewis' arguments in their portrayal of native-born minority communities as negative influences on immigrants.

In contemporary discussions of immigrants and incorporation there is a realization that today's immigrants and their children, most of whom hail from Latin America, the Caribbean, Asia, and Africa, are racialized into the lower rungs of the U.S. racial hierarchy. Denied the level of acceptance offered to earlier waves of white ethnics (Sacks 1994; Ignatiev 1995), today's immigrants of color seek new paths to declare their arrival in and ownership of their new homeland. The current literature on the new racialized second-generation immigrants focuses on the identity choices they must make in order to achieve a level of upward mobility. What experiences inform these choices? To what extent can we say that today's second generation chooses an identity that encompasses other Latino and Black categories? Is this identity choice necessarily a retreat into perpetual poverty and complacency with one's marginalized status? And, finally, can we determine the degree to which these coalitional identities mark a new oppositional identity in the making—not the negative construct of oppositional identity appearing in the segmented assimilation literature, but one that questions the conditions that create poverty and injustice?

Racializing Dominican Youth

Ascribed identities affect members of the second generation and limit the choices they can make, as well as their social and economic mobility. Dominicans have been racialized in popular media, popular and academic discourse, and everyday settings (see López 2003). Literature on Washington Heights, particularly on Dominican youth, abounds with vivid portraits of violence, drugs, and gangs (see, for example, Williams 1989; O'Shaughnessy 1992; McAlary 1992b; Gonzalez 1993; Arce 1996; Jackall 1997). One *New York Daily News* cover page article (May 14, 1992) was headlined: "Bodega Terror: Dominican Gangs Rape, Rob and Torture Their Own in City," rearticulating a stereotypical and racist image of Dominicans and their supposedly self-imposed, ruthless, unnecessary violence. In a more recent *New York Daily News* article, the headline promises the reader a "Cocaine Crackdown" in Washington Heights. Although the article emphasizes the New York Police Department seizure of narcotics from a home in the area, it begins with a vivid description of the "front line" of the new army of drug monsters:

> A 13-year-old boy stood on the corner of 150th St. and Amsterdam Ave., his skinny arms folded across his chest as he paced in front of a busy bodega, staring at passersby. Directly across the street, another teen, 17, stood in the same position, his eyes darting up and down the busy block, scanning for *las moscas*, or the flies—slang for undercover cops. The teens were lookouts for a cocaine-dealing gang, The 500 Crew, which took its name from the building where it operated: 500 W. 150th St. Inside the lobby of that building, another man, known as the Crew's manager, took orders for $20 tins, a half-gram of cocaine slipped to customers by a different dealer in neatly folded foil gum wrappers. Upstairs, in a third-floor apartment, was the Crew's stash. There an enforcer stood

guard, protecting the drugs from both the cops and rival dealers. (Mc-Phee 2002)

This depiction of the new drug wars racializes young Dominicans, particularly Black males (see also López 2003). The *New York Daily News* report refers to the young men as a "pack of pigeons." In the 2000 Paramount Pictures motion picture *Shaft*, young Dominicans were once again portrayed as greedy, violent young drug lords against whom society must fight. The heroics of Shaft, the unorthodox crime fighter, are championed as he tries to outsmart [and kill] the young, murderous, gold-chain-wearing, dark-skinned Dominican men. That no other major motion picture features the Dominican experience and that mainstream media accounts continue to focus on Dominicans' involvement with the drug trade point to the way this society has generally seen Dominican youth as a pathological population that must be controlled and rehabilitated.

Martín Guevara, director of Quisqueya United's Beacons Initiative site, is a thirty-one-year-old Dominican-American. He doesn't describe himself as dark skinned or light skinned, but rather as in between these codes of color. He often talks about the many issues that young people in Washington Heights have to deal with. As part of his work at the organization, he has tried to bring youth together with local law enforcement to foster mutual collaboration. Although he believes improvement in the relationship between Dominican youth and law enforcement is possible, he nevertheless recognizes the effects of individual and institutional racism:

> We have friends who are good people, they are open-minded, but you can tell that they walk around with the privilege because they're light [white]. And they can open doors, go to Yonkers, to the wealthy communities and apply for houses and no one will question them. But as soon as my wife and I try that—and we have the same positions, the same salaries, same everything—we don't have that luxury. This country has never made me feel welcome.

Racialization in the Dominican Republic

In an article describing the prospects for first- and second-generation Dominicans, Grasmuck and Pessar (1996: 290) identify race as a fault line between the generations, stating that race "will undoubtedly remain salient for second-generation Dominicans, who are likely to experience both color discrimination and racial pride in the United States in a way different from that experienced by their parents coming from the Dominican Republic."

Race and racialization processes in the Dominican Republic privilege whiteness, as is the case elsewhere in Latin America, the Caribbean, and the United States (Torres-Saillant 1999a, 2000; Safa 1998). The roots of the Dominican version of racialization are found in the colonial era and the Haitian slave revolts (Franco-Pichardo 1996; Sagás 2000). The invention of the Dominican nation-state as a white, or at the very least a non-Black, nation is the product of a long history of political manipulations of race by a powerful white ruling class.

In the late eighteenth century, slaves on the Haitian side of the island of Hispaniola organized the largest and most successful slave revolution in history, revolting against the French colonial government. Sagás (2000: 26) describes the revolution as "a true social revolution, the first one in the Americas." In 1804 Haiti became the first free, Black-ruled nation in the Western Hemisphere, as Blacks and mulattos replaced the white colonial administration. Initially, Toussaint-Louverture, one of the leaders of the Haitian Revolution, found support in the Dominican colony.[2] Once the Haitian Revolution showed signs of victory and a Black government was in place, however, white Dominican elites resisted efforts to unify under Black rule. Many whites fled the island. In 1822 Jean-Pierre Boyer, president of the Haitian Republic, annexed the Spanish colony. Boyer declared the entire island the Republic of Haiti. Sagás (2000) notes that the lower class and the Black masses were in favor of unification under Black Haitian rule. The white elite, having lost administrative posts and privileges based on race, resisted Haitian rule, however. In the early 1840s they began organizing revolts against the Haitian Republic, attempting to unify inhabitants on the eastern portion of the island by highlighting their "Hispanic" origins and values. But it wasn't until Black figures joined the Dominican movement that the country unified against Haiti and drove Haitian authorities from the future Dominican Republic.

In 1844, after the Dominican Republic declared itself sovereign from the unified, Black-controlled government, "U.S. Secretary of State John C. Calhoun spoke of the need for the fledgling Dominican state to receive formal recognition from the U.S., France, and Spain in order to prevent 'the further spread of the Negro influence in the West Indies'" (Torres-Saillant 2000b: 1087). In much of the discourse that followed, elite and ruling Dominicans placed themselves in opposition to Haitians. In their attempts to solidify a national Dominican identity, the ruling elite created the channels through which all

Dominicans would claim their national identity and "race" in contradistinction to Haitians. Dominican identity was Hispanic and Catholic, whereas Haitians became the measure of Blackness. Sagás (2000: 4) defines this *antihaitianismo* as "a set of socially reproduced anti-Haitian prejudices, myths, and stereotypes prevalent in the cultural makeup of the Dominican Republic. These are based on presumed racial, social, economic, and national-cultural differences between the two peoples."

The Dominican ruling elite made strenuous efforts to subsume all Dominicans within the language of Dominican national identity, identifying all Dominicans—Black, white, and mulatto—as part of the Dominican nation. All those who were part of the Dominican nation could claim Hispanic roots and culture and were conditioned to understand that they were "not Black," as Haitians were the true measure of Blackness. With an elite class of whites and mulattos leading the Dominican Republic, the racial hierarchy, though not rigid, did nonetheless place Blackness on the lowest rung of the social order. In efforts to solidify a national Dominican identity, however, the Dominican state created mechanisms whereby the Black masses could claim a measure of superiority over their Haitian neighbors through decades of institutionalized forms of *antihaitianismo* and the privileging of a history that championed white European lineages and cultural inheritances in the Dominican Republic.

In the twentieth century race continued to be a central component in conceptualizations of Dominican national identity. Dominican dictators and leaders such as Rafael Trujillo and Joaquín Balaguer continued to assert the superiority of the "Dominican race" over the "Haitian race." Just six years after becoming president of the Dominican Republic, Trujillo ordered the mass murder of Haitians who resided or worked along the Dominican border. Thousands of Haitians were massacred. He attempted to solidify a Dominican national identity that to some extent included the country's Black masses in order to build loyalty to his regime. He organized intellectuals to provide credibility for Dominican claims of Iberian lineage and superiority over Haitians (and their African past). Sagás (2000: 46) explains, "The regime's intellectuals transformed popular anti-Haitian prejudices, and the elite's Hispanophile ideas, into a complex, yet historically flawed, dominant ideology." *Antihaitianismo* became state-sponsored ideology. One of the most important tools in this agenda was the education system. Under Trujillo, history books were rewritten to highlight Spanish and indigenous presences and influences in the Dominican Republic. Sagás writes,

The ideology of *antihaitianismo,* as promoted during the Trujillo era, operated on simple principles: Haitians were an inferior people, the pure descendants of Black African slaves who were illiterate, malnourished, disease-ridden, and believed in voodoo; Dominicans, on the other hand, were portrayed as the proud descendants of the Catholic Spanish conquistadors and the brave Taino Indians. (Sagás 1993: 47)

Under Trujillo the population was socialized into a national identity that denied their Blackness. The Catholic Church seemed to further this process by admonishing the Haitian "pagans" and underscoring the Hispanic-Catholic character of the Dominican Republic. Trujillo used the church to instill fear of God among the masses, along with respect, obedience, and fear of the Dominican authorities. He also attempted to unite Dominicans by reasserting *antihaitianismo.* "Dominicans were socialized to think and act as a sole entity with a single purpose: to passively accept the authority of General Trujillo" (Sagás 2000: 61).

Dominican citizens were encouraged to reject the racial category of Blackness. Central to Dominican national identity was a social distancing from the blackness identified with Haitians and toward the whiteness identified with the country's elite. In fact, under Trujillo, state documentation, such as census reports and identification cards, did not include the category of Black. Instead, the term *indio* (Indian) was used as a catchall category for all nonwhites. Negrophobia, a sentiment to which the country's white elite adhered, permeated national ideology. Identifications of the Dominican nation as anything but Black prevailed in state-sponsored education, policy, and religion. Trujillo and his administration erased all contributions and influences of people of African descent in Dominican history. The "Black Eve," to use Torres-Saillant's (2000b) terminology, was written out of history and out of the national conscience.

The omission of the majority of the Dominican masses from the discourse of white national identity and history was solidified under Trujillo and continues in the present. The oppression of Haitians also continues to this day, as evidenced by the government's expulsion of Haitians from the country during the 1990s.

Dominican-American Conceptions of Race

The denial of Blackness in the Dominican Republic is countered with different experiences and readings of race by Dominicans living in the United States.

Many Dominican immigrants talk about how they did not discover they were Black until they came to the United States. In the United States, one cannot "escape" into categories meant to hide one's roots, explains Abraham Pierino: "You can't insulate yourself ever from it, not to mention the fact that wherever you go people will remind you . . . aha, so that's who you are!"

Second-generation Dominican-Americans say that their views on race differ from those of their parents in a way that critiques and challenges Dominican racist views. Racialized into the most marginalized sectors of this society—immigrant and Black—many second-generation Dominicans have begun to confront the racial dilemmas their histories present.

Youth Experiences

Experiences with and issues of race and racism have arisen in both the public and the private realms. Second-generation Dominican-Americans have encountered racism in both. During my time in the field, informants spoke primarily of racism experienced in the public sphere, particularly in individual interactions throughout the city and in institutional settings—such as schools or with the New York Police Department. The private spheres of racialization include peer groups and their families. Youths' experiences around race have also been shaped by both these groups. Most of my informants have established friendships or participated in collaborative organizing across ethnic and racial lines (see chapter 7 for examples). These experiences have often led them to reformulate their perceptions of race and ethnicity, as well as their own identities. They have also allowed many to create perspectives around race that contradict and challenge the ideas the first generation brought over from the Dominican Republic. They often contend with and contest concepts of race and racism in this society and within their own families.

Experiencing Race with the Supralocal

In New York, as in many other major U.S. cities, young people of color have called attention to local forms of institutionalized racism and racist practices. Police brutality and unemployment are two issues with particular relevance for second-generation Dominican-American youth in Washington Heights. In 2000, youth of Quisqueya United tackled these issues in their annual youth conference, entitled "Youth, Jobs, and Justice." They focused the conference on the shooting of Amadou Diallo by police, other police brutality, and the erosion of Summer Youth Employment (SYEP) opportunities.

On February 4, 1999, four officers of the New York Police Department's Street Crimes Unit fired forty-one gunshots at Amadou Diallo, an unarmed African immigrant. As Jemima Pierre (2004) explains, Diallo's immigrant identity mattered little in the face of the officers who saw him as Black and suspect as they proceeded to murder him. He died instantly in the vestibule of his apartment building.[3] In early 2000, around the same time as the trial of the officers who killed Mr. Diallo, the New York State Assembly debated eliminating funding for the state's SYEP. This program provided summer jobs and internships for youth ages fourteen through twenty-one throughout the state. In past years Quisqueya United had received funding through the program to employ approximately five hundred area youth every summer either as staff assistants or as participants in daily skill-building seminars.

In 1999 more than 80,000 youth applied for the 40,000 SYEP jobs statewide. Kenneth Fisher, chair of the city council's Youth Services Committee stated, "These are kids who want to work. They are poor but they are ambitious and they do meaningful work and get real-world experience." In a *New York Amsterdam News* story on the issue (March 2–March 8, 2000), David R. Jones wrote, "The losers will be kids from poor neighborhoods who are eager for experience in real jobs."

Youth from Washington Heights were concerned about the effects of these job cuts. On March 29, 2000, the director of the after-school program at Quisqueya United arranged for approximately twelve youth from the youth council to join him on a morning trip to Albany. The group left at 5:30 a.m., traveling from their Washington Heights school site to Albany, where they rallied for support of SYEP. They met with their assemblyman, Adriano Espaillat, to talk about the significance of the program for youth in Washington Heights. As the director of Quisqueya United related, "They met with our assemblyman and he was really impressive, and the youth were able to go into the building and meet with the assemblyman." The fact that Espaillat had a friendly working relationship with the leadership of Quisqueya United no doubt facilitated the youths' access to him and his offices. One former SYEP participant told me later,

> So what would I be doing if I didn't go to SYEP? Okay, so maybe I could make some money in Mickey D's [McDonald's], but that's if they're hiring a lot of people. But it's better for me to come here [to SYEP work at Quisqueya United]. It's different. It's like, you're gonna learn something and you're with people who care. It's the money, no doubt, but it's something else, too. It does something to you, working with other

people who give a shit about what happens to us and here in our [neigh-borhood].

In mid-April the New York State Assembly approved the 40,000 positions in the SYEP, now renamed the Youth Employment Program. Staff at Quisqueya United informed its youth membership and began helping youth council members compile their information in preparation for the April 24 applica-tion release date. Despite the late application process, more than 54,000 youths applied for the slots available that summer. In late May, there were a number of days when the line of youths waiting to apply for the slots avail-able through Quisqueya United stretched down an entire city block and around the corner.

The youth of Quisqueya United had numerous discussions about SYEP and the budget cuts. They felt that people outside the community did not really care about what happened to young people there. Marta, a fourteen-year-old in the leadership group, explained how she learned "a lot of stuff with the SYEP thing. You don't see anybody doing nothing about it, so you take it into your own hands. Since you know ain't nobody gonna do nothing and you know it's gonna affect you, you take it into your own hands." Jesse, a sixteen-year-old in the same program explained, "We kept them from making jails for young people like us. Yeah, cause they was gonna play us. They were gonna take our summer youth jobs, they were gonna take that money and make jails. They were gonna cut schools funds too." Marta said that it's important to keep fight-ing against these injustices: "With each step we can do something, and then maybe one day it can be a giant step. . . . We have to take [it] because you don't see anyone else fighting for you. It's just the opposite. It's like people want to see us fail. Or they make us fight really hard for even the most basic thing. Like respect and jobs and just, really, I mean, just for a chance."

Many of the youth share similar experiences with and interpretations of everyday forms of racism. Henry, a seventeen-year-old college-bound senior related his experience with peers in Quisqueya United, from whom he received an important level of understanding:

I had this friend. He's white. My friend, he was chillin' on the corner [by my apartment]. He's white, chillin' where there are Dominicans. And the cops stopped, like, asking the kid if we're doing something wrong to him. Just because he's chillin' with Dominicans, you know what I mean? It's like, automatically, just because he's chillin' with us, that means we're hurting him or something?

Yudelkis Pérez, a fifteen-year-old Quisqueya United youth council leader, responded, "And that's in our own community. It's not like we're taking a train" and going to another neighborhood. Berto, another youth council leader, responded, "That bugs me out. It shouldn't, but no matter how many times I hear [stories like that], it just bugs me out."

Participating in programs such as those offered in Quisqueya United, including the opportunity to be employed through SYEP, allows youth to share a space with peers who share their frustrations. Many attempt to move toward creating a dialogue around these issues.

Developing Race through Peers

Second-generation Dominican-Americans develop important systems of support with peers. It appears that peer groups composed of fellow Dominicans and people of color allow youths to develop a community in which frustrations over issues of race and racism can be channeled and identities developed.

A sense of solidarity and mutual support is often developed in friendships among second-generation Dominican-Americans and other people of color encountering racism. Such is the case for Dinorah Rosa, a twenty-six-year-old leader of Dominican Nation. She describes herself as privileged. Though she was born in Washington Heights, her grandparents raised her in the Dominican Republic until she reached high school age. She lived in the capital city, in a wealthy neighborhood called *Ensanche Piantini*, or the "family compound," as she likes to call it, because her great-uncle used to own most of the area during the time of Trujillo, and many family members still reside there. In the Dominican Republic, Dinorah is considered white: She is fair skinned and has straight brown hair. Growing up in Santo Domingo, she attended a private school with children from many different countries. Her experience had always been one in which she was one of the many different faces that made up a multicultural group. Her concepts of race, specifically her perception of her own racial identity, changed when she arrived in the United States. Here, she has found friendship and support among peers from different backgrounds but says that a Black friend, Brandy, was most helpful in figuring out issues of race:

[As a senior in high school] I had my first encounter with skinheads. I didn't know what a skinhead was. . . . This kid was harassing me in high school. . . . And nobody really protected me except Brandy. And Brandy was the only Black person in the group, so they had issues with her, too.

So one day I remember going into my house and . . . my aunt was going, "What's wrong with you? Are you stressed? What's going on in school?" And then I started to cry. I was, like, "There's these girls and they're really ugly and they have their head[s] shaved." My father was like, "Oh-oh, my God. Those are skinheads." And I was, like, "Oh, what's a skinhead?" And they explained the whole thing of what a skinhead was. . . . That was, like, my first experience with outright racism that . . . I didn't process until years later.

Brandy was around to protect Dinorah during the school day, and after school her father and uncles accompanied her home. Dinorah continued to develop friendships she calls multicultural, but she continued to experience her "Blackness" through college.

Many second-generation Dominicans develop other important friendships and collaborations across racial and ethnic lines in their college years. These friends often challenge their perceptions and identifications around race. Dinorah explained how her friends questioned her self-identification as being only Latina:

My Black friends [would] say, "You're Black. You're Black. 'Cause you got African blood in you and you got big, thick lips and you got a big Black butt and, like, you're Black." And, [I'm] going, "Yeah, I do have all that, but I'm not [phenotypically] Black." . . . All of that . . . made me kind of come to terms with who I was. It made me really think.

The identity issue that most second-generation Dominicans engage with is "what kind" of Black identity they embody. That is, like Dinorah, many people I worked with feel that others tried to pressure them to make a choice between being Dominican and Latino or being Black. They do not see the two as separate but feel that Black friends would often urge them to identify themselves as Black. The question for many was, Does this embody all of who they are? They acknowledge membership in the Black diaspora, but they infuse this with Latino or Dominican elements of identity. Nocena Domínguez-Fernández, a twenty-eight-year-old organizer for Dominican Nation, expresses this Dominican-American consciousness quite clearly. Nocena developed an identity around Blackness that distinguishes between Blackness as experienced by individuals in the United States versus by individuals in Latin America. She developed this identity as a response to the issues raised during conversations with peers in college:

Well, I just have had that conversation with many people about how . . .
I think a lot of African-American people at [college] that I was with felt
that there was this thread of Africanness that joined everybody. But they
wanted to define what those things were. And I had a problem with that
because to them, you know, if I said I would have more in common with
a person from Puerto Rico who might not look like me in terms of language and culture than I may have with you, and they would say, "Well,
no. You're Black. You look Black. You have that skin tone. So you would
have more in common with me and my experience." And so if I don't
have that, then I'm not African enough. So what am I saying? So I had a
lot of conversations trying to explain to people it's not that I'm denying
that there is a[n] . . . ethnic and racial composition in me that can be
labeled as Black. All I'm saying is that my experience and your experience as an African person have other things added to them. You know,
and I always used to use the example of, you know, you're a first world
African person. I'm a third world African person.

Although Nocena acknowledges her African roots and her Blackness, she
distinguishes those from what she feels African-Americans experience. Her
position does not suggest a distancing from African-Americans; it is, rather,
an affirmation of her place in the African diaspora that includes acknowl-
edgment of roots in the Caribbean.

Contesting Race within the Family

The second generation's definitions of race and Blackness in the United States
contend with their parents' perceptions of race. Racial discourse in the Dominican Republic privileges whiteness. As noted earlier, Dominican elites have
constructed the nation in a way that highlights whiteness and degrades the
population's African roots. Racial codes in the Dominican Republic have been
normalized to the extent that the majority of the country's population can
deny their Blackness, even though their African roots are visible (Torres-
Saillant 2000b; Sagás 2000). When they do acknowledge their African roots, or
Blackness, they claim that they "may be Black, but at least they're not Haitian."

My first encounter with this racialized national identity occurred when I
was living in the Dominican Republic in 1997 in the home of an older, dark-
skinned Dominican woman. She and her husband had lived in New York,
where they raised their daughters. After both daughters graduated from college, the couple returned to live in the Dominican Republic. With money they

had saved over the years and with help from their daughters, they purchased a home in a new urban development in the eastern part of Santo Domingo. During my time there, the homeowner hired a young Dominican woman as a live-in housekeeper. On numerous occasions the older woman would talk about the problems she was experiencing with this young maid. She attributed many of them to the young woman's poverty and, indirectly, to attributes laced with racial codes: "esa cultura de esa gente" [the culture of those people], "la ignorancia de la raza" [the ignorance of the race], "Esa gente es mala . . . se aprovechan. No, no, no, uno no puede darle mucho la mano, se aprovechan de ti" [Those people are bad . . . they take advantage of you. No, no, no, you can't give them much of a hand, they'll take advantage of you]. She and I sat one afternoon watching music videos on television. There was a young Black woman in a hip-hop video that reminded me very much of one of her daughters. I asked if she were presented with two identically dressed Black women— one Dominican, one African-American—would she be able to distinguish between the two? She answered affirmatively, that you can tell, that they were raised differently. I probed, asking if the two were not only dressed alike, but had the same hairstyles and makeup and did not speak, would she still be able to tell? She responded that without question she would be able to tell the difference. When I asked how that could be, if they looked exactly the same, she replied, "Es que la piel de nosotros tiene otro brillo. Tu ves la piel de ellos, como los haitianos, es muy distinto." [Our skin has another shine. You see, their skin, like the Haitians', is very distinct.] As she told me this, she rubbed the skin on her arm, as if to prove that she did, in fact, "have a different shine to her skin."

Categories of skin color in the Dominican Republic allow people to identify themselves as other than white without having to self-identify as Black. Such is the case with the infamous racial code *indio*. Whereas in much of Latin America *indio* is a term describing indigenous peoples, in the Dominican Republic its use is most similar to that of the term *mulatto*, a mix. Anyone not phenotypically white—from light-skinned Blacks to "charcoal black," as Torres-Saillant (1998a) explains—place themselves in this category. The continuum of *indio* runs from *indio claro*, light, to *indio oscuro*, dark. In one census, the Dominican government created the term *color teléfono*, (black) telephone colored, to describe people who were darker than the term *indio* would allow. Again, this terminology allowed people to identify an ambiguous Blackness without ever subscribing to the term *negro* (black).

For Dominicans in the United States, these color codes are not relevant. But perhaps more important, second-generation Dominicans do not find the ideologies behind these codes relevant. Young second-generation participants of one program discussed their parents' ideologies around race and criticized the racism inherent in these modes of thought:

> Well, my mom, she says she's not racist. My grandmother, she's half French and half Spanish. But she's like mad tinted, you know, she's mad tan, Black. So next thing you know, there's Black Dominicans, white Dominicans, every kind of Dominicans you could think of. But then when you're talking about "another race," they freak out. I'm serious, they do freak out. And it's hard for me. My point was that sometimes parents impose these stupid beliefs on us, and we take [them] out onto the streets. But some of us are smart enough not to be guided by that, but some of us are stupid enough to fall for that.

Second-generation Dominican youth identify and challenge what they perceive as the explicit and masked racism carried over from the Dominican Republic:

> My mother, she may sound racist; my mother's not racist, but I think she is in a way. . . . My mother will be, like, "Damn, está tan prieto que es azul." I'll be like, "Mami, how you gonna say that? That he's so Black that he's blue?" That's some messed-up evil. . . . I'm like, "Mami, we're Dominican. Why you gonna say things like that?" And then you wonder why we're divided. And then we wonder why even in our own [families] we're divided. My mother's like that. Because one day I took my boyfriend to my house, right? And he was dark. She was like, "Why you bring this dark nigger to my house?" whatever, whatever. And I'm like, "What? You want me to bring a light-skinned guy, a white boy?" And she's like, "Yeah, it looks better." And I was like, "Well, I like my dark-skinned people." And she was like, "Well, it would look better and people talk too much." And I was like them people don't pay my rent and they don't do nothing for me. My mother, was, like, "Well, people don't like that and they talk."

Youth, Race, and Politics

Second-generation Dominicans living in New York have developed numerous reactions to racialization processes. Many have developed identities and ideologies of race and politics that allow for organizing with other people of color. Speaking of African-American women and their resistance to the popular mammy image, Leith Mullings gives an explanation that applies well to the

Dominican situation: "Despite minimal control of the institutions that produce and reproduce these images, people develop alternative beliefs that grow out of their own experience. In their everyday lives people accommodate, resist, and transform hegemonic models" (Mullings 1997: 119–20). We need to understand this resistance and see it for "what it is (the power to oppose) and what it is not (submission)" (Gáspar de Alba 1995: 104).

Thomas, a young second-generation, light-skinned Dominican who often sported an afro, indicated that he attended the youth program at Quisqueya United as a means of protection from the effects of everyday forms of racism:

> The reason I come here. It might sound kind of selfish. But I do a lot of fucked-up shit and if I was caught for half the things I did, I could get in trouble. But things happen no matter what [I do]. There's times that I'm tired and I'm trying to get home and I take a cab. [On one occasion a] cop follow[ed] me all the way from the Bronx all the way to the front of my building. My neighbors are all chillin' outside. I pay the cab driver. They [the cops] see the money in my hand. They make me get out, take everything out of my pockets. They search me right there in front of my neighbors. Now you don't do that. You followed me. Why? Just because [of] where I was at. Just because I'm Hispanic. Just because of where I live. . . . I'm here minding my own business and you're harassing me. At least being here, I'm not around cops or nobody like that. And if shit happens, then [people in the organization] got my back.

Gabriel Aponte, a twenty-seven-year-old assistant director of Quisqueya United's Beacons site, explained that even though he believes that teenagers of all backgrounds face issues of drugs, unemployment, teen pregnancy and, for youth of color, police brutality, he recognizes the important role of institutionalized racism:

> [The problems are] universal. They're definitely universal. It just affects certain groups in different ways, you know, because if you're, if you're Dominican in this country, you're going to get certain help and you're going to be treated a certain way, you know, and you're going to go to certain schools. If you're white, you're going to go to certain schools, you're going to get treated differently. You're going to have more resources. This community, you know, now is getting more and more resources. But before, I'm pretty sure that other libraries downtown had computers before we had [them] up here in these libraries or in these schools. You know, it's taken a while for us to reach that, but it just shows

that when, when something comes out, before it gets here, it's going to go through so many levels first. I haven't mentioned Blacks because they're a minority like us.

This understanding has led many to take action. Second-generation Dominicans are developing a level of consciousness and action in attempts to counteract the racism and racial disparities they experience growing up in New York. Teen leaders of Quisqueya United's youth programs explain why they feel it is important to participate in local organizations:

We do not like what we see. And adults have this view of us that maybe we've led them to believe or maybe we haven't stood up [to them about it]. . . . But the parents are a tiny portion of it 'cause school también [also], you know. I mean, seriously, think about it. If you hear a teacher call somebody a *plátano* [plantain],[4] what are you supposed to do? You gotta stand up somehow.

Others affirmed the need to organize and make demands:

If you see all the other people who got something in this country, it's not like anyone just gave it to them. That's not what it's like. Nobody's gonna give you nothing for free. You gotta work hard. I mean, you gotta fight to get recognized, to get respect. When we saw the Young Lords' movie [*¡Pa'lante Siempre Pa'lante!*], I felt like they could've been talking about us. We have all those same issues. We should do like they did and organize. They inspired me. We're all here, but we need to do something. Things have to change.

Dominican youths' experiences have shaped not only the way they envision "doing something" about the issues they confront, but their identities as well. Dinorah Rosa said,

Understanding that all of that had been done by society [the good-hair, bad-hair, light-skinned, dark-skinned thing], and so all that, sort of brought me into figuring out what being Latino was and whether I wanted to [identify as] Latin American, Caribbean, whether I was Dominican-American or Dominican, and recognizing that I was American. . . . So that was sort of an identity I'd always had, but redefined Dominican style. Since I was little I always questioned these social inequalities. . . . I remember asking my grandfather why there were these poor people and why, like, maids [in the Dominican Republic] were Black and all these random things and never really getting a straight answer. But realizing all this in college . . . if there was a cause, I was there. And if there was any cause of social inequality, I was there. And anything that I felt was, like, unfair or anything, I was signing a petition or, like, leading a demonstration or whatever. I felt, like, this was sort of my calling or something that I needed to do, [to] just always be involved. And it included Blacks, it included Latinos and it also included the Asians and other groups of color. I'm a part of that no matter how you slice the pie.

While in graduate school, Dinorah belonged to SADA, the Students of African Descent Association. While pursuing her master's degree in public policy, she worked with an African-American professor, Dr. Walter Stafford. Dinorah explains,

[Dr. Stafford] would send me to work with Richie Perez [a recently deceased Puerto Rican organizer in New York, formerly of the Young Lords Party], and he would send me to work with Reverend Rawlins at the Catholic Church Charity. And so through him I got all these gigs and, also, he was one of the founders of the Roundtable of Institutions of People of Color, and through him I met all these really great folks from all these institutions and so, sort of that dream of connecting all these people was, like, yeah, it's really great, that's what it's all about. And so that's how I met and worked with really fabulous people from all groups of color and saw, like, the old guard that had been the young guard. 'Cause all these folks that were in the Roundtable were all friends in the sixties and the seventies, and these were all people who organized at one point, and now they were leading, like, organizations, and they were trying to see how to coalesce and I was, like, this is so cool. I'm going to be there some day. I want to do this. . . . I want to be nurtured and sustained in a community of color. And that, I guess, is one of the things that makes me really happy about coming to [Dominican Nation], that although I have friends of all backgrounds and I love it and it's wonderful, it's just, there's a real nurturing sense. . . . It was sort of an extension of family.

Joaquín Alexander Robles, a Dominican Nation organizer, also saw Dominican-American organizing connected to other communities. He explained how he connected progressive movements throughout Latin America to local action and how that empowered him to take action:

Just to bring out *el orgullo latino* [Latin pride], like the different struggles that we've been involved [in] not only in the U.S. but *otros lugares* [in other places]: El Salvador and Colombia and Santo Domingo and Puerto Rico, and just to make it, to bring it out there, this is a collective movement that's been happening in different countries and different continents with the purpose of self-determination. Knowing all of this, *yo creo que a pesar de estar en un lugar que no somos blancos* [I think that despite being in a place where we're not white] it gives you more sense of pride to be Latino, or Latina, and a person of color. . . . There were some issues where people felt that there were some type[s] of discrimination going on at the school, and so we got involved in outreach, getting people involved, and that was good.

Second-generation Dominicans' experiences of racism and marginalization have clearly allowed some to create a political space that examines and challenges racial ideologies. Dinorah says,

I just think that if we all did it, then that would really contribute to, like, popular growth in the community, in all the communities we're a part of. And maybe even to this society. We all know that real democracy and real civil rights and equality can only happen if we decide to do something and take action.

7

Expanding the Movement

Second-generation Dominicans I interviewed recognize that they wear markers of race in public spaces, no matter how they choose to identify themselves. In this chapter, I point out the ways in which second-generation Dominican-Americans challenge racialization processes. This includes an understanding of why and how they organize with other people of color. Not only does this sort of collaboration demonstrate a connection to native-born people of color, but it also suggests an alliance built on the prospects for social change and social justice—a fluctuating sense of self and community that permits people to work together to obtain resources and rights from the nation or to challenge the state. It also exposes and speaks against three ever-present myths: (1) that primordial ties ultimately bind people to an ethnic group; (2) that a bound, homogeneous, essentialized ethnic group exists; and finally, (3) that those who take refuge in the presumably nonracialized bosom of an ethnic group are promised success.

What kinds of alliances do Dominican-Americans forge with other people of color in New York? What political prospects should we envision for this new generation? This chapter focuses on second-generation organizers' perspectives and activities in order to answer these questions. I present two examples of the ways in which these organizers organize around Blackness and take on racial demarcations in politics in both New York and the Dominican diaspora.

Remapping Ethnic and Racial Identity

In our attempt to understand the significance of second-generation Dominicans' perspectives on race and identity, it is perhaps fitting to highlight the work of some Latino studies scholars. Discussing immigrants and racism in the United States, Candace Nelson and Marta Tienda (1997: 9) state,

> Europeans settled in large Eastern and Western cities during a period of industrial expansion. . . . Predominantly white Europeans gave birth to the melting pot metaphor while the very different experience of Hispanics continues to destroy it. That most Hispanics have not assimilated and occupy the lower ranks of the stratification hierarchy brings into focus the issue of the convergence of ethnicity and low socio-economic position—an issue that needs to be explored in both theoretical and empirical terms.

Felix Padilla (1995) criticizes the vast body of new social science literature that has focused analysis on the separate experiences of individual ethnic groups, claiming that these approaches have ignored the relationships that exist between and among these groups. The issue at hand is not whether various ethnic groups have assimilated, but rather the ways in which members associate with one another in "a conscious attempt to use ethnicity for the purpose of empowerment and entitlement" (Torres and Ngin 1995: 65). But it is important not to assume that an alternative or unexpected ethnic or racial identification automatically suggests protest, resistance, or a social movement. Mullings (1997: 121) states, "What appears as accommodation may be resistance, but it does not lead to transformation. Resisting one set of oppressions may produce or reproduce another; dominant ideology may be replaced with alternative rather than oppositional forms." For the Dominican-American organizers in my research, however, oppositional identities and collaborative organizing are intended to resist dominant discourses of race and oppression.

The meaningful coexistence of various communities of color leads us into a new territory of panethnic/pan-racial theorizing. Though identity choices are infused with deeper power relations and political processes, the notions of heterogeneity and mobilization are very useful in this analysis. Ethnic and racial identity, in this argument, is not inherited or static; it is a social product resulting from a mix of history, politics, and experiences in particular economic and social locations. I do not mean to suggest that people can always choose their ethnic signifiers at will, that all groups have the same prospects, nor that these choices alone can determine socioeconomic and political outcomes, particularly for communities of color.

In his research on new immigrants and second-generation youth, Juan Flores (1993, 1996) discusses the interaction among various Latin-American immigrant groups in New York, arguing, "the individual and interweaving cultures involved are expressions of histories of conquest, enslavement and forced incorporation at the hands of the prevalent surrounding society. As such, the main thrust . . . is toward self-affirmation and association with other cultures caught up in comparable processes of historical recovery and strategic resistance" (1993: 185).

Collaborative organizing and racial and ethnic identity are "collective generated behavior which [transcend] the individual national and cultural identities of the various . . . units and [emerge] as a distinct and separate group identification and consciousness" (Padilla 1995: 442).

Because panethnic/pan-racial identity is situational, Dominican-American individuals can see themselves as a Latino/a at some times and as Dominican or Black at others. By identifying as a person of color, one takes on a consciousness, or at least an understanding, that one shares an experience and a link with other groups of color. At the very least it is an awareness of racialization and one's position in the hierarchy. From this interaction and consciousness, however, may come the beginnings of a movement that attempts to foster positive change in communities of color in the United States. Such is the case with many of my informants. Dinorah Rosa, a self-proclaimed Dominican, of Dominican and Puerto Rican descent, explains that her identity is rooted in the belief that her experiences here in the United States are very similar to those that other women of color face. Guadalupe Palmas, a second-generation Dominican, identifies with the newly arrived Dominican youth because that's how she identifies her family. But growing up in New York also "puts [me] close to Black people and other Hispanics. I mean, I go to school with people and they're all my friends. We've been hanging out since we were little and they're like sisters. . . . Yeah, it's like there's a group of us that's I guess pretty multicultural. I mean, we're probably all Hispanic and Black but we know what we're about." Rosa's and Palmas' conscious attempts to link themselves to these other groups allow them to envision a different means of resistance and affecting change.[1] We need to keep in mind that when people begin to utilize a self-ascribed identity more regularly and consciously, more fruitful social and political prospects enter our field of vision.

Identities such as Latino and person of color, as social categories, are embedded within a larger system and a longer history. We "need to look much more carefully into the social conditions that create the situation for the emergence or construction of this group form" (Padilla 1995: 448). Identity formation is not merely a reactive force among exploited, impoverished groups that occupy lower rungs of political and economic hierarchies. It can be a strategy to achieve various resources and rights for a group. A self-conscious frame of reference as person of color, a Latino, or a member of the African diaspora carries with it strong proactive possibilities. "Rather than deriving from historically fixed and primordial ties, the collective representations . . . and consciousness derive from the observation of the strategic reactions of disadvantaged peoples to their assignment to underprivileged statuses offered within the context of this society's political economy" (Padilla 1995: 451).

From Amadou to the Heights: The New Generation

The issues around which much coalition work has occurred have also permeated the work of younger members of Quisqueya United. In the beginning of the last chapter I highlighted the rallying cry issued by Quisqueya United's youth council in their 2000 conference: "Youth, Jobs, and Justice." Conference flyers announced this demand and asked people, particularly youth in the Washington Heights community, to "be part of the solution!"

In 1990, one year after opening its doors as an incorporated, funded nonprofit organization, Quisqueya United held its first annual youth conference. Every year since then, youth leadership from the organization, under the supervision of staff and with final approval from the organization's executive director, have drafted ideas for workshops and themes for their conference. The annual conference, which targets issues that affect youth in the community, generally draws between two hundred and four hundred area youth. The conferences always run one full day, usually on a Saturday.

The year 2000 marked the conference's tenth anniversary, and the youth council wanted to make this conference a memorable one. That spring their meeting, pre-meeting, and post-meeting time was dedicated to conference planning, particularly as the day of the conference drew near. Planning for the Quisqueya United Tenth Annual Youth Conference took most of the spring. The entire youth council, composed of fifteen youth, met two days every week to discuss the issues being raised for the conference: police brutality and jobs for youth. Police brutality weighed heavily on the minds of the youth in the council, who asked themselves, "How many more [times] will I have to sit there and watch this happen?" Police brutality against Dominicans was not a new theme in the community. In the early 1990s New York police murdered José "Kiko" García in Washington Heights. Many from the old and new guards of activists recalled the uprisings that occurred after police shot Kiko on the street:

It was a time when we all had to come together. It didn't matter that someone was a dealer or not. The issue was how much we were not respected, we were like animals to [the police]. They couldn't care less about what happened to us so we had to speak out. And we shut down the [George Washington] bridge and just made everyone listen. We weren't going to play the silent victims. We were here and we were going to be treated with dignity. . . . And we demanded justice.

For every reported abuse, another handful goes unreported and uninvestigated; the Dominican youth in Washington Heights know this. In April 1997, members of Dominican Nation videotaped an afternoon in their neighborhood. In it they questioned the police-community liaison about the death of a teenage girl. Eyewitnesses (including a Dominican Nation member who lived in the building) said that police officers had chased her up to the roof of a building, handcuffed her, watched her fall, raced to the bottom, and removed the handcuffs. The liaison insisted that the girl's death was a suicide and that neither handcuffs nor force were ever used with the young woman. Yet several eyewitnesses, including young girls ages six to ten, witnessed the event differently.

On various occasions, in my own walks through Washington Heights, I observed police arrests, surrounded by groups of neighborhood residents. During one incident, I stopped and asked an older community member what had happened. She said that the police simply stopped a man as he was walking, reached into his pocket, removed some money, and then handcuffed him. They did not take him away, but rather held him while they radioed for backup. It took about ten minutes for an unmarked van with no windows to arrive and take the man away. In those ten minutes a group of at least twenty-five or thirty people arrived, to "watch over [the situation] and make sure the police don't do anything" according to one woman.

In 1996, Mayor Rudolph Giuliani and police commissioner Howard Safir made strong efforts to establish a contingent of the New York City Police Department in the Dominican Republic. One of the goals of this department was to capture drug dealers from Washington Heights vacationing or taking refuge with family in the Dominican Republic. Organizers with whom I worked perceived this move as adding to the criminalization of young Dominicans in New York City. To many activists, Giuliani and Safir seemed to be more intent on expanding the reach of the police department into the Dominican Republic than on investigating and curbing police brutality in Washington Heights, providing adequate housing for impoverished Dominicans, or establishing guidelines and budgets to support a decent educational system for the growing Dominican/Latino population.

A 1997 Federal Bureau of Investigation report concluded that of all the major U.S. cities, New York City had the lowest crime rate, with the homicide rate down 50 percent and overall crime down 36 percent. Yet complaints and cases of police brutality were on the rise. Iris Baez, mother of Anthony Baez (killed by an illegal police choke hold), observed, "now you can't even stand on your stoop because they [police] can harass you" (June 2, 1997, Channel 11 news report). Young second-generation Dominicans concerned about issues rooted in their New York experience have developed a new kind of identity and organizing—a kind that says little of assimilation and ethnic divisions, but much of resistance to mainstream hype and of empowerment alongside other people of color. Many Dominican Nation members and other Dominican youth have collaborated with other Latinos and African-Americans to confront police brutality and racism. After Kevin Cedeno, another young Black male, was murdered by police officers, there were numerous community protests. One protest took place at the ceremony where the accused officer received a merit award from the thirty-third police precinct. The presence of Dominican and other Black youth was obvious.

Michael Robles, a twenty-seven-year-old pilot and volunteer organizer for Dominican Nation, frequently informed Dominicans about marches in support of Mumia Abu-Jamal. On December 5, 1999, in one of Dominican Nation's open community meetings, he talked about Mumia and why so many people have rallied for his release from prison. He invited people to participate in a meeting with ProLibertad, a progressive Puerto Rican organization, to talk about Mumia and political prisoners in Puerto Rico. The following Saturday, December 11, 1999, I joined members of Dominican Nation at 5:00 a.m. to go to a rally in Philadelphia for Mumia. We took the subway over to a CUNY campus on the Upper East Side of Manhattan. There, we joined dozens of other young people from around New York City on chartered buses.

What propels youth to work against racism? As one second-generation Dominican-American organizer stated, "Yes, we have to work for a better future, but don't forget we're here now, and we have to make the present a place with more justice and opportunity."

This sentiment is what propelled the youth council of Quisqueya United to move forward with their conference agenda. The flyers they distributed declared, "This year we want to address the most important issues that concern young adults, which are Police Brutality and Summer Jobs." When they first talked about the conference and its main objective of demanding justice in areas such as police brutality and youth employment, the youth discussed staging a march around the area of the conference, near 181st Street. Trinidad, one of the more senior members of the council, stood up during one meeting and said,

> You know, we always say how people don't listen to us, so let's make them hear us this time. A conference is good, but let's do something different. We can't just keep our voices locked up inside, inside a school, in a conference. Well, it's good to get together and talk about this but, okay, then what? What are we gonna do? We have to get out there, make people hear us.

It is clear that these activists identify with broader coalitions while simultaneously addressing Dominican-American politics; the two are intimately connected.

Challenging Racial Discourse: Second-Generation Projects

Azabache

In 1995 a group of young activists from Puerto Rican, Black, and Dominican-led organizations began discussing the possibility of collaborating on one project. They envisioned an organization of people who shared political ideologies that demanded justice for Black and Latino populations and for the Black diaspora in general. They called the group Azabache.[2] Many Latino parents have their children wear the *azabache,* a black stone, to protect them from *mal de ojo,* or the evil eye, caused by the envious or ill-intentioned stares of others (see Burk, Weiser, and Keegan 1995; Mikhail 1994).

Members of Azabache hailed from Muévete! (a Puerto Rican youth organization founded in 1993 by twenty-something Puerto Rican activist Gina Amaro and the National Latinas Caucus); from numerous Black and West Indian organizations in Brooklyn, such as the Malcolm X Grassroots Movement; and from the after-school program of Quisqueya United. Among Azabache's members were Martín Guevara, current director of the Quisqueya United Beacons site, and Farabundo Márquez, former codirector of the same program. Many in the organizing committee of Azabache had also been involved in solidarity movements with Cuba; the two members representing

Quisqueya United had actually been the organizing leaders for the New York contingent of the Venceremos Brigade, a U.S.-based organization that assembles groups of young activists from around the country to participate in work and training in Cuba every summer. The Venceremos Brigade represents yet another political coalition with an ideology and goal shared by Dominican activists; furthermore, it is the kind of anti-imperialist project that involves progressive people of color and whites. Martín Guevara said,

> Of course it's connected if you see people that look like you as the constant target. We're targets for police, our communities, our poor. We have overcrowded schools and live in the worst conditions. That's not an accident. Not if you look around and it's happening to all us Black and brown people. . . . And we have to address this together. The divide-and-conquer tactics have to be left behind. We need to address all these political, these real issues together.

All the organizing committee members were aware of the various social justice projects of their peers. And all had organized various rallies protesting police brutality in the city of New York. A flyer announced a rally to protest the light sentence given police officer Frank Speringo, convicted of the wrongful death of María Rivas, a young Dominican woman. Though Speringo was sentenced to four years in prison, the parole board was opting to place him in a work release program:

> This decision is an insult against the Dominican and Latino community, and against the family of María Rivas, which confirms that the judicial system and the police are all part of the same structure of domination and oppression. We must continue the struggle for social justice and to end police brutality, and with that goal we call on women, youth and workers, and the community at large, to join us in this protest.

Collaborations around police brutality have also been apparent during New York's Racial Justice Day, an annual event in which Quisqueya United and Azabache took part. A flyer for the 1997 rally announced a "Rally for Racial Justice: Against Racial Violence and Police Brutality." Held on the steps of New York's City Hall, the rally was spearheaded by the National Congress for Puerto Rican Rights, led by former Young Lords Party member Richie Pérez. The event was cosponsored by Quisqueya United, Azabache, Alianza Islamica, the Almighty Latin King and Queen Nation, the Audre Lorde Project, the Center for Puerto Rican Studies at Hunter College, the Committee Against Anti-Asian

Violence, Jews for Racial and Economic Justice, Malcolm X Grassroots Movement, Muévete!, Mosque of Islamic Brotherhood, and other organizations. The rally was led by the families of victims of police brutality. But the organizers went on to say,

> It's not only about those who have been killed. All our young people are at risk because of government policies and police action. We're marching because it seems that society has no use for its youth, especially youth of color. Education, youth services, and job programs have been cut drastically. There are no jobs for young people and the doors of the colleges are slamming shut in their faces. What is the message when the only increased spending is for prison construction? With dignity, discipline, and militancy, thousands of us will send our own message: INVEST IN OUR YOUTH! JOBS & EDUCATION—NOT PRISONS! PROTECT OUR YOUTH! STOP RACIAL VIOLENCE AND POLICE BRUTALITY! JUSTICE NOW! (Emphasis on flyer)

People, including members of Azabache, organized against the treatment of youth by the state apparatus, particularly Mayor Rudolph Giuliani's crackdown on youth of color, activity that echoes the same kind of organizing ideology as Quisqueya United's youth, described in the last chapter. During the mayor's first year in office, juvenile arrests increased nearly 50 percent, with "four of five arrests . . . for non-violent offenses such as disorderly conduct and drug possession, and half were violations so minor that they did not require fingerprints, just a summons." An Amnesty International report also denounced police practices toward youth of color in Giuliani's New York. As members of Azabache began to meet and organize more continuously, they were given a home in the Caribbean Cultural Center in Midtown Manhattan. Marta Moreno Vega, the center's director and a professor of anthropology at Baruch College of CUNY, had been involved with many of the Azabache activists for years. In public forums, she has expressed the pride she feels in having seen so many of today's leaders grow and flourish (public forum, Baruch College, fall 1997). The selection of the cultural center as their headquarters is highly indicative of the emphasis of the organization. Based in a center that showcases Afro-Caribbean cultures and artistic representations, the group's attachment to the Caribbean and to the African diaspora is striking. Not only do people go to work together around common goals of racial and economic justice, but they do so with a sense of common heritage, a bond created through their roots in the Black diaspora. The selection of the *azabache* as an organizational symbol also signals a connection to Latin America, but in a way that emphasizes Blackness. This is no small divergence from the more common racialized discourse over Blackness, particularly for those coming from the Dominican Republic.

For many second-generation Dominicans, including those who are members of Azabache, the examination of racial discourse and an affirmation of one's Blackness or allegiances to Black populations has been important. This is evident in Azabache's mission statement:

Who We Are: We are a collective of African (Black/New Afrikan) and Latino grassroots community activists desirous of radical social change and the development of a politics of human liberation. We reject capitalism, white supremacy, patriarchy and homophobia as it is these institutions which have constantly oppressed us. We are students, New Afrikan nationalist, socialist, youth organizers, cultural and educational institutions. Collectively we understand that we are responsible for forging this new change in society, [in] our communities and in ourselves. We are dedicated to the defense of human rights globally.

Why We Exist: We exist to initiate a proactive movement for the benefit of our communities. We recognize that a reactive pattern of organizing has had limited success in transforming the overall economic and political condition of People of Color—domestically and internationally. We exist to create new alternatives for strengthening and empowering our communities for self-determination, self-preservation, and self-defense.

What We Will Do: We will organize to bring political power to our communities and improve their social and economic conditions.

We will build truly democratic mass organizations.

We will design and build a citywide network that will unify our actions as a larger community.

We as a collective have taken on the charge of empowering our communities with information needed to effectively mobilize our communities, through organizer training sessions.

We will continue to organize political education sessions for grassroots organizations and activists.

We will articulate the need for the larger masses of our communities to understand their/our responsibility to move forward. (Azabache organizational literature)

The two key points this agenda addresses are (1) unity in Blackness and in experiences of socioeconomic and political oppression; and (2) the need for ongoing collective action among communities of color.

During its relatively short existence (the organization came to an informal and slow end in 1998), Azabache held monthly organizers' training sessions at the Caribbean Cultural Center, where they "continued the dialogue on crucial organizational issues, such as political prisoners and legal defense, organizational security, grassroots utilizations of the Internet, sexism within the ranks, independent educational institutions, etc." (Azabache organizational literature). Between 1995 and 1996, the coalition established a "'Charge for New York City,' that sought to address the position of the African (Black/New Afrikan) and Latino grassroots community and the challenges we face, as well as the direction we must take to effect substantive change" (Azabache organizational literature). In New York City, Latino, Black, and Asian organizing had often taken place around rallies against police brutality (Sales and Bush 2000; Jennings 1994). Azabache was an attempt to continue this coalition on a number of fronts.

In June 1996, the Azabache organizing committee held its second annual roundtable conference in the school where Quisqueya United holds its after-school program. Martín Guevara, director of the Quisqueya United Beacons Initiative, stated, "It's important for this to be included in what we do. We can't build a real movement separately. I want these kids [in the youth programs] to see us working together." In the conference flyer the coordinating committee summarized the first conference as "a 'call to action' to mobilize, educate and organize our communities with the goal of radical social change and the development of a politics of human liberation." They called on organizers to meet to discuss these issues further and create action plans. During the second conference, representatives from all organizations participated in three "think tank microgroups" that focused on the topics of "(1) Defining a common vision, (2) Defining common principles, and (3) Developing common organizing strategies" (Azabache Roundtable Agenda 1996). The conference brought together the new leadership with "veterans from traditional resistance organizations like the Black Panther Party, the Young Lords, SNCC (Student Nonviolent Coordinating Committee), The East, and trade unions" (Sales and Bush 2000: 33).

The involvement of Dominicans, Puerto Ricans, and African-Americans in this collaborative project represents the way some contemporary Dominican-American activists imagine themselves as part of a larger network of people of color in the United States. That this identification is part of political efforts and grassroots mobilization suggests a serious limitation in Alejandro Portes and colleagues' framework of downward assimilation for the new second generation. Second-generation Dominican activists' involvement in organizations such as Azabache indicates not only that they are identifying with and working beyond their national ethnic group, but also that they are doing so consciously, with goals of empowerment and social justice. They question social and political issues in the United States then use the wider network to attempt not merely a modest degree of upward mobility, but more important, to question the practices of policy and race in this country and to demand change. In this way, they create a new level of consciousness. Dominican-Americans' involvement in solidarity efforts with Haitian organizations highlights the importance of this work.

Movimiento de Mujeres Dominico-Haitiana (MUDHA)

The second generation has altered their work and meanings around the Black diaspora in ways that extend beyond the local New York scene, shifting the definitions of Blackness in relation to Haitians. Dominicans have questioned and attempted to change the racialization of Haitians by organizing to change the lived experiences of state-sanctioned racism hiding behind the guise of nation and citizenship. This was evident in the issues the Quisqueya United youth council highlighted for the conference and in the program of Azabache. And, as I will attempt to demonstrate, it was also the driving force behind second-generation Dominicans' involvement with a Haitian organization, Movimiento de Mujeres Dominico-Haitiana or MUDHA (Movement of Dominican-Haitian Women).

Haitians have consistently been racialized in the Dominican Republic as the "savage race." Their stay in that country has been historically tolerated by the state for the cheap and nearly slave labor they provide in the country's sugar and tobacco fields. This racism is often shrugged off in the Dominican Republic as simply the country's consistent adherence to *antihaitianismo* (Sagás 2000).

Founded in 1983, MUDHA works with Dominican-Haitian populations throughout the Dominican Republic. Composed of Dominican women of Haitian descent, it is "una organización No Gubernamental sin fines de lucro, que impulsa el desarrollo democrático, equitativo, solidario, sostenible y el respeto a los Derechos Humanos. . . . Trabaja desde una perspectiva de genero y etnia con la población dominicana de ascendencia haitiana y haitiano con énfasis en las mujeres, niñas y niños" [a nonprofit, nongovernmental organization that advances the development of democracy, egalitarianism, solidarity, sustainable work, and the respect of human rights. . . . It works from a gender and ethnic perspective with Dominicans of Haitian descent, with an emphasis on women and children] (MUDHA document, translated by author). MUDHA's mission statement reads as follows:

> MUDHA, como institución integrada por mujeres dominicanas de ascendencia haitiana, que forman parte de un grupo étnico: promueve la integración y participación de las mujeres dominicanas de ascendencia haitiana y haitianas en los procesos sociales que se desarrollan en sus respectivas comunidades, con la finalidad de contrarrestar el *sexismo, el racismo y el antihaitianismo* que permea amplios sectores de nuestra sociedad; asimismo para defender y salvaguardar los *derechos civiles, políticos, económicos, sociales, culturales y humanos* de la población dominicana de ascendencia haitiana.
>
> [MUDHA, as an institution made up of Dominican women of Haitian descent who form part of an ethnic group, promotes the integration and participation of Dominican women of Haitian descent in the social processes that develop in their communities, with the goal of eradicating the *sexism, racism, and antihaitianismo* that permeates many sectors of our society; to defend the *civil, political, economic, social, cultural, and human rights* of Dominicans of Haitian descent.] (MUDHA, organizational literature, translation by author)

Disdain for Haitians is still state-sanctioned in the Dominican Republic, where children born there to Haitian parents were not, until recently, legally eligible for citizenship. These children have no country to call their own. In 1999 Dominican President Leonel Fernández began to round up Haitians and bus them to the Haitian side of the island. Many were taken away from their families; many children who knew no other country than the Dominican Republic and no other language than Spanish were forced to abandon their lives there. This violent rupture did not go unchallenged by Haitians and Dominicans living in the United States. On a number of occasions in late fall 1999, Dominican and Haitian activists joined forces in rallies in front of the Dominican Consulate in New York City, located in the heart of Times Square, to protest the Dominican government's treatment of Haitians. Among this group was Leticia Reyna, then a law student at Columbia University, who began organizing with Dominican Nation in 1997.

During her tenure at Columbia, Reyna became involved with MUDHA in the Dominican Republic. She began to work with the director of MUDHA, Sonia Pierre, inviting her to speak at Dominican Nation's first national conference in 2000. Conference participants' response to and dialogue with Pierre were so fruitful that in 2001, during planning for Dominican Nation's second national conference, which was to focus on community empowerment through civic participation, one organizer nominated Pierre as the keynote speaker. Another organizer noted that Pierre is "the epitome of civic participation." Organizers also began to work on a lawsuit challenging President Fernández's policies toward Haitians. A legal team from Columbia led the legal assault on the Dominican government. Two renowned authors, Dominican-American Junot Díaz and Haitian-American Edwidge Danticat, joined forces to write an article on the issue. Members of the diaspora of each country met to tackle an issue that was taboo in the Dominican Republic. With dozens of Haitian and Dominican activists coming together, including those from Dominican Nation, these protests marked a time when the two sides of the island joined to demand an end to the racial discourse and racist practices underlying many Dominican state projects. Dominican-Americans took their past successes of bridging presumed ethnic and racial divides to change what racial justice meant for all people of color.

Conclusion

Literature on contemporary immigrant groups places many in a paradigm defined as "betwixt and between." That is, immigrants, particularly the children of immigrants, find themselves straddling their home and U.S. societies. Gerd Baumann (1996) critiques this notion of ambiguous social existence. Referring to the way social scientists have defined South Asian youth living in London, he tells us,

> I could not work out why they should be suspended between, rather than be seen to reach across two cultures. More importantly, which two cultures were involved? Was there a homogeneous British culture on the one hand, perhaps regardless of class or region, and on the other hand some other culture, perhaps one which was shared with their parents? If so, how were these parental cultures defined: was it on the basis of regional origin or religion, caste or language, migratory path or nationality? Each of these could define a community, culture, and an ethnic iden-

tity in the same breath, it seemed. So between which two cultures was any young Southallian suspended? (2)

Are we to retain this language of duality in which cultures are seen as static, bound entities that one can never really transcend? Or should we examine the manner in which people travel through different identities and social locations, altering them in the process? These questions are central to a study on second-generation youth; "what is at stake . . . is the claim to cultural citizenship, as new categories of citizens or social movements organized by disenfranchised citizens demand both state 'recognition' and 'redistribution of resources'" (Maira 2002). Second-generation Dominicans involved in organizations like Quisqueya United, Azabache, Dominican Nation, and MUDHA challenge definitions of ethnicity and race, working across prescribed roles to confront the state and to demand justice. Second-generation Dominican-American organizers can be said to have gone through a three-pronged process to reach their oppositional or progressive stance: (1) They experience daily and institutionalized racism in both the public and private realms; (2) they develop ideologies and identities in response; and (3) they use these identities or ideologies to organize collaborations with other people of color to challenge racist constructs. This "oppositional stance" is crucial as Dominicans attempt to change the structures that have thus far racialized them and limited their opportunities. Guillermo Linares, former city council member for the district that includes Washington Heights, stated,

> Since the very beginning, I understood the importance of making alliances and connections with other communities. I also recognized that the group that is pushing you ahead is your own ethnic group at the immediate level. But you also have potential allies with whom you are struggling together and [with] whom you unite [in political] efforts and [to] promote collective agendas. The results are more effective and viable solutions and with a wider outreach. (Quoted in Ricourt 2002: 77)

Conclusion

Renewing Political Cartographies

In April 2003, the Dominican presidential elections were two months away. They were taking place in a country miles from my field site. Yet there I was in the Dominican Republic, with the organizers of New York–based Dominican Nation, having dinner with one of the presidential candidates and his family. Amid talk of the recent conference in New York, the local (Dominican) elections, and the candidate's and New York organizers' families, I could not help but see the connections between political organizing in Washington Heights and in the Dominican Republic. As the night progressed and the festivities continued, the connections between Dominicans in New York and Dominicans on the island became even more apparent. It was late evening. The power had been temporarily cut off in parts of Los Minas, a neighborhood on the eastern end of Santo Domingo. Nevertheless, food, drink, and *pa'lo* (a Dominican musical style with African roots) continued. I sat with the New York organizers on the veranda of a two-story home belonging to the family of one of the organizers, and we planned for the next day of newspaper interviews and appearances. Although a transnational political connection seemed to be operating, it was not the focus of this trip—at least not in the way current literature on the subject would suggest.

We were there to discuss the New York conference that Dominican Nation had held two months earlier to build a Dominican-American national agenda (see chapter 4). The Dominican Nation representatives had traveled to the Dominican Republic to speak about the conference and the organization and to request support from island leadership in their development efforts in New

York. Our visit just happened to coincide with the Dominican presidential campaign. We had already met with reporters from two national newspapers and the president of the senate. The next day we were to appear on *Hoy Mismo,* the Dominican equivalent of the *Today* show. I tried to understand how this connection and dialogue between leaders in the Dominican Republic and U.S. activists figured into my understanding of the development of local leadership in New York.

I did not intend to ignore what would easily be categorized as a transnational connection. This type of political organizing has been extensively documented and highlighted as proof of the transnational identity and political life of contemporary immigrants. It was not something I would overlook, because it was still an element of Dominican organizing in Washington Heights. Immigrants do maintain important ties to home country politics. And at first glance, Dominican Nation did appear to conform to the transnational paradigm. Although the goal of the 2000 conference in New York was to build a national agenda in the United States, the conference included invited speakers from the island. And there we were, in the Dominican Republic, discussing future plans for collaboration with Dominican leaders.

One point that organizers from Dominican Nation stressed to reporters and to the president of the Senate was that support from politicians in the Dominican Republic was necessary in getting the majority of Dominicans to participate in the 2000 U.S. Census. The leaders of the organization clearly understand that many Dominican immigrants do maintain some identification with and connection to the republic. They watch television programs recorded in the Dominican Republic via satellite, they frequent local businesses to send money and to speak to relatives in the island country, and they read newspapers exported from Santo Domingo to newsstands across Washington Heights.

Dominican Nation leaders explained that based on the 2000 census count, political and financial decisions would be made that might benefit local residents; this could only occur if a majority of Dominicans participated in the count. They enlisted the help of island-based Dominicans in their effort to get the message out to U.S.-based Dominicans that it was safe—even if one were undocumented—to fill out census forms accurately and that all information would be used for purposes of the census count *only*. While this case points to the role those living in the Dominican Republic have in the lives of some Dominicans in the United States, it also highlights another important trend:

that U.S.-based activists and organizations educate politicians in the Dominican Republic on issues that affect Dominicans living in the U.S. and then actively recruit them to support activities and agendas initiated by those living in the U.S.

The goal of this shift in transnational efforts is to have those in the Dominican Republic contribute to the political efforts based in and for Dominican communities in the U.S. Individuals based in the U.S. can and do use the transnational network available as they actively confront the political machinery in local and national settings in the United States, because they believe that in recruiting the support of members of the Dominican Republic's political and media sectors, they might reach more Dominicans, garnering more support and political power in the United States. Similar to the cash remittances from the United States that provide a major source of financial support, this New York–based political capital was finding its way back to the Dominican Republic. Dominican-American organizers are attempting to address a new series of issues, born in New York, with island leaders. Theirs is a call for a renewal of collaborative efforts benefiting Dominicans living in New York. It was, at its most basic level, a move away from the negative "Dominicanyork" stereotype that still prevails among Dominicans on the island. The desired end result of this flow of ideas and dialogue would be a strengthening of the political power of the Dominican community living in New York.

It is at this point that I diverge from the contemporary immigration literature that, as Silvio Torres-Saillant states, lingers on and overdramatizes the transnational condition. I suggest that in the work of Dominican Nation and other organizations in Washington Heights, we are witnessing a political strategy not sufficiently explored in the current literature. Sitting there, speaking of what New York–based leaders were taking to share with island leaders, I sensed a political and personal connection that might never disintegrate, along with a renewed commitment to building the network of empowerment for Dominicans living in New York. That Dominican Nation uses a network of politicians in the Dominican Republic is understandable as they try to expand their collaborations with groups that will help them attain power and rights in the United States.

The identities and networks from which Dominican organizers draw strength are numerous. The ways in which they organize suggest a very strategic manipulation of historical memory, racial politics, and identity shifts. Rooted in all of the activism I witnessed was a desire to effect change in social and political discourse in New York. Dominicans have not simply arrived in Washington Heights; they have also initiated a process of local ownership; they challenge the state, and use Dominican, Latino, and Black identities—racially laced identities they can no more ignore than escape—and coalitions to claim rights and power in the New York political landscape. Although many who carry out this work now are the second generation, first-generation Dominican immigrants also participate in this demand for power. The issue at hand is therefore not about intergenerational difference or fault lines, for as Lisa Lowe (1996: 63) reminds us, "The reduction of ... politics of racialized ethnic groups ... to first-generation/second-generation struggles displaces social differences into a privatized familial opposition, ... denying ... immigrant histories of material exclusion and differentiation."

This study has been about the ways in which immigrants and the second generation have mobilized locally to challenge macro-level politics and obtain power. The roots of identity from which Dominicans pull strategically are multiple and cry out for examination. The routes of Dominican politics, however, are clearly etched in the geography of New York and U.S. politics. It is important to understand the diverse tools with which Dominicans carve their new agenda.

Priority of Local Concerns

There are a number of conclusions to be drawn from this work. First, ethnographic and archival research has demonstrated that in their current organizational activities Dominican-American leaders in Washington Heights prioritize New York–based concerns over home country issues. For the past two decades, Washington Heights community organizers have been mobilizing around problems such as underemployment, government disinvestment in public education, police brutality, and the lack of political representation. Their organizational activities center on educational, economic, and political empowerment in the United States, with home country issues being raised much less frequently. This observation complicates the current trend in popular immigration literature that emphasizes the transnational, or home country politics, aspects of immigrant community politics over local activity (see also Hernández and Jacobs 2001). In this study I offer a critical perspective on the history and continuing development of immigrant-community organizing and empowerment and the role of the second generation in this process.

The Role of the Second Generation

The second conclusion to be gathered from this work is that the second generation plays a significant role in shaping contemporary racial discourse and politics. The literature on migration has often failed to analyze the role of young or second-generation immigrants in shaping the new immigrant politics. Scholars writing on the new second generation have attempted to understand this growing population, focusing much attention on their identity choices and the implications of these choices for the future of immigrant communities. However, this body of literature also omits the second generation from the political landscape. I have attempted to understand the ways in which identity and politics are practiced in Washington Heights, making a concerted effort to document first- and second-generation involvement in local politics. In the process, I have moved away from the assumption of a zero-sum game in which the two generations stand at polar ends of the transnational-local dichotomy. Understanding the continuum of activism, the reasons behind these organizing choices, and the ways in which racialized immigrants use numerous identities, networks, and coalitions to initiate or participate in political projects requires a more nuanced analysis. The task of identifying oneself and others in a particular economic and political context is more than an act of classification or a choice; it is a process of social imagination that forces individuals to search for a new ethos (Flores 1997). This new ethos often leads to a shift in how one organizes collectively, how one (re)presents and (re)envisions cultural practices, and ultimately, how one relates to the state and its institutions. The relationship between the state (its policies and everyday practices) and immigrants is often contentious and plagued with rigid power imbalances; one need only observe recent changes in U.S. immigration and welfare policies to recognize the detrimental effects of such an imbalance. Second-generation Dominican activists confront these issues regularly, and they have altered local politics accordingly.

Race, Identity, and Politics

The third conclusion involves a nuanced understanding of identity politics. Individually and collectively, individuals develop new strategies through which they creatively manipulate or alter state-imposed regulations. These transformations from the margins (of discourse and politics) can serve as vehicles for resistance as well as accommodation. This research documents and places identity formation and manipulation at the center of the discussion of immigrant politics, with attention to racialization and questions of power. Social scientists have begun to understand how marginalized or racialized individuals and groups "selectively appropriate, contest, and transform" cultural and racial meanings (Gregory 1994: 366; see also Darder 1995; Duany 1994; Flores 1993; Fox 1996; Kelley 1997; Mullings 1997; Torres and Ngin 1995). The role of individuals as active agents in such processes is at the forefront of current theories. However, investigations into the roles that contemporary racialized youth play in these processes of reconfiguration and transformation are scarce (Amit-Talai and Wulff 1995; Gilroy 1981–82; Solomos and Back 1995; Willis 1977), as are ethnographies of coalition building across racial and ethnic lines (notable exceptions include Jennings 1992, 1994; Henry 1980, 1994; Tchen 1990; Yun 1993).

When people take control of the representations of themselves, their communities, their cultures, and their histories, they can begin to fashion a more just present and a more empowered future for themselves. From this vantage point, power relations can begin to shift. Frantz Fanon (1963) points out that as long as the dominant group's power to represent the history and cultures of subaltern groups persists, the tools to maintain its domination grow stronger. Once a group begins to break from this structure, it can begin to create new spheres of struggle. Those who control the interpretation of history have in their power the tools necessary for charting the future. Contemporary immigrants and their children, the new second generation, face a deindustrialized, racialized labor market (Kasinitz 1992; Sassen 1991; Sharff 1998) that may curtail their social, economic, and political mobility. Contemporary scholars have demonstrated that people use various strategies to survive economically and socially under such conditions (Jones 1993; Sharff 1998; Sacks 1988; Susser 1982). Excluded from (or forced into) certain social spheres and labor markets, marginalized ethnic and racial populations select, modify, develop, and act upon different modes of identification (Bonus 2000; Goode 2000; Espiritu 1992; Torres and Ngin 1995).

The issue at hand is the extent to which the networks and modes of identification of racialized ethnic groups presuppose "a conscious attempt to use ethnicity for the purpose of empowerment and entitlement" (Torres and Ngin 1995: 65). In a racialized society such as the United States, organizing mobilization around these identities and networks is not only necessary and useful but proactive. It is with these tools and this sense of empowerment that a number of Dominican-American activists have organized. The leaders and members of the organizations that form the subject of this research see their lives very much rooted and routed in the United States (and, for most, in New York).

Community organizations have a long history in Washington Heights; political activism and civic participation have an even longer history in the Dominican Republic. Scholars of transnationalism theorize that involvement in home country politics is a way in which immigrants, denied power in the political mainstream of the host country, choose to exercise some claim to power. Being disenfranchised from the political discourse in the host country, their choice to maintain some engagement with home country politics serves as a tool for regaining a sense of power and control and, in some cases, a rise in social status. In fact, the Dominican organizing that took place in New York City in the 1960s would support the transnational or home politics theory. Underlying this particular transnational work was the political climate in the Dominican Republic at the time and the manner in which many activists were also involved in solidarity movements in multiple countries throughout Latin America, regardless of their country of origin. Political developments would later alter the sense of urgency with which the Dominican expatriate community addressed international solidarity issues. Over the past twenty years, Dominican-Americans' work with other racialized groups has focused on poor educational services, state violence, and racial and social injustice. The ever-changing nature and long-term effects of such politics merit further inquiry.

Limitations of Segmented Assimilation Theory

The fourth conclusion questions the assumptions Portes and others set forth in the segmented assimilation model. The co-ethnic theory is bound and static and does not account for the ways people strategically and successfully organize across ethnic and racial lines. In addition, organizing with native-born minorities has been a crucial step toward empowerment for Dominicans; this collaboration has helped catapult the Dominican-American community onto New York's political landscape. On the surface, it does appear that the organizations I studied retain the co-ethnic identity that Portes endorses. They do not remain bounded within such an identity, however. Many Dominican-Americans collaborate with other groups of color in their efforts to build power in the Dominican community, recognizing their shared status in a racial hierarchy that is both inescapable and static.

As one of Duany's (1994: 34) interviewees stated, "It's difficult to feel American . . . because there's a lot of discrimination against Hispanics." Common experiences of racism and discrimination, coupled with geographic proximity to other communities of color, have led to an ideological and organizational shift among the new generation of Dominican-American activists. That is, the Dominican-American organizers who participated in this study intertwine their Dominican identities and networks with alliances to other marginalized groups in the United States.[1] Members of the new generation are actively engaged in reidentifying themselves and constructing a strategic and empowered sense of community (Hernández and Torres-Saillant 1998). In this process, they are developing an identity, perhaps a worldview, that does not fit with any of the melting pot, cultural pluralist, transnational, or co-ethnic models (Fox 1996; Haslip-Viera and Baver 1996).

During their early years of large-scale participation in local politics in New York, the young Dominican population reached out to other, more established communities of color for support; many leaders of all these populations met in the New York City public schools, including CUNY. By allying with Puerto Ricans in the early years, the Dominican leadership was able to gain a degree of political visibility. Relationships and ties to native minority groups were an important and empowering option for the Dominican community in these years of political growth in Washington Heights. Alliances with Puerto Ricans and with key leaders in the African-American community continued after the 1970s and 1980s. These alliances are still called upon for major events (conferences), fundraising, and political support.

Theories of segmented assimilation and downward assimilation, as proposed by Portes and others, predict that immigrant youth who choose to identify with Black, Puerto Rican, or Mexican-American youth will develop an oppositional identity and spiral down a path of decreased opportunity and life chances. This perspective resonates with elements of the culture of poverty arguments made more than half a century ago while ignoring larger economic and political occurrences that affect the choices and life chances youth of color face in the United States. It also fails to capture the opportunities for empowerment that affiliation with other people of color present for the political growth of populations like Dominicans in Washington Heights.

Far from disengaging from U.S. politics or from other people of color, the local Dominican-American activists described in this book have mapped very complex paths of involvement with other Latinos and with African-Americans in order to secure a space in national politics. Rather than being divisive, identities such as Latino, Dominican, person of color, and Black are used by local organizers to create a political unit that organizes collectively, if only for specific events or around a particular issue. Such identities promote mobilization across multiple boundaries, allowing for the possibility of a larger, more diverse, and potentially more powerful political community. I am not suggesting, however, that activists simply replace one identity with another for political gain nor that these self-ascribed identities and organizational tactics alone can channel resources and power to the Dominican-American community. To make such assumptions would lead away from the complexities of Dominican political organization in Washington Heights. Dominicans wear various markers of identity simultaneously. They are at once Black, Latino, Dominican, Dominican-American, Caribbean, and people of color, even in moments when they are not explicitly defining themselves as such. The issue therefore is not what Dominicans "are," per se, but rather how, when, and why certain identities emerge at specific points in history. Why would an individual carry a Dominican flag at a festival in el Alto Manhattan or northern Manhattan, embrace collective identity and action with a wider Latino coalition on a college campus, and then organize alongside African-American, Asian-American, and Latino youth to protest police brutality? Rick Bonus explains that ethnicity is "a contingent, unstable, and open-ended site of convergence between individuals and society, structure and agency, theory and practice, and accommodation and resistance" (Bonus 2000: 22).

Developing Political Routes in the United States

At the root of U.S. racial hierarchies and ethnicity are issues of division of labor and allocation of resources (Mullings 1978). The way in which people determine when, where, and how one status is articulated over another reveals as much about their individual political strategies as it does about the society in which they operate. Joan Vincent (1974) explains that these choices of ethnicity are embedded in structures and ideologies of domination and power; for racialized subjects of a society, the conventional notion of choosing an identity is obsolete, as their options are circumscribed by a hierarchical system that codifies them as occupants of the lowest rungs. We must study these processes over time, and we must document the relationships and the processes in which these constructs become important.

We must also acknowledge that Dominican leaders are using a Dominican network. Within this network they challenge what it means to belong to the diaspora; they also question and attempt to change racial discourse in Dominicanidad. The organizations I studied do not identify themselves solely with

the Dominican Republic. It is true that family links to the republic are important, as are Dominicans' identification and struggle with other Latinos and
Blacks in the United States and, in some cases, with the Black diaspora in general. But local organizing seems to supersede transnational organizing when
the time comes for the new generation of activists to take action, in school
settings, in social and political meetings, in theater and arts productions, and
in mobilized, organized demonstrations and other political forums. This illu-
minates and complicates our efforts at representing this group. We must continue to investigate the ways in which immigrants and their children play an
active role in trying to change their economic,[2] social, and political situations
in the United States. Their dedication to developing political routes in the
United States continues to grow, with a growing population of youth continually taking the reins. As one organizer stated, "There's always been some organizing in the community. [However,] activism in and of itself is not enough.
There's a role and a purpose for activism. But I've always been clear that activism has to lead toward infrastructure. And the role of activism here is to create
conditions to increase resources to deal with issues here."

Dominicans have been doing this in Washington Heights—some through
social-service delivery, others through grassroots or electoral politics in the
city of New York, and yet others by calling on the Dominican diaspora to lend
a hand in establishing Dominican power in the United States.

There are differences and conflicts between and within the various organizations with which I have worked; however, major shifts are similar, with
funding and political orientation and fervor being the primary differences.
Although financial, logistical, and political difficulties have challenged their
efforts, the Dominican activists and institution builders of Washington
Heights are creating a new sense of community empowerment. Some attempt
to accomplish this by maintaining a Dominican identity, while others reach
out to other communities of color. Some established vertical networks of solidarity, while others garner power with a horizontal network of collaborators.
Some attempt to obtain resources to provide more services, while others challenge the state and its policies. Dominican-American organizing, therefore,
cannot be simply and quickly defined as co-ethnic, transnational, or local. It is,
rather, politically astute and strategic. In any analysis we must recognize the
local and national political climates in the United States, in the Dominican
Republic, and in New York and how they affect community organizing in general, and immigrant community organizing in particular.

We must understand the ways in which local populations and organizations work within the context of and in relationship with larger, macro-level processes. People are not passive or simply reactive in their organizing, but rather are proactive and strategic agents of change in dialogue with political, social, and economic developments around them. It is not difficult to imagine that people will ultimately organize around the concerns and issues they face in their daily lives. People are not isolated; instead, they have a direct and powerful relationship to things external to community life. Community and community organizing are not homogenous, unchanging, bound entities. They change, people renegotiate relationships—both productive and contentious—with one another and with supralocal institutions. Furthermore, communities are riddled with internal politics and structural changes very much related to larger processes. The transnational literature follows community studies in challenging notions of bound communities as passé and inaccurate interpretations of immigrant life. What I suggest is that this understanding be extended to an analysis of the ways in which immigrant politics incorporates multiple communities—Latino, Black, diaspora—in the process of securing political citizenship and empowerment in the United States.

I have attempted to document the numerous and diverse ways that Dominicans have challenged their marginalization and exclusion by organizing to take ownership of their neighborhoods and challenge state policies. That they do so in consultation with non-Dominicans is crucial. And that the second generation is involved in important ways in local politics is not to be ignored. Young émigrés and second-generation immigrants are an integral part of the current social capital in any community. This is particularly the case in Washington Heights, as this population founded and continues to develop some of the most prominent organizations in the neighborhood.

The organizational identities and networks of Dominican activists in Washington Heights do not follow a linear model, but are constantly shaped and reconfigured in response to micro- and macro-level sociopolitical and economic developments. Although it can be argued that the second generation will be more influenced by their peers and by life in the United States than by their parents, and that the first generation will have far greater interest in maintaining some connection to friends, family, and organizational compatriots back home, we must sidestep simplistic zero-sum assumptions and examine the history of Dominican organizing based in New York alongside other, larger political and economic occurrences. And we must do so utilizing the memories and interpretations of those who form a part of this community.

Their individual perspectives and identities may differ radically, as may their political orientations. But the political cultures and communities of which they are all a part have been etched from longer trajectories of activism and will continue to change, as will the actors involved. And it is clear that their involvement and interest in U.S. or New York politics will continue to develop alongside other people of color.

In this study I have explored the dynamics and histories of contemporary organizing and identity politics among Washington Heights' Dominican population. Dominicans are positioned into certain locations and, as I have attempted to document, they organize in diverse ways to position themselves into alternate spaces of empowerment. Many immigrants of color are excluded from full citizenship (Haney López 1996; Takaki 1989; Maira 2002; Espiritu 1992). Excluded from certain spheres, they work to create new forms of empowerment. Bonus (2000: 28) tells us that immigrants "want a different kind of inclusion and they want to transform the ways in which the nation incorporates them."

The political and racial ideologies that motivate many contemporary Dominican activists have been central to the development of local Dominican politics. An Azabache conference flyer quotes Shawna Maglangbayan:

> In essence, an ideology is a set of principles drawn from the historical experience of a given people, a people submitted to the same general social, economic and cultural realities, in a common historical situation. ... The aim of this set of principles is to explain to this given people the causes of their past situation and their present situation, and the ways and means to bring about a future situation consistent with their desire for an independent and free existence.

Dominican activists in Washington Heights are clearly involved in reformulating the political ideologies and practices that are undeniably catapulting this community onto a path leading to empowerment. The tools with which they carve this new path are multiple. The manner in which we describe their efforts must reflect the diverse and powerful ways in which they create community and challenge hegemonic discourses of race, ethnicity, and nation. In the end, scholars must see the diaspora and the connections and disconnections that have made it what it is (Hyppolite 2001: 11)—a community organizing an active citizenry in the United States, demanding resources from the state and inclusion in local politics.

Power in Quisqueya Heights: Concluding Thoughts
for a Renewed Scholarship

I began my official period of fieldwork in the summer of 1999. It was the summer the lights went out in Washington Heights and a storm of activism united many local officials, activists, business owners, and residents. That June, major electrical arteries supplying power to Washington Heights disintegrated because of poor maintenance by Consolidated Edison, New York City's major energy provider. Washington Heights residents and businesses went without electricity for three days. Local residents and business owners demanded explanations and just treatment from the city and from Con Edison. Even Mayor Rudolph Giuliani, not usually sensitive to the issues facing people of color in New York, condemned Con Edison for not preventing this kind of electrical power outage. I very quickly entered the political spheres in which issues of marginalization, disrespect, disenfranchisement, racism, activism, identity, and coalition building took center stage. Local activists with whom I had been involved since 1996 were at the forefront of the community outcry and organizing that took place that summer. People with whom I worked continue to participate in channeling activism into local politics. The power I have seen emanating from the community and its activists has not been sufficiently or adequately documented.

As I complete this book, the activists with whom I worked are still positioning themselves in multiple racial and ethnic networks, coalitions, and political spheres. With a U.S. war targeting the Middle East and civil rights and freedom everywhere, many have taken to the streets in protest. They associate the U.S. military invasion of Iraq with the U.S. invasion of the Dominican Republic in the 1960s and with many other instances where U.S. imperialism has infringed on the basic human rights of people—particularly Black and brown people—throughout the world. One Dominican Nation organizer wrote,

> In case you haven't noticed, we are under siege and our community and its apathy is ill-equipped to deal with these Patriot Games, Mind Games, and the War Games of an unelected President and his unelected Vice President. For some of us born under dictators and other violent, cultish phenomena, this new post 9/11 system resonates with the familiarity of danger. (Reynoso 2003)

Dominican-Americans' understanding of how global events and processes affect individuals' lives has been at the center of the vision of activism they are constructing in New York. Theirs is not an activism bound to co-ethnics, to the neighborhood, to the Dominican diaspora, or even to other people of color. It is an activism that embraces all these identities and all those who use these identities in their cries for justice. In a recent article on her protest against the U.S. attacks on Iraq, one young Dominican Nation organizer simultaneously identifies as an immigrant, a Dominican, a person of color, and an American:

> You see, my existence in this country is a product of 'the American Empire building. . . .' My country's attempts at democracy and some form of economic justice were derailed by the U.S.-backed coups that put my people under dictatorships. . . . So, I—a subject of the American Empire—came knocking at its door. And they inside its walls were shocked . . . stunned to this day as if they just can't figure out where folks like me are coming from—why are folks like me populating the crown's inner-cities and ghettos? Yo—Does America remember what it did to my country's self-determination? So I am a part of you, America. I will not become your house Negro. Or more appropriately your house mulatta. I will not stand by and participate in your colonialism. . . . I will learn your language beautifully and devour the knowledge that you offer. I will do my part to teach you, America, the values and culture of consciousness. And through you, America, the multilingual voices of your empire will be heard. Beware, my America, I might be your future President. (Reynoso 2003)

In my long journey with organizers in Washington Heights I have come to admire the many ways they attempt to create a more empowered citizenry. And I have come to respect the many young people who initiate and labor over these attempts. I began this research during a hot summer, one heated by political debates around local issues. I end in a time when war and U.S. imperialism place a heavy weight on all, including the many activists working from Washington Heights. Through it all, these activists have provided me with a sense of hope. As they work tirelessly to infuse the local and the global with their sense of politics and empowerment, they create possibilities for change.

Notes

Introduction

1. In order to protect the anonymity of all who participated in this research, I have used pseudonyms for individuals and organizations with whom I conducted research. I use the actual names of organizations and individuals whose information I obtained via public channels, such as local media, public records, and archival data sources.

2. Interviewees' and local activists' words are presented in the language they spoke them. That is, if they delivered their thoughts in English, the quotation appears in English in this text. If they chose to speak Spanish, I have retained their words in Spanish. In those cases, I have translated their words following the quotation.

3. The understanding of identity in this study is not based in the discipline of social psychology, but rather, is one of politicized identities. I employ an understanding of the politics of identity as a social construct, the parameters of which are constantly changing. Identity shifts in this case are to be understood in the context of politics, economic conditions, racialization, and power.

Chapter 1. Scholarly Demarcations: New Typologies

1. This interpretation does not imply that the sending and receiving countries had not been linked in other (and in the case of the United States and the Dominican Republic, more exploitative and interdependent colonial) ways, though researchers of transnationalism rarely point out this long-standing relationship of transnational power.

2. Such perspectives resonate in popular discourse as well. In May 2004, at the NAACP gala to celebrate the fiftieth anniversary of the Brown v. Board of Education ruling, Bill Cosby vehemently blamed and chastised poor Blacks for what he suggested was a lack of education, culture, pride, and for general behavior:

It's standing on the corner. It can't speak English. It doesn't want to speak English. I can't even talk the way these people talk. "Why you ain't where you is go, ra." I don't know who these people are. And I blamed the kid until I heard the mother talk. Then I heard the father talk. This is all in the house. You used to talk a certain way on the corner and you got into the house and switched to English. Everybody knows it's important to speak English except these knuckle-heads.

Cosby used high school dropout rates, incarceration rates, and teenage pregnancy rates among Blacks as evidence of the failures of the Black family. After much critique, Cosby stood by his comments and further reprimanded Black impoverished families during his appearance at the Rainbow Push conference in Chicago that same year.

On NPR's *Talk of the Nation*, Michael Eric Dyson (2005b) called Cosby's comments "classist, elitist, and rooted in generational warfare" and stated that Cosby was "ill-informed on critical and complex issues that shape people's lives [and that his words] reinforce suspicions about black humanity." He elaborated his critique of Cosby's moral ideological stance as unbalanced analysis that levels a direct assault on poor Black people in his recent book, *Is Bill Cosby Right? (or Has the Black Middle-Class Lost Its Mind?)* (2005a). There is no question that Cosby's perspective is entrenched in cul-ture-of-poverty and culture-of-pathology theories that fail to consider the complex condition of the lives of the people he so angrily reproaches. Cosby's underlying as-sumptions about impoverished Black populations mirror those found in the literature on the second generation, when it refers to native-born minorities.

3. Leeds defines the supralocal as follows: "Supralocal structures confront any local-ity, any socio-geographical subunit of the total system or its subdivisions, with uni-form, generalized, organizational and operational norms or equipment. Supralocal in-stitutions refers to principles and manners of operation of supralocal structures. Any structure whose form is not governed by, or related to, a given locality, and which con-fronts a number of localities identically, is a supralocal structure operating with supra-local institutions" (Leeds 1973: 27). The state operates as a key set of supralocal institu-tions, "first, because it is a channel and coordinator for the rest of the supralocal institutions of society at large, and second, because it does not necessarily depend di-rectly on the masses for its resources but can exercise control over resources, numbers, and organizations by virtue of its public polity purposes, in a relatively autonomous and indirect way" (Leeds 1973: 30).

Chapter 2. El Alto Manhattan: The Setting and ResearchContext

1. For a comprehensive study of this historical development see Graham (1997).
2. For a more detailed and comprehensive reading of Washington Heights' urban development and its historical class and race-based geographic and social divisions, see

Ira Katznelson (1981), *City Trenches: Urban Politics and the Patterning of Class in the United States.*

3. Each borough of New York City is divided into numerous community planning boards. The city council member with jurisdiction over the corresponding district appoints voting members of these local boards. These boards then deliberate and decide on local matters, such as building planning in their districts.

4. In recent years the media have drawn attention to Dominicans attempting to reach U.S. shores by boat, or *yola*. Given dire economic prospects in the Dominican Republic, many risk their lives in the hope that they might build a life of self-sufficiency and opportunity for their children. Many never make it to their destination: either they are caught and sent back or they lose their lives at sea.

5. CCNY is part of CUNY, a system of public institutions of higher education in the city of New of York. This system spans the five boroughs of New York City and includes community colleges and universities granting bachelor's, master's, doctoral, medical, and law degrees.

6. Osiris Robles, former general coordinator of Dominican Nation, was instrumental in obtaining this space for students at CCNY. As a student at CCNY in the late 1980s and early 1990s, he was a key player in student mobilizations against CUNY cutbacks. After much struggle, CCNY administration granted some concessions, one of which was this office space. Osiris, along with other CCNY student-activists, named the office the Assata Shakur–Guillermo Morales Student Center. Since 1996, however, Dominican Nation has been its main occupant.

7. Some school administrators have recognized the work the teachers do in this program and have offered them a small salary. The instructors have often opted to donate these funds to the organization.

8. Muévete! was born in 1993 after several meetings between Gina Amaro, a young Puerto Rican recently graduated from SUNY Binghamton, and the National Latinas Caucus.

9. Though the Beacons Initiative is the name used for the city-wide program, people typically refer to one of its local programs as "the Beacon" or "the Beacon site." My early encounter with this initiative made me aware of the cyclical nature of networks in Washington Heights. During our first meeting in 1996, I told one of the directors of the Quisqueya United Beacons site that I had become interested in doing work with Dominican political institutions. He gave me contact information for people he thought I should speak with; among them was the principal of a local high school. As it turned out, this educator has been a key figure in the development of both organizations with which I worked in Washington Heights, serving on the board of directors or advisory board of each organization. He also continues to direct his progressive politics beyond the Dominican community. In the mid-1990s, he organized a program that took New York City public school teachers to Cuba for summer training.

Chapter 3. Politics and the Dominican Exodus

1. Popular political movements in the Dominican Republic affected the way in which the Dominican and U.S. governments structured formal and informal policy, particularly immigration policy, during the 1960s and 1990s. This is obviously not specific to the Dominican case but is important to note when discussing the mass migration of this population.

2. When discussing the concept of transnationalism, one can easily view the United States, its policies (such as Operation Bootstrap, NAFTA) and its sponsored businesses (such as United Fruit Company) as the incomparable and ever-powerful neocolonial transmigrant, extending its reach and influence over multiple nation-states.

3. The Dominican Republic's relationship with Haiti has been conflictual. I will discuss the nature of these historic and contemporary issues later in this book.

4. Scholars and activists have noted the probable role of the U.S. government in either planning or assisting with Trujillo's assassination.

5. Numerous authors have documented the feminization of international migration (see, for example, Hernández 2002; Grasmuck and Pessar 1991). More than 50 percent of the Dominican immigrant population is women. For many families, women begin the chain of migration, as was the case with this organizer. Although I do not address migration and gender in this study, an examination of this issue would shed light on the role of women and the politics of gender in establishing the Dominican community and power in New York.

Chapter 4. Setting Down Roots, Expanding Routes

1. Under Trujillo, only a select few from the elite sectors of Dominican society were granted passports by the Dominican government.

2. During the 1960s many Dominicans resided in buildings located on the Upper West Side of Manhattan, joining the Puerto Rican population already living in that neighborhood. Soon thereafter, the gentrification process effectively pushed the new arrivals into a niche on the northernmost tip of Manhattan, Washington Heights and Inwood.

3. This seemed to follow a trend in the city's ethnic and racial political divisions, a product of a long history of politics in New York and Mayor Ed Koch's attempts to solidify divisions along racial lines (see Mollenkopf 1992).

4. During Koch's third term as mayor, he and his associates were investigated for gross abuses of political office and financial misconduct and corruption. Hundreds of people from his administration left in disgrace or were indicted and imprisoned. During this time it was revealed that Koch's close friend and business partner Donald Manes, borough president of Queens, had looted millions from the city's Parking Vio-

lation Bureau. In 1986 Manes committed suicide, never facing investigators' questioning regarding his own involvement in city corruption.

5. See Audrey Singer, October 1999, "U.S. Citizenship Applications at All-Time High," *Population Today* (Washington, D.C.: Population Reference Bureau). This account documents the increased citizenship application rates nationwide. With Greta Gilbertson, Singer also published a piece on Dominican immigrant citizenship rates: "Naturalization in the Wake of Anti-Immigrant Legislation: The Case of Dominican Immigrants in New York City," Carnegie Endowment Working Paper #10 (New York: Carnegie Endowment for International Peace, 2000). The authors cite many reasons for the increase in New York Dominicans, among them access to services such as college financial aid and political promise (when the Dominican government recognized dual citizenship, it encouraged Dominicans in the diaspora to participate in the political life of their host countries). In 2000, one of the founders and continuous leaders of Dominican Nation became a U.S. citizen.

6. In many instances, even within this conference, Dominican-Americans cited examples that illustrated the negative stereotypes Dominicans in the island country have of the "diaspora." The clearest example of such stereotyping lies in the use of the term *Dominicanyork*, a derogatory coinage used by some islanders to describe Dominicans living in New York. The leadership of the Dominican Nation demonstrates a desire to involve island compatriots along the road to building a Dominican-American national agenda; intrinsic to this call for support is the goal to erase negative stereotypes.

7. These alliances are rarely used to establish collaborative institutions. Recently, however, there has been a surge in the antiwar movement, in which Dominicans are organizing with progressive Black, Latino, and white constituents.

Chapter 5. The Leadership

1. I do not mean to suggest that the two generations are distinct entities with their own ideologies. This would imply that political and ideological differences were primarily generation based. As I demonstrate in this chapter, organizers from both generations can be seen operating in overlapping ways. Their modus operandi is not necessarily contingent on their place of birth nor age of migration.

2. Abraham Pierino often says he is the founding executive director and that he created Quisqueya United. Numerous accounts—newspaper and city accounts primarily, but also a few academic accounts—place Pierino in this position. He is to be credited for developing the organization into a multimillion-dollar, multiservice nonprofit organization in Washington Heights. It is, in fact, the largest Dominican-run organization in the state. As discussed elsewhere in the text, the founding board of directors hired Pierino to build the organization, but the founding executive director, Michael Ocampo, was part of the original group of organizers that established the organization.

Ocampo resigned shortly after the organization began to acquire funding. Ocampo is now a member of the local community planning board and is the founding director of an economic development organization in Washington Heights (a program fashioned in concert with the Empowerment Zone project that has transformed Harlem's 125th Street).

3. Minerva, Dedé, Patria, and Maria Teresa Mirabal, more often referred to as *las hermanas Mirabal* or *las Mariposas*, the butterflies, were sisters who worked actively against the Trujillo dictatorship. The Mirabal sisters' work alongside revolutionary groups such as Movimiento Popular Dominicano (MPD) was as well known as Trujillo's ruthless repression. For many Dominicans, the point at which quiet opposition became intolerable was after Trujillo ordered the murder of three of these young activists: Minerva, Patria, and Maria Teresa. On November 20, 1960, they traveled to Puerto Plata on the northern coast of the country to visit Minerva and Patria's husbands, who were being held as political prisoners for their involvement with the June 14, 1959 revolt. Trujillo had ordered executioners to stop the sisters on a deserted road as they made their way away from the prison in Puerto Plata. Trujillo's henchmen mutilated the sisters and their friend, Rufino de la Cruz, and later, pushed their car into a ditch to make it appear an accident. Accounts of the execution fueled mass revolt.

Manuel Aurelio Tavárez Justo, more commonly referred to as Manolo, was another revolutionary figure during the era of Trujillo. While studying at the Universidad Autónoma de Santo Domingo, he maintained a strong presence in anti-Trujillo militant movements. It was during this time that he met and married Minerva Mirabal. Manolo is often recognized as the principal leader of the June 14, 1959 militant attack on the Trujillo government. (This attack never came to fruition, as an infiltrator informed the government, effectively quashing all plans.) In January 1960, Trujillo's Servicio de Inteligencia Militar (SIM), the Military Intelligence Service, arrested and imprisoned Manolo. A few months later, he and other prisoners were relocated from a prison in Santo Domingo to one in Puerto Plata. It was during a visit to this prison, to see Manolo and others that the Mirabal sisters were murdered. Manolo was released from prison two months after Trujillo's assassination in 1961. He formally established the Agrupación Política 14 de Junio, the June 14 political group, and became its founding president. He continued to speak out against imperialism and dictatorships, criticizing Joaquin Balaguer and the government of Juan Bosch. In November 1963 he led an armed revolt, and on December 21, 1963, he was assassinated in Manaclas.

4. Riverbank State Park was initially offered by the city as a concession to area residents. In 1962 city planners began drafting plans for the North River Sewage Treatment Plant, what later became known as the North River Water Pollution Control Plant

(NRWPCP). The plant treats millions of gallons of raw sewage. It was originally slated for construction along the Hudson River on 72nd Street, a predominantly white, upper- and middle-class neighborhood. As a result of community resistance and technical issues, the city altered its plans and built the plant in 1985 alongside the river from 137th Street to 145th Street, an area officially part of West Harlem, a predominantly black neighborhood that Dominicans were also beginning to claim as part of Washington Heights.

The site selected for the NRWPCP was adjacent to dozens of residential buildings. The city and the commission involved in overseeing the planning and construction of this plant did not seek input from area residents, their community boards, or their elected officials. Area residents were concerned over the likely effects of such a plant: pollution, health hazards, and chronic and potentially deadly health problems. The West Harlem Environmental Action Group initiated a court case in 1985 to prevent plant construction, and many other community members protested the building of the plant in the neighborhood, with one protest stopping traffic on the West Side Highway. In an attempt to placate local residents, the state committed itself to building a park on top of the NRWPCP. Area politicians welcomed this park, which would have landscaped areas for leisure activities and events, as well as facilities for swimming, skating, fieldgames, and other sports.

Although odor and health complaints were registered only months after the NRWPCP opened, the city didn't acknowledge such problems until 1991, and the plant nonetheless continues to operate, the rooftop park attracting many to indoor and outdoor recreational facilities. Local residents, advocacy groups, and health institutions continue to draw attention to odor and health concerns, such as increasing asthma rates in the neighborhood.

5. This principal has actively supported the efforts of both Dominican Nation and Quisqueya United, serving on their advisory board and board of directors, respectively. He has a long history of activism stretching to his youth in the Dominican Republic and has been at the helm of many groups that established major organizations in Washington Heights. His politics and strategic community planning skills have consistently found their way into the ongoing programming of Dominican Nation. This principal's support has proved instrumental in the growth of Dominican Nation. In its early years, Dominican Nation held its Saturday programs at this local high school. Most of the program's youth constituents were students in this school as well. And for a short while when some of the leaders were teachers at this school, this principal offered two Dominican Nation leaders overtime pay for their Saturday work with Dominican Nation; until 2000, with the exception of volunteers provided for two years under AmeriCorps, this has been the only salary-type support the staff of Dominican Nation have received.

Chapter 6. Race, Identities, and the Second Generation

1. It is quite ironic that this body of work was published at a time in U.S. history when many impoverished groups were organizing mass movements to address the inequities in U.S. society (Piven and Cloward 1971; Valentine 1968).

2. The Spanish colony offered Toussaint-Louverture refuge and supplied food and other essential resources to those opposing the French. They were motivated in large part by dislike of the French, a political sentiment handed down from the Spanish government (which had recently been defeated by the French in Europe).

3. The police claim they had mistakenly identified him as a suspect and fired when Diallo reached for his pocket to produce identification.

4. *Plátano* is a racial slur used to refer to someone from the Dominican Republic, where plantains abound. In recent years, however, some participants in local parades have begun to pin plantains to their caps and call themselves *plátanos*, turning this into a source of pride. Some might argue that this play on a racist slur is similar to the use of the term *nigga'* by Black youth (particularly those of the hip-hop generation). It also suggests that subjugated people maintain an acute awareness of racism and its drivel and make a conscious attempt to invert and control the language so often used to racialize them.

Chapter 7. Expanding the Movement

1. Many people who are not affiliated with any organization may also identify themselves as Latino or a person of color. We need not assume that they are addressing political issues or trying to overcome disadvantages or gain political, economic, or social empowerment. Certain events—such as the Puerto Rican Day Parade or Dominican Day Parade—may instill ethnic pride for short intervals during the year. "Ethnic fads" also occur, spurred by Hollywood or advertising; at times it has been fashionable to be Latino (for example, Madonna's and Hollywood's obsession and influence in creating popular/mainstream Latino images; Dávila 2001).

2. Azabache is a fossilized carbon that, over millennia, turns into a brilliant black stone. In Latin America it is commonly carved into a charm in the shape of a fist, which is placed on a gold bracelet or necklace. ·

Conclusion: Renewing Political Cartographies

1. I wish to point out here that the youth I worked with did not express the strongly antagonistic feelings toward Puerto Ricans that popular lingo and media stereotypes claim to exist.

2. "Even though Dominicans came predominantly from an urban, middle-sector class/educational background, that is, a higher class background than that of Puerto

Rican migrants, it was not an accident that Dominicans came to occupy the same economic niche [as] the Puerto Ricans in the racial/ethnic division of labor of New York City. As racialized non-citizens, Dominicans were an even cheaper source of labor than were Puerto Ricans. Dominicans replaced the so-called 'expensive' Puerto Rican labor force in the manufacturing sector. Many Dominicans worked in New York City's sweatshops, earning wages below the federal minimum wage. . . . By 1980 Dominicans had formed their own ethnic community in Washington Heights. They started to be identified by whites as a 'racialized other' distinct from Puerto Ricans. However, the 'Puerto Ricanization' [read "Latinization"] of the Dominican migration in New York's racial/ethnic division of labor was an accomplished fact by then. Around 50 percent of the Dominican work force worked as cheap labor in manufacturing" (Grosfoguel and Georas 1996: 196–97).

Bibliography

Alba, Richard D. 1985. "The Twilight of Ethnicity among Americans of European Ancestry: The Case of Italians." In *Ethnicity and Race in the U.S.A.,* ed. Richard Alba. Boston: Routledge and Kegan Paul.

Amit-Talai, Vered, and Helena Wulff, eds. 1995. *Youth Cultures: A Cross-Cultural Perspective.* New York: Routledge.

Anderson, Benedict. 1983. *Imagined Communities: Reflections on the Origin and Spread of Nationalism.* New York: Verso.

Anzaldúa, Gloria. 1987. *La Frontera/Borderlands.* Consortium Books.

Badillo, Cassandra. 2001. "Only My Hairdresser Knows for Sure: Stories of Race, Hair and Gender." *NACLA Report on the Americas* 34 (6): 35–37.

Báez, Josefina. 1999. *Aquí Ahora Es Manhattan, Allá Antes La Romana: Manhattan Here Now, There La Romana.* Colección Tertuliando no. 3. New York: Ediciones Alcance.

Báez Evertsz, Franc. 1978. *Azúcar y dependencia en la República Dominicana.* Santo Domingo: Universidad Autónoma de Santo Domingo.

Balibar, Etienne, and Immanuel Wallerstein. 1991. *Race, Nation, and Class: Ambiguous Identities.* London: Verso.

Barth, Frederick. 1969. *Ethnic Groups and Boundaries: The Social Organization of Cultural Difference.* London: Allen and Unwin.

Basch, Linda. 1987. "The Politics of Caribbeanization: Vincentians and Grenadians in New York." In *Caribbean Life in New York City: Sociocultural Dimension,* ed. Constance Sutton and Elsa Chaney. New York: The Center for Migration Studies of New York.

Basch, Linda, Nina Glick Schiller, and Cristina Szanton Blanc. 1994. *Nations Unbound: Transnational Projects, Postcolonial Predicaments and Deterritorialized Nation-States.* Australia: Gordon and Breach.

Baumann, Gerd. 1996. *Contesting Culture: Discourses of Identity in Multi-Ethnic London.* Cambridge: Cambridge University Press.

Beck, Bertram. 1982. "New Patterns of Service." *Social Policy* 13 (2): 2–3.

Biles, Roger. 2001. "Mayor David Dinkins and the Politics of Race in New York City." In *African-American Mayors: Race, Politics, and the American City,* ed. David Colburn and Jeffrey Adler. Urbana: University of Illinois Press.

Bonus, Rick. 2000. *Locating Filipino Americans: Ethnicity and Cultural Politics of Space.* Philadelphia: Temple University Press.

Burk, M. E., P. C. Weiser, and L. Keegan. 1995. "Cultural Beliefs and Health Behaviors of Pregnant Mexican-American Women: Implications for Primary Care." *Advances in Nursing Science* 7 (4): 37–52.

Candelario, Ginetta. 2000. "Situating Ambiguity: Dominican Identity Formations." Ph.D. diss., CUNY Graduate School and University Center, New York.

Cardwell, Diane. 2002. "Bloomberg's Trip to Caribbean Points to Rising Stature of Latinos." *New York Times,* July 26.

Casimir, Leslie. 2000a. "Dominicans Map National Agenda." *New York Daily News,* February 25.

———. 2000b. "A Little Bit of Home on the Hudson." *New York Daily News,* August 14, 22.

Cassá, Roberto. 1982. *Capitalismo y dictadura.* Santo Domingo: Universidad Autónoma de Santo Domingo.

Castells, Manuel. 1982. "Squatters and Politics in Latin America: A Comparative Analysis of Urban Social Movements in Chile, Peru, and Mexico." In *Towards a Political Economy of Urbanization in Third World Countries,* ed. Helen Safa. New York: Oxford University Press.

———. 1983. *The City and the Grassroots: A Cross-Cultural Theory of Urban Social Movements.* Berkeley and Los Angeles: University of California Press.

———. 1984. "Squatters and the State in Latin America." In *The Urbanization of the Third World,* ed. Joseph Gugler. New York: Oxford University Press.

———. 1997. *The Power of Identity.* Malden, Mass.: Blackwell.

Cox, Oliver. 1948. *Caste, Class and Race: A Study in Social Dynamics.* New York: Modern Reader Paperbacks.

Cruz, José E. 1998. *Identity and Power: Puerto Rican Politics and the Challenge of Ethnicity.* Philadelphia: Temple University Press.

Darder, Antonia, ed. 1995. *Culture and Difference: Critical Perspectives on the Bicultural Experience in the United States.* Westport, Conn.: Bergin and Garvey.

Dávila, Arlene. 2001. *Latinos, Inc.: The Marketing and Making of a People.* Berkeley and Los Angeles: University of California Press.

Day, Barbara. 1990. "New York: David Dinkins Opens the Door." In *Fire in the Hearth: The Radical Politics of Place in America,* ed. Mike Davis, Steven Hiatt, Marie Kennedy, Susan Ruddick, and Michael Sprinker. New York: Verso.

del Castillo, José, Miguel Cocco, Walter Cordero, Max Puig, Otto Fernandez, and Wilfredo Lozano. 1974. *La Gulf y Western en la República Dominicana.* Santo Domingo: Universidad Autónoma de Santo Domingo.

DeWind, Josh, Charles Hirschman, and Philip Kasinitz, eds. 1997. "Immigrant Adaptation and Native-Born Responses in the Making of Americans," special issue, *International Migration Review* 31 (4).

Dietz, James. 1986. *Economic History of Puerto Rico: Institutional Change and Capitalist Development.* Princeton, N.J.: Princeton University Press.

Drake, St. Claire, and Horace Cayton. 1945. *Black Metropolis.* New York: Harcourt, Brace.

Duany, Jorge. 1994. *Quisqueya on the Hudson: The Transnational Identity of Dominicans in Washington Heights.* Dominican Research Monograph series. New York: CUNY Dominican Studies Institute.

————. 1998. "Reconstructing Racial Identity: Ethnicity, Color, and Class among Dominicans in the United States and Puerto Rico." *Latin American Perspectives* 25 (3): 147–72.

DuBois, W.E.B. [1899] 1961. *The Souls of Black Folks.* Greenwich, Conn.: Fawcett Publications.

————. 1935. *Black Reconstruction in America: An Essay toward a History of the Part Which Black Folk Played in the Attempt to Reconstruct Democracy in America, 1860–1880.* New York: Harcourt, Brace.

Dyson, Michael Eric. 2005a. *Is Bill Cosby Right (or Has the Black Middle Class Lost Its Mind?).* Philadelphia: Civitas Books.

————. 2005b. "Is Bill Cosby Right or Is the Black Middle Class Out of Touch?" Broadcast commentary. *Talk of the Nation,* NPR, May 3.

Escobar, Gabriel. 1999. "Dominicans Face Assimilation in Black and White." *Washington Post,* May 14: A21–22.

Espiritu, Yen Le. 1992. *Asian American Pan-Ethnicity: Bridging Institutions and Identities.* Philadelphia: Temple University Press.

Fainstein, Susan, and Norman Fainstein. 1991. "The Changing Character of Community Politics in New York City: 1968–1988." In *Dual City: Restructuring New York,* ed. John Mollenkopf. New York: Russell Sage Foundation.

Fanon, Frantz. 1963. *The Wretched of the Earth.* New York: Grove.

Fiscal Policy Institute. n.d. "Immigrant Workers and Minimum Wage in New York City." Prepared for the New York Immigration Coalition. http://www.fiscalpolicy.org/ImmigrantWorkers&MimimunWage.pdf.

Flores, Juan. 1993. "Que Assimilated, Brother, Yo Soy Asimila'o: The Structuring of Puerto Rican Identity." In *Divided Borders: Essays on Puerto Rican Identity,* ed. Juan Flores. Houston: Arte Público Press.

————. 1996. "Pan-Latino/Trans-Latino: Puerto Ricans in the 'New Nueva York.'" *Centro de Estudios Puertorriqueños* 8 (1–2): 170–86.

————. 1997. "The Latino Imaginary: Dimensions of Community and Identity." In *Tropicalizations: Transcultural Representations of Latinidad,* ed. Frances R. Aparicio and Susana Chavez-Silverman. Hanover, N.H.: University Press of New England.

Foner, Nancy. 2000. *From Ellis Island to JFK: New York's Two Great Waves of Immigration.* New Haven: Yale University Press.

Fox, Geoffrey. 1996. *Hispanic Nation: Culture, Politics, and the Construction of Identity.* New York: Carol Publishing Group.

Franco-Pichardo, Franklin. 1996. *Sobre racismo y antihaitianismo (y otros ensayos).* Santo Domingo: Impresora Vidal.

Frankenberg, Ruth. 1993. *White Women, Race Matters: The Social Construction of Whiteness.* Minneapolis: University of Minnesota Press.

Gans, Herbert. 1962. *The Urban Villagers: Group and Class in the Life of Italian-Americans.* New York: Free Press.

Gáspar de Alba, Alicia. 1995. "The Alter-Native Grain: Theorizing Chicano/a Popular Culture." In *Culture and Difference: Critical Perspectives on the Bicultural Experience in the United States,* ed. Antonia Darder. Westport, Conn.: Bergin and Garvey.

Georges, Eugenia. 1984. "Dominican Diaspora: Putting Down Roots?" *Hispanic Monitor* May: 6.

———. 1987. "A Comment on Dominican Ethnic Associations." In *Caribbean Life in New York City: Sociocultural Dimensions,* ed. Constance Sutton and Elsa Chaney. New York: Center for Migration Studies of New York.

———. 1988. *Dominican Self-Help Associations in Washington Heights: Integration of a New Immigrant Population in a Multiethnic Neighborhood.* Working Paper No. 1. New York: New Directions for Latino Public Policy Research.

Gilbertson, Greta. 1992. "Women's Labor and Enclave Employment: The Case of Dominican and Colombian Women in New York City." *International Migration Review* 29 (3):657–70.

Gilbertson, Greta, and Douglas T. Gurak. 1993. "Broadening the Enclave Debate: The Labor Market Experiences of Dominican and Colombian Men in New York City." *Sociological Forum* 8 (2): 205–20.

Gilroy, Paul. 1981–82. "You Can't Fool the Youths . . . Race and Class Formation in the 1980s." *Race and Class* 23 (2–3): 207–22.

Glazer, Nathan, and Daniel P. Moynihan. 1963. *Beyond the Melting Pot: The Negroes, Puerto Ricans, Jews, Italians, and Irish of New York City.* Boston: The Joint Center for Urban Studies of the Massachusetts Institute of Technology and the President and Fellows of Harvard University.

Gonzalez, David. 1993. "Unmasking the Roots of Washington Heights Violence: Residents Point to Overcrowding, Distrust of Police, Poverty and Thriving Drug Trade." *New York Times,* October 17: 29, 34–35.

Gonzalez, Nancie. 1976. "Multiple Migratory Experiences of Dominicans in New York." *Anthropological Quarterly* 49 (1): 36–43.

Goode, Judith. 2000. "Immigration and Ethnicity: Shifting Boundaries." In *Cultural Diversity in the United States: A Critical Reader,* ed. Ida Susser and Thomas Patterson. Oxford: Blackwell.

Graham, Pamela. 1997. "Reimagining the Nation and Defining the District: Dominican Migration and Transnational Politics." In *Caribbean Circuits: New Directions in the Study of Caribbean Migration,* ed. Patricia Pessar. New York: Center for Migration Studies.

Grasmuck, Sherry, and Patricia Pessar. 1991. *Between Two Islands: Dominican International Migration.* Berkeley and Los Angeles: University of California Press.

———. 1996. "Dominicans in the United States: First- and Second-Generation Settlement, 1960–1990." In *Origins and Destinies: Immigration, Race, and Ethnicity in America,* ed. Silvia Pedraza and Ruben Rumbaut. New York: Wadsworth.

Greenbaum, Susan D. 2002. *More Than Black: Afro-Cubans in Tampa.* Gainesville: University Press of Florida.

Gregory, Steven. 1994. "Race, Rubbish, and Resistance: Empowering Difference in Community Politics." In *Race,* ed. Steven Gregory and Roger Sanjek. New Brunswick, N.J.: Rutgers University Press.

———. 1998. *Black Corona: Race and the Politics of Place in an Urban Community.* Princeton, N.J.: Princeton University Press.

Grosfoguel, Ramon, and Chloe Georas. 1996. "The Racialization of Latino Caribbean Migrants in the New York Metropolitan Area." *Centro de Estudios Puertorriqueños* 8 (1–2): 190–201.

Guest, Kenneth, and Peter Kwong. 2000. "Ethnic Enclaves and Cultural Diversity." In *Cultural Diversity in the United States: A Critical Reader,* ed. Ida Susser and Thomas Patterson. Oxford: Blackwell.

Gupta, Akhil, and James Ferguson. 1992. "Beyond Culture: Space, Identity and the Politics of Difference." *Cultural Anthropology* 7 (1): 6–23.

Gutierrez, David G. 1995. *Walls and Mirrors: Mexican Americans, Mexican Immigrants and the Politics of Ethnicity.* Berkeley and Los Angeles: University of California Press.

Hale, Charles. 1997. "Cultural Politics of Identity in Latin America." *Annual Reviews of Anthropology* 26: 567–90.

Handlin, Oscar. 1951. *The Uprooted: The Epic Story of the Great Migrations That Made the American People.* Boston: Little, Brown.

———. 1959. *The Newcomers: Negroes and Puerto Ricans in a Changing Metropolis.* New York: Doubleday.

Haney López, Ian. 1996. *White by Law: The Legal Construction of Race.* New York: New York University Press.

Haslip-Viera, Gabriel, and Sherrie Baver, eds. 1996. *Latinos in New York: Communities in Transition.* Notre Dame: University of Notre Dame Press.

Henry, Charles P. 1980. "Black-Chicano Coalitions: Possibilities and Problems." *Western Journal of Black Studies* 4: 222–32.

———. 1994. "Urban Politics and Incorporation: The Case of Blacks, Latinos, and Asians in Three Cities." In *Blacks, Latinos, and Asians in Urban America: Status and Prospects for Politics and Activism,* ed. James Jennings. Westport, Conn.: Praeger.

Hernández, Ramona. 2002. *The Mobility of Workers under Advanced Capitalism: Dominican Migration to the United States.* New York: Columbia University Press.

Hernández, Ramona, and Glenn Jacobs. 2001. "Beyond Homeland Politics: Dominicans in Massachusetts." In *Latino Politics in Massachusetts: Struggles, Strategies, and Prospects,* ed. Carol Hardy-Fanta and Jeffrey Gerson. New York: Garland.

Hernández, Ramona, and Francisco Rivera-Batiz. 1997. *Dominican New Yorkers: A Socioeconomic Profile, 1997.* Dominican Research Monographs series. New York: CUNY Dominican Studies Institute.

———. 2003. *Dominicans in the United States: A Socioeconomic Profile, 2000.* Research Monographs series. New York: CUNY Dominican Studies Institute.

Hernández, Ramona, and Silvio Torres-Saillant. 1996. "Dominicans in New York: Men, Women, and Prospects." In *Latinos in New York: Communities in Transition,* ed. Gabriel Haslip-Viera and Sherrie Baver. Notre Dame: University of Notre Dame Press.

———. 1998. *The Dominican Americans.* Westport, Conn.: Greenwood.

Hyppolite, Joanne. 2001. "Dyaspora." In *The Butterfly's Way: Voices from the Haitian Dyaspora in the United States,* ed. Edwidge Danticat. New York: Soho Press.

Ignatiev, Noel. 1995. *How the Irish Became White.* New York: Routledge.

Jackall, Robert. 1997. *Wild Cowboys: Urban Marauders and the Forces of Order.* Cambridge, Mass.: Harvard University Press.

Jennings, James. 1992. "Blacks and Latinos in the American City in the 1990s: Toward Political Alliance or Social Conflict." *National Political Science Review* 3: 158–63.

———. 1994. "Changing Urban Policy Paradigms: Impact of Black and Latino Coalitions." In *Blacks, Latinos, and Asians in Urban America: Status and Prospects for Politics and Activism,* ed. James Jennings. Westport, Conn.: Praeger.

———. 2003. *Welfare Reform and the Revitalization of Inner-City Neighborhoods.* East Lansing: Michigan State University Press.

Jennings, James, and Monte Rivera, eds. 1984. *Puerto Rican Politics in Urban America.* Westport, Conn.: Greenwood.

Jones, Delmos J. 1982. "Are Local Organizations Local?" *Social Policy* 13 (2): 42–45.

———. 1987. "The Community and Organizations in the Community." In *Cities of the United States: Studies in Urban Anthropology,* ed. Leith Mullings. New York: Columbia University Press.

———. 1993. "The Culture of Achievement among the Poor: The Case of Mothers and Children in a Head Start Program." *Critique of Anthropology* 13 (3): 247–66.

Kasinitz, Phillip. 1992. *Caribbean New York.* New York: Cornell University Press.

Katznelson, Ira. 1981. *City Trenches: Urban Politics and the Patterning of Class in the United States.* New York: Pantheon Books.

Kelley, Robin. 1996. *Race Rebels: Culture, Politics, and the Black Working Class.* New York: Free Press.

———. 1997. *Yo' Mama's Disfunktional!: Fighting the Culture Wars in Urban America.* Boston: Beacon Press.

Kohl, Phillip. 1998. "Nationalism and Archaeology: On the Constructions of Nations and the Reconstructions of the Remote Past." *Annual Review of Anthropology* 27: 223–46.

Kozol, Jonathan. 1991. *Savage Inequalities: Children in America's Schools.* New York: Crown Publishers.

Kwong, Peter. 1979. *Chinatown, New York: Labor and Politics, 1930–1950.* New York: Monthly Review Press.

———. 1996. *The New Chinatown.* New York: Hill and Wang.

———. 1997. "Manufacturing Ethnicity." *Critique of Anthropology* 17 (4): 365–87.

LaGuerre, Michel. 1984. *American Odyssey: Haitians in New York City.* New York: Cornell University Press.

Leacock, Eleanor, ed. 1971. *The Culture of Poverty: A Critique*. New York: Simon and Schuster.

Leeds, Anthony. 1973. "Locality Power in Relation to Supralocal Power Institutions." In *Urban Anthropology: Cross-Cultural Studies of Urbanization*, ed. Aidan Southall. New York: Oxford University Press.

Lescaille, Fernando. 1992. "Dominican Political Empowerment." New York: Dominican Public Policy Project.

Levitt, Peggy. 2001. *The Transnational Villagers*. Berkeley and Los Angeles: University of California Press.

Levitt, Peggy, and Mary Waters, eds. 2002. *The Changing Face of Home: The Transnational Lives of the Second Generation*. New York: Russell Sage Foundation.

Lewis, Oscar. 1965. *La Vida: A Puerto Rican Family in the Culture of Poverty—San Juan and New York*. New York: Random House.

———. 1966. "The Culture of Poverty." *Scientific American* 215 (4): 3–9.

Linares, Guillermo. 1989. "Dominicans in New York: Superando los Obstáculos y Adqui-riendo Poder. The Struggle for Community Control in District 6." *Centro Bulletin* 2 (5): 77–84.

Lipsitz, George. 1998. *The Possessive Investment in Whiteness: How White People Profit from Identity Politics*. Philadelphia: Temple University Press.

Lopez, David, and Yen Le Espiritu. 1990. "Panethnicity in the United States: A Theoretical Framework." *Ethnic and Racial Studies* 13 (2): 198–224.

López, Nancy. 2003. *Hopeful Girls, Troubled Boys: Race and Gender Disparity in Urban Education*. New York: Routledge.

Lowe, Lisa. 1996. *Immigrant Acts: On Asian American Cultural Politics*. Durham: Duke University Press.

Lowenstein, Steven. 1989. *Frankfurt on the Hudson: The German-Jewish Community of Washington Heights, 1933–1983, Its Structure and Culture*. Detroit: Wayne State University Press.

Mahler, Sarah. 1995. *American Dreaming: Immigrant Life on the Margins*. Princeton, N.J.: Princeton University Press.

Maira, Sunaina. 2002. *Desis in the House: Indian American Youth Culture in New York City*. Philadelphia: Temple University Press.

Malinowski, Bronislaw. 1922. *Argonauts of the Western Pacific*. New York: Dutton.

Marable, Manning. 1994. "Building Coalitions among Communities of Color: Beyond Racial Identity Politics." In *Blacks, Latinos, and Asians in Urban America: Status and Prospects for Politics and Activism*, ed. James Jennings. Westport, Conn.: Praeger.

———. 2002. *The Great Wells of Democracy: The Meaning of Race in American Life*. New York: Basic Civitas Books.

Marable, Manning, and Leith Mullings. 1995. "The Divided Mind of Black America: Race, Ideology and Politics in the Post-Civil-Rights Era." In *Beyond Black and White: Transforming African-American Politics*, ed. Manning Marable. New York: Verso.

———, eds. 2000. *Let Nobody Turn Us Around: Voices of Resistance, Reform, and Renewal: An African American Anthology*. Lanham, Md.: Rowman and Littlefield.

Martin, John Bartlow. 1966. *Overtaken by Events: The Dominican Crisis from the Fall of Trujillo to the Civil War.* New York: Doubleday.

Marx, Anthony. 1998. *Making Race and Nation: A Comparison of the United States, South Africa, and Brazil.* New York: Cambridge University Press.

Maxwell, Andrew. 1993. "The Underclass, 'Social Isolation,' and 'Concentration Effects': The 'Culture of Poverty' Revisited." *Critique of Anthropology* 13 (3): 231–45.

McAlary, Mike. 1992a. "Tragic Legacy of 'Narco Village.'" *New York Daily News,* April 20.

———. 1992b. "Washington Heights' Deadly Dominican Connection: One Town's Poor Happily Kill Here for Drug Millions (Exclusive)." *New York Post,* September 16, 3, 13.

McPhee, Michelle. 2002. "Cocaine Crackdown." *New York Daily News,* July 21.

Mead, Margaret. 1949. *Coming of Age in Samoa.* New York: Mentor Books.

Mikhail, B. 1994. "Hispanic Mothers' Beliefs and Practices Regarding Selected Children's Health Problems." *Western Journal of Nursing Research* 16 (6): 623–38.

Miller, D. W. 1999. "Scholars of Immigration Focus on the Children." *Chronicle of Higher Education* 45 (22): A19.

Mills, C. Wright. 1959. *The Sociological Imagination.* New York: Grove.

Mitchell, Christopher. 1992. "U.S. Foreign Policy and Dominican Migration to the United States." In *Western Hemisphere Immigration and United States Foreign Policy,* ed. Christopher Mitchell. University Park: Penn State University Press.

Mollenkopf, John. 1992. *A Phoenix in the Ashes: The Rise and Fall of the Koch Administration.* Princeton, N.J.: Princeton University Press.

Mollenkopf, John, and Manuel Castells. 1991. *Dual City: Restructuring New York.* New York: Russell Sage Foundation.

Moya Pons, Frank. 1995. *The Dominican Republic: A National History.* New York: Hispaniola Books.

Moynihan, Daniel Patrick. 1965. *The Negro Family: The Case for National Action.* Washington, D.C.: Office of Policy Planning and Research, U.S. Department of Labor.

Muller, Thomas. 1993. *Immigrants and the American City.* New York: New York University Press.

Mullings, Leith. 1977. "The New Ethnicity: Old Wine in New Bottles." *Reviews in Anthropology* 4: 615–24.

———. 1978. "Ethnicity and Stratification in the United States." *Annals of the New York Academy of Sciences* 318: 10–22.

———. 1997. "Images, Ideology, and Women of Color." In *On Our Own Terms: Race, Class, and Gender in the Lives of African-American Women,* ed. Leith Mullings. New York: Routledge.

———, ed. 1987. *Cities of the United States: Studies in Urban Anthropology.* New York: Columbia University Press.

Mumford Center for Comparative Urban and Regional Research. 2001. "New York, NY PMSA: Hispanic Population Data for the Metropolitan Statistical Area." New York: State University of New York, Albany.

Nelson, Candace, and Marta Tienda. 1997. "The Structuring of Hispanic Ethnicity: Historical and Contemporary Perspectives." In *Challenging Fronteras: Structuring Latino*

Lives in the United States, ed. Mary Romero, Pierrette Hondagneu-Sotelo, and Vilma Ortiz. New York: Routledge.

New York City Department of City Planning. 1999. *District Profiles.* New York: Author.

Nugent, David. 1982. "Closed Systems and Contradiction: The Kachin in and out of History." *Man* 17: 508–27.

Oboler, Suzanne. 1995. *Ethnic Labels, Latino Lives: Identity and the Politics of (Re)Presentation in the United States.* Minneapolis: University of Minnesota Press.

Ong, Aihwa. 1991. "The Gender and Labor Politics of Postmodernity." *Annual Review of Anthropology* 20: 279–309.

O'Shaughnessy, Patrice. 1992. "Brutalized Bizman vs. Dominican Gang." *New York Daily News,* May 14, 3.

Padilla, Felix. 1995. "On the Nature of Latino Ethnicity." In *Historical Themes and Identity: Mestizaje and Labels,* ed. Antoinette Sedillo López. New York: Garland.

Park, Robert Ezra. [1915] 1969. "The City: Suggestions for the Investigation of Human Behavior in the Urban Environment." In *Classic Essays on the Culture of Cities,* ed. Richard Sennett. New York: Appleton-Century-Crofts.

Pérez-Firmat, Gustavo. 1994. *Life on the Hyphen: The Cuban-American Way.* Austin: University of Texas Press.

Pierre, Jemima. 2004. "Black Immigrants in the United States and the 'Cultural Narratives' of Ethnicity." *Identities: Global Studies in Culture and Power* 11: 141–70.

Piven, Frances Fox, and Richard Cloward. 1971. *Regulating the Poor: The Functions of Public Welfare.* New York: Pantheon.

———. 1977. *Poor People's Movements: Studies from the Contemporary United States.* New York: Pantheon.

Plant, Roger. 1987. *Sugar and Modern Slavery: A Tale of Two Countries.* Atlantic Highlands, N.J.: Zed Books.

Portes, Alejandro, ed. 1996. *The New Second Generation.* New York: Russell Sage Foundation.

Portes, Alejandro, and Robert Bach. 1985. *Latin Journey: Cuban and Mexican Immigrants in the United States.* Berkeley and Los Angeles: University of California Press.

Portes, Alejandro, and Dag MacLeod. 1996. "What Shall I Call Myself? Hispanic Identity Formation in the Second Generation." *Ethnic and Racial Studies* 19 (3): 523–47.

Portes, Alejandro, and Ruben Rumbaut. 2001a. *Ethnicities: Children of Immigrants in America.* Berkeley and Los Angeles: University of California Press; New York: Russell Sage Foundation.

———. 2001b. *Legacies: The Story of the Immigrant Second Generation.* Berkeley and Los Angeles: University of California Press; New York: Russell Sage Foundation.

Portes, Alejandro, and Min Zhou. 1993. "The New Second Generation: Segmented Assimilation and Its Variants." *Annals of the American Academy of Political Social Science* 530 (November): 74–96.

Prashad, Vijay. 2001. *Everybody Was Kung Fu Fighting: Afro-Asian Connections and the Myth of Cultural Purity.* Boston: Beacon Press.

Reynoso, Julissa. 2003. "From a Cabaret on War: Yo, la Loca." *Brooklyn Rail: Critical Per-*

spectives on Arts, Politics, and Culture. April. http://www.thebrooklynrail.org/theater/
april03/yolaloca.html.

Ricourt, Milagros. 2002. *Dominicans in New York City: Power from the Margins.* New York:
Routledge.

Ricourt, Milagros, and Ruby Danta. 2002. *Hispanas de Queens: Latino Panethnicity in a
New York City Neighborhood.* Ithaca, N.Y.: Cornell University Press.

Rischin, Moses. 1962. *The Promised City: New York's Jews, 1870–1914.* Cambridge, Mass.:
Harvard University Press.

Rivera, Raquel Z. 2003. *New York Ricans from the Hip Hop Zone.* New York: Palgrave.

Robotham, Don. 1996. "Transnationalism in the Caribbean: Formal and Informal."
American Ethnologist 25 (2): 307–21.

Roediger, David. 1999. *The Wages of Whiteness: Race and the Making of the American
Working Class.* New York: Verso.

Rosaldo, Renato. 1993. *Culture and Truth: The Remaking of Social Analysis.* Boston: Beacon Press.

Sacks, Karen Brodkin. 1988. *Caring by the Hour: Women, Work, and Organizing at Duke
Medical Center.* Chicago: University of Illinois Press.

———. 1994. "How Did Jews Become White Folks?" In *Race,* ed. Steven Gregory and
Roger Sanjek. New Brunswick, N.J.: Rutgers University Press.

———. 1999. *How Jews Became White Folks and What That Says About Race in America.*
New Brunswick, N.J.: Rutgers University Press.

Safa, Helen, ed. 1982. *Towards a Political Economy of Urbanization in Third World Countries.* New York: Oxford University Press.

———. 1998. "Race and National Identity in the Americas," special issue, *Latin American
Perspectives* 25 (3).

Sagás, Ernesto. 1993. "A Case of Mistaken Identity: Antihaitianismo in Dominican Culture." *Latinamericanist* (University of Florida) 29 (1):1–5.

———. 2000. *Race and Politics in the Dominican Republic.* Gainesville: University Press
of Florida.

Sagás, Ernesto, and Sintia E. Molina, eds., 2004. *Dominican Migration: Transnational Perspectives.* Gainesville: University Press of Florida.

Sainz, Rudy Anthony. 1990. "Dominican Ethnic Associations: Classification and Service
Delivery Roles in Washington Heights." Ph.D. diss., Columbia University.

Sales, William W., and Roderick Bush. 2000. "The Political Awakening of Blacks and
Latinos in New York City: Competition or Cooperation?" *Social Justice* 27 (1): 19–42.

Sánchez, George. 1993. *Becoming Mexican American: Ethnicity, Culture, and Identity in
Chicano Los Angeles, 1900–1945.* New York: Oxford University Press.

Sanders, J. M., and Victor Nee. 1987. "Limits of Ethnic Solidarity in the Enclave
Economy." *American Sociological Review* 52: 745–73.

Sanjek, Roger. 1998. *The Future of Us All: Race and Neighborhood Politics in New York City.*
Ithaca, N.Y.: Cornell University Press.

Santiago-Valles, Kelvin. 1994. *"Subject People" and Colonial Discourses: Economic Transformations and Social Disorder in Puerto Rico, 1898–1947.* Albany: State University of
New York Press.

Sassen, Saskia. 1987. "Formal and Informal Association: Dominicans and Colombians in New York." In *Caribbean Life in New York: Sociocultural Dimensions,* ed. Constance Sutton and Elsa Chaney. New York: Center for Migration Studies of New York.

———. 1991. *The Global City: New York, London, Tokyo.* Princeton, N.J.: Princeton University Press.

Schiller, Nina Glick, Linda Basch, and Cristina Blanc-Szanton. 1992a. "Towards a Definition of Transnationalism: Introductory Remarks and Research Questions." In *Towards a Transnational Perspective on Migration: Race, Class, Ethnicity and Nationalism Reconsidered,* ed. Nina Glick Schiller, Linda Basch, and Cristina Blanc-Szanton. New York: New York Academy of Sciences.

———. 1992b. "Transnationalism: A New Analytic Framework for Understanding Migration." In *Towards a Transnational Perspective on Migration: Race, Class, Ethnicity and Nationalism Reconsidered,* ed. Nina Glick Schiller, Linda Basch, and Cristina Blanc-Szanton. New York: New York Academy of Sciences.

Schiller, Nina Glick, Josh DeWind, Marie Lucie Brutus, Carolle Charles, Georges Fouron, and Antoine Thomas. 1987. "All in the Same Boat? Unity and Diversity in Haitian Organizing in New York." In *Caribbean Life in New York: Sociocultural Dimensions,* ed. Constance Sutton and Elsa Chaney. New York: Center for Migration Studies of New York.

Schlesinger, Arthur M., Jr. 1992. *The Disuniting of America.* New York: W. W. Norton.

Scott, James C. 1985. *Weapons of the Weak: Everyday Forms of Peasant Resistance.* New Haven, Conn.: Yale University Press.

———. 1990. *Domination and the Arts of Resistance: Hidden Transcripts.* New Haven, Conn.: Yale University Press.

Sharff, Jagna Wojcicka. 1998. *King Kong on 4th Street: Families and the Violence of Poverty on the Lower East Side.* Boulder, Colo.: Westview Press.

Solomos, John, and Les Back. 1995. *Race, Politics, and Social Change.* New York: Routledge.

Stack, Carol. 1974. *All Our Kin: Strategies for Survival in a Black Community.* New York: Harper and Row.

———. 1995. "Writing Ethnography: Feminist Critical Practice." In *Feminist Dilemmas in Fieldwork,* ed. Dian L. Wolf. Boulder, Colo.: Westview Press.

Steinberg, Stephen. 1989. *The Ethnic Myth: Race, Ethnicity, and Class in America.* Boston: Beacon Press.

Sunshine, Catherine. 1988. *Caribbean: Survival, Struggle and Sovereignty.* New York: Epica Task Force.

Suro, Roberto. 1998. "New York: Teetering on the Heights." In Roberto Suro, *Strangers among Us: How Latino Immigration Is Transforming America.* New York: Alfred A. Knopf.

Susser, Ida. 1982. *Norman Street: Poverty and Politics in an Urban Neighborhood.* New York: Oxford University Press.

———. 1986. "Political Activity among Working-Class Women in a U.S. City." *American Ethnologist* 13 (1): 108–17.

———. 1996. "The Construction of Poverty and Homelessness in U.S. Cities." *Annual Review of Anthropology* 25: 411–35.

Susser, Ida, and John Kreniske. 1987. "The Welfare Trap: A Public Policy for Deprivation." In *Cities of the United States: Studies in Urban Anthropology,* ed. Leith Mullings. New York: Columbia University Press.

Takaki, Ronald. 1989. *Strangers from a Different Shore.* New York: Penguin.

Tchen, J. Kuo Wei. 1990. "The Chinatown-Harlem Initiative: Building Multicultural Understanding in New York City." In *Building Bridges: The Emerging Grassroots Coalition of Labor and Community,* ed. Jeremy Brecher and Tim Costello. New York: Monthly Review Press.

Thomas, J. Phillip. n.d.a. "Has Liberalism Lost Its Mind? Race and Local Democracy." Seminar paper originally posted online through Harvard University's Kennedy School of Government, Multidisciplinary Program in Inequality and Social Policy. http://www.ksg.harvard.edu/inequality/. Accessed March 9, 2001.

———. n.d.b. "The Politics of Building Regional Multi-Racial Political Coalitions." Seminar paper originally posted online through Harvard University's Kennedy School of Government, Joblessness and Urban Poverty Research Program. http://www.ksg.harvard.edu/urbanpoverty/. Accessed December 2001.

Torres, Andrés. 1995. *Between Melting Pot and Mosaic: African Americans and Puerto Ricans in the New York Political Economy.* Philadelphia: Temple University Press.

Torres, Andrés, and José E. Velázquez, eds. 1998. *The Puerto Rican Movement: Voices from the Diaspora.* Philadelphia: Temple University Press.

Torres, Rodolfo D., and ChorSwang Ngin. 1995. "Racialized Boundaries, Class Relations, and Cultural Politics: The Asian-American and Latino Experience." In *Culture and Difference: Critical Perspectives on the Bicultural Experience in the United States,* ed. Antonia Darder. Westport, Conn.: Bergin and Garvey.

Torres-Saillant, Silvio. 1989. "Dominicans as a New York Community: A Social Appraisal." *Punto 7 Review* 2 (1): 7–25.

———. 1992–93. "El concepto de la dominicanidad y la emigración." *Punto y Coma* 4 (1–2): 161–69.

———. 1997. "Diaspora and National Identity: Dominican Migration in the Postmodern Society." *Migration World Magazine* 25 (3): 18–22.

———. 1998a. "The Tribulations of Blackness: Stages in Dominican Racial Identity." *Latin American Perspective: A Journal on Capitalism and Socialism* 25 (3): 126–46.

———. 1998b. "Visions of Dominicanness in the United States." In *Borderless Borders: U.S. Latinos, Latin Americans, and the Paradox of Interdependence,* ed. Frank Bonilla, Edwin Melendez, Rebecca Morales, and Maria de los Angeles Torres. Philadelphia: Temple University Press.

———. 1999a. *Introduction to Dominican Blackness.* Dominican Studies Working Papers series No. 1. New York: CUNY Dominican Studies Institute.

———. 1999b. "La dominicanidad en la diaspora." *El Diario/La Prensa,* December 1: 14.

———. 1999c. "Nothing to Celebrate." *Culturefront: A Magazine of the Humanities* 8 (2): 41–44. (Available: http://www.it.murdoch.edu.au/~sudweeks/b329/readings/Torres-Saillant.html.)

———. 2000a. *Diasporic Disquisitions: Dominicanists, Transnationalism, and the Com-*

munity. Dominican Studies Working Papers series. New York: CUNY Dominican Studies Institute.

———. 2000b. "The Tribulations of Blackness: Stages in Dominican Racial Identity." *Calalloo* 23 (3): 1086–1111.

Trueba, Henry T. 1999. *Latinos Unidos: From Cultural Diversity to the Politics of Solidarity.* Lanham, Md.: Rowman and Littlefield.

Valentine, Charles A. 1968. *Culture and Poverty: Critique and Counterproposals.* Chicago: University of Chicago Press.

Valenzuela, Abel. 1999. "Gender Roles and Settlement Activities among Children and Their Immigrant Families." *American Behavioral Scientist* 42 (4): 720–45.

Vincent, Joan. 1974. "The Structuring of Ethnicity." *Human Organization* 33 (4): 375–79.

———. 1990. *Anthropology and Politics: Visions, Traditions, and Trends.* Tucson: University of Arizona Press.

———. 1993. "Framing the Underclass." *Critique of Anthropology* 13 (3):215–30.

Wacquant, Loic J., and William Julius Wilson. 1989. "The Cost of Racial and Class Exclusion in the Inner City." *Annals of the American Academy of Political Social Science* 501: 10–26.

Waldinger, Roger. 1989. *Through the Eye of the Needle: Immigrants and Enterprise in New York's Garment Trades.* New York: New York University Press.

Warner, W. Lloyd, and Leo Srole. 1945. *The Social Systems of American Ethnic Groups.* New Haven, Conn.: Yale University Press.

Waters, Mary. 1996. "Ethnic and Racial Identities of Second-Generation Black Immigrants in New York City." In *The New Second Generation,* ed. Alejandro Portes. New York: Russell Sage Foundation.

———. 1999. *Black Identities: West Indian Immigrant Dreams and American Realities.* Cambridge, Mass.: Harvard University Press; New York: Russell Sage Foundation.

Whyte, William. 1943. *Street Corner Society: The Social Structure of an Italian Slum.* Chicago: University of Chicago Press.

Williams, Terry. 1989. *The Cocaine Kids: The Inside Story of a Teenage Drug Ring.* New York: Addison-Wesley.

Willis, Paul. 1977. *Learning to Labor: How Working-Class Kids Get Working-Class Jobs.* New York: Columbia University Press.

Wolf, Eric. 1982. *Europe and the People without History.* Berkeley and Los Angeles: University of California Press.

Yun, Grace. 1993. *Intergroup Cooperation in Cities: African, Asian, and Hispanic American Communities.* New York: Asian-American Federation of New York.

Zhou, Min. 1992. *Chinatown: The Socioeconomic Potential of an Urban Enclave.* Philadelphia: Temple University Press.

Zhou, Min, and Carl Bankston. 1996. "Social Capital and the Adaptation of the Second Generation: The Case of Vietnamese Youth in New Orleans." In *The New Second Generation,* ed. Alejandro Portes. New York: Russell Sage Foundation.

Zhou, Min, and John Logan. 1989. "Returns on Human Capital in Ethnic Enclaves: New York City's Chinatown." *American Sociological Review* 54: 809–20.

Index

Abu-Jamal, Mumia, 110, 151

Accommodation, 10, 147, 165

ACDP (Asociación Comunal de Dominicanos Progresistas): activists, 75, 76–77; electoral politics, 79; founding, 70; leftist exiles, 61; origins, 101; Puerto Rican help, 77

Acosta, Rolando, 81

Activism: contexts, 112; as continuum, 165; global vision, 173–74; history of, 53, 112–13; local ownership, 164; people of color collective mobilizations, 168–69; role of immigrant organizations, 6–7; role and purpose, 93, 170; social change, 163–64, 174

Activists: changing strategies, 89; conference (2000) planning, 83; new ethos, 165; as political brokers, 96; stories of, 53; U.S. roots or return migration, 70–71; younger than thirty, 75–76

Advisory Council on Hispanic Affairs, 77

African Americans: alliances with leaders, 168; Black identity and immigrants, 138–39; culture of poverty thesis, 28, 29; Dominican peers and, 1–2; history, 100; identifying with, 30; Linares campaign, 80; mammy image, 141–42; political-ideological connection, 2; political ideologies, 100; political representation, 115; as torchbearers, 104; use of term, 15

Afro-Caribbean cultures, 154–55

Agency, 6, 20; ethnic identification, 26; literature on, 21, 166; politics and, 46, 170–71

Agency for Children's Development, 102

Agency for Children Services, 106

Agrupación Política 14 de Junio, 180n3

Alianza Islámica, 153

Alliances with people of color. *See* People of color alliances

Almighty Latin King and Queen Nation, 153

Alto Manhattan, 34–37, 55

Amaro, Gina, 152, 177n8

Amaro, Miguel, 73–74

Amnesty International, 154

Anonymity of informants, xii, 175n1

Anthropology, fieldwork experience, 53

Antihaitinismo, 131–32, 139, 140, 157–58

Antiwar movement, 179n7, 173

Aponte, Gabriel, 48, 88–89

April War, 61, 65

Aquí-allá (here-there) debate, 69

Archival research, 52

Area Policy Board 12, 77

Ascribed identities, 129

Asociación Comunal de Dominicanos Progresistas. *See* ACDP

Asociación Dominicana, 65

Aspira of New York, 111

Assassinations, political, 67–68

Assata Shakur-Guillermo Morales Student Center, 75, 177n6

Ana Aparicio is assistant professor of anthropology and research associate of the Mauricio Gastón Institute for Latino Community Development and Public Policy at the University of Massachusetts, Boston. She has organized with and served on the boards of various Latino, youth, and advocacy organizations in New York and Massachusetts. She is a coeditor with Philip Kretsedemas of *Immigrants, Welfare Reform, and the Poverty of Policy* (Praeger 2004).